Postwar America

Readings and Reminiscences

Prentice-Hall, Inc., *Englewood Cliffs, New Jersey*

EMILY S. ROSENBERG
Macalester College

NORMAN L. ROSENBERG
Macalester College

Postwar America

Readings and Reminiscences

Library of Congress Cataloguing in Publication Data
Main entry under title:
Postwar America.

  Includes bibliographical references.
  1. United States—History—1945-   —Addresses:
essays, lectures. I. Rosenberg, Emily S., 1944-
II. Rosenberg, Norman L., 1942-
E741.P67   973.92   75-42424
ISBN 0-13-685495-8

© 1976 by Prentice-Hall, Inc., Englewood Cliffs, New Jersey

Printed in the United States of America

10 9 8 7 6 5 4 3 2

PRENTICE-HALL INTERNATIONAL, INC., *London*
PRENTICE-HALL OF AUSTRALIA PTY. LIMITED, *Sydney*
PRENTICE-HALL OF CANADA, LTD., *Toronto*
PRENTICE-HALL OF INDIA PRIVATE LIMITED, *New Delhi*
PRENTICE-HALL OF JAPAN, INC., *Tokyo*
PRENTICE-HALL OF SOUTHEAST ASIA PRIVATE LIMITED, *Singapore*

for Sarah Ann Rosenberg

contents

part VI   THE NIXON YEARS

We have planned this reader for students who want to discover the excitement and diversity of postwar America. Although the students of the 1970's have lived through many events of recent American history, they frequently express surprise when confronted by "all those things we didn't know were going on." Most concede that they have great difficulty understanding how they were involved in or affected by fundamental changes which have overtaken American society since 1945. These selections have been chosen in order to highlight much discussed events like the Vietnam War and to introduce more subtle influences like the revolt against technological society.

Some of the readings are primary documents—like Joe McCarthy's Wheeling speech and the Watergate tapes. Others are secondary accounts which historians will treat as primary evidence—such as Tom Hayden's document of the SDS or John A. Williams' account of the civil rights activities of Martin Luther King, Jr. These attempts by contemporaries to write the history of their own time, we believe, provide students with material that can be used on at least two levels. First, these accounts provide illuminating records of what happened: Frances FitzGerald vividly describes the effects of the war on the Vietnamese people and their culture; Barry Commoner traces technological changes since World War II; Peter Drucker writes of the radicals of the 60's becoming the conservatives of the 70's. Students reading the selections can obtain new insights and gather important information. But they can also examine these documents on a second level, analyzing the authors' motives, use of evidence, and point of view. People like Betty Friedan, Richard J. Barnet, Michael Harrington, and others, were not only trying to observe their times but were trying to influence the direction of historical change. Students can subject these materials to close scrutiny and discover a whole new dimension in historical analysis. The comments which introduce each selection place it in historical perspective and suggest analytical problems.

No readings book can be successful unless the selections will catch students' attention and raise interesting questions. We have used most of these selections in our own teaching and have found that they spark interest and stimulate discussion. These are not esoteric historical articles or snippets from specialized monographs; all are works which were aimed at a broad audience; all are works which display an important perspective on the history of our times.

We would like to thank Cathie Mahar, our editor at Prentice-Hall, for her assistance.

EMILY S. ROSENBERG
NORMAN L. ROSENBERG

preface

Postwar America
Readings and Reminiscences

1

the cold war

Writing under the pseudonym Mr. X, the experienced foreign service officer, George Kennan provided the classic statement for the policy of "containment." His recommendations about applying "counterforce" against Soviet expansionism provided the intellectual basis of America's postwar foreign policy and, some people would claim, substantially contributed to cold war tensions. Kennan's views, however, were usually judicious; the problem with "containment" arose less from its initial rationale than from its aggressive implementation.

What does Kennan believe to be the Soviet goal in the world? How does he think American policy should respond? Compare Kennan's statement of "containment" with that of Dean Acheson in a following selection. What are the similarities and differences?

George Kennan

The Sources of Soviet Conduct

It is clear that the main element of any United States policy toward the Soviet Union must be that of a long-term, patient but firm and vigilant containment of Russian expansive tendencies. It is important to note, however, that such a policy has nothing to do with outward histrionics: with threats or blustering or superfluous gestures of outward "toughness." While the Kremlin is basically flexible in its reaction to political realities, it is by no means unamenable to considerations of prestige. Like almost any other government, it can be placed by tactless and threatening gestures in a position where it cannot afford to yield even though this might be dictated by its sense of realism. The Russian leaders are keen judges of human psychology, and as such they are highly conscious that loss of temper and of self-control is never a source of strength in political affairs. They are quick to exploit such evidences of weakness. For these reasons, it is a *sine qua non* of successful dealing with Russia that the foreign government in question should remain at all times cool and collected and that its demands on Russian policy should be put forward in such a manner as to leave the way open for a compliance not too detrimental to Russian prestige.

In the light of the above, it will be clearly seen that the Soviet pressure against the free institutions of the western world is something that can be contained by the adroit and vigilant application of counterforce at a series of constantly shifting geographical and political points, corresponding to the shifts and manœuvres of Soviet policy, but which cannot be charmed or talked out of existence. The Russians look forward to a duel of infinite duration, and they see that already they have scored great successes. It must be borne in mind that there was a time when the Communist Party represented far more of a minority in the sphere of Russian national life than Soviet power today represents in the world community.

But if ideology convinces the rulers of Russia that truth is on their side and that they can therefore afford to wait, those of us on whom that ideology has no claim are free to examine objectively the validity of that premise. The Soviet thesis not only implies complete lack of control by the west over its own economic destiny, it likewise assumes Russian unity, discipline and patience over an infinite period. Let us bring this apocalyptic vision down to earth, and suppose that the western world finds the strength and resourcefulness to contain Soviet power over a period of ten to fifteen years. What does that spell for Russia itself? . . .

The future of Soviet power may not be by any means as secure as Russian capacity for self-delusion would make it appear to the men in the Kremlin. That they can keep power themselves, they have demon-

George Kennan, "The Sources of Soviet Conduct," Reprinted by permission from *Foreign Affairs* (July, 1947). Copyright 1947 by Council on Foreign Relations, Inc., 575-582.

strated. That they can quietly and easily turn it over to others remains to be proved. Meanwhile, the hardships of their rule and the vicissitudes of international life have taken a heavy toll of the strength and hopes of the great people on whom their power rests. It is curious to note that the ideological power of Soviet authority is strongest today in areas beyond the frontiers of Russia, beyond the reach of its police power. This phenomenon brings to mind a comparison used by Thomas Mann in his great novel "Buddenbrooks." Observing that human institutions often show the greatest outward brilliance at a moment when inner decay is in reality farthest advanced, he compared the Buddenbrook family, in the days of its greatest glamour, to one of those stars whose light shines most brightly on this world when in reality it has long since ceased to exist. And who can say with assurance that the strong light still cast by the Kremlin on the dissatisfied peoples of the western world is not the powerful afterglow of a constellation which is in actuality on the wane? This cannot be proved. And it cannot be disproved. But the possibility remains (and in the opinion of this writer it is a strong one) that Soviet power, like the capitalist world of its conception, bears within it the seeds of its own decay, and that the sprouting of these seeds is well advanced.

It is clear that the United States cannot expect in the foreseeable future to enjoy political intimacy with the Soviet régime. It must continue to regard the Soviet Union as a rival, not a partner, in the political arena. It must continue to expect that Soviet policies will reflect no abstract love of peace and stability, no real faith in the possibility of a permanent happy coexistence of the Socialist and capitalist worlds, but rather a cautious, persistent pressure toward the disruption and weakening of all rival influence and rival power.

Balanced against this are the facts that Russia, as opposed to the western world in general, is still by far the weaker party, that Soviet policy is highly flexible, and that Soviet society may well contain deficiencies which will eventually weaken its own total potential. This would of itself warrant the United States entering with reasonable confidence upon a policy of firm containment, designed to confront the Russians with unalterable counterforce at every point where they show signs of encroaching upon the interests of a peaceful and stable world.

But in actuality the possibilities for American policy are by no means limited to holding the line and hoping for the best. It is entirely possible for the United States to influence by its actions the internal developments, both within Russia and throughout the international Communist movement, by which Russian policy is largely determined. This is not only a question of the modest measure of informational activity which this government can conduct in the Soviet Union and elsewhere, although that, too, is important. It is rather a question of the degree to which the United States can create among the peoples of the world generally the impression of a country which knows what it wants, which is coping successfully with the problems of its internal life and with the responsibilities of a World Power, and which has a spiritual vitality capable of holding its own among the major ideological currents of the time. To the extent that such an impression can be created and maintained, the aims of Russian Communism must appear sterile and quixotic, the hopes and enthusiasm of Moscow's supporters must wane, and added strain must be imposed on the Kremlin's foreign policies. For the palsied decrepitude of the capitalist world is the keystone of Communist philosophy. Even the failure of the United States to experience the early economic depression which the ravens of the Red Square have been predicting with such complacent confidence since hostilities ceased would have deep and important repercussions throughout the Communist world.

By the same token, exhibitions of indecision, disunity and internal disintegration within this country have an exhilarating effect on the whole Communist movement. At each evidence of these tendencies, a thrill of hope and excitement goes through the Communist world; a new jauntiness can be noted in the Moscow tread; new groups of foreign supporters climb on to what they can only view as the band wagon of international politics; and Russian pressure increases all along the line in international affairs.

It would be an exaggeration to say that American behavior unassisted and alone could exercise a power of life and death over the Communist movement and bring about the early fall of Soviet power in Russia. But the United States has it in its power to increase enormously the strains under which Soviet policy must operate, to force upon the Kremlin a far greater degree of moderation and circumspection than it has had to observe in recent years, and in this way to promote tendencies which must eventually find their outlet in either the break-up or the gradual mellowing of Soviet power. For no mystical, Messianic movement—and particularly not that of the Kremlin—can face frustration indefinitely without eventually adjusting itself in one way or another to the logic of that state of affairs.

Thus the decision will really fall in large measure in this country itself. The issue of Soviet-American relations is in essence a test of the over-all worth of the United States as a nation among nations. To avoid destruction the United States need only measure up to its own best traditions and prove itself worthy of preservation as a great nation.

Surely, there was never a fairer test of national quality than this. In the light of these circumstances, the thoughtful observer of Russian-

American relations will find no cause for complaint in the Kremlin's challenge to American society. He will rather experience a certain gratitude to a Providence which, by providing the American people with this implacable challenge, has made their entire security as a nation dependent on their pulling themselves together and accepting the responsibilities of moral and political leadership that history plainly intended them to bear.

George Kennan's argument that the United States should develop a "containment" policy against Soviet expansionism was widely accepted in official circles, but it did not go unchallenged elsewhere. Walter Lippmann, who had been an influential newspaper columnist and political theorist for decades, wrote a series of articles for the New York Herald Tribune which criticized the policy enunciated by Mr. X." Later published in The Cold War: A Study in U.S. Foreign Policy, Lippmann's articles foreshadowed many later critiques of American postwar policy: that containment could lead to American support for unpopular puppet regimes and possibly to military intervention in undesirable or unwinnable places.

Did Lippmann believe that containment would, in the long run, command support from most Americans? What were his arguments against containment? Have subsequent events shown that containment was a successful or an unsuccessful foreign policy?

Walter Lippmann

The Cold War

If then the Kremlin's challenge to American society is to be met by the policy which Mr. X proposes, we are committed to a contest for ten or fifteen years with the Soviet system which is planned and directed from Moscow. Mr. X is much mistaken, it seems to me, if he thinks that a free and undirected economy like our own can be used by the diplomatic planners to wage a diplomatic war against a planned economy at a series of constantly shifting geographical and political points. He is proposing to meet the Soviet challenge on the ground which is most favorable to the Soviets, and with the very instruments, procedures, and weapons in which they have a manifest superiority.

I find it hard to understand how Mr. X could have recommended such a strategic monstrosity. For he tells us, no doubt truly, that the Soviet power "cannot be easily defeated or discouraged by a single victory on the part of its opponents," and that "the patient persistence by which it is animated" means that it cannot be "effectively countered" by "sporadic acts." Yet his own policy calls for a series of sporadic acts: the United States is to apply "counterforce" where the Russians encroach and when they encroach.

On his own testimony no single victory will easily defeat or discourage the patient persistence of the Kremlin. Yet Mr. X says that the United States should aim to win a series of victories which will cause the Russians to "yield on individual sectors of the diplomatic front." And then what? When the United States has forced the Kremlin to "face frustration indefinitely" there will "eventually" come "either the breakup or the gradual mellowing of the Soviet power."

There is, however, no rational ground for confidence that the United States could muster "unalterable counterforce" at all the individual sectors. The Eurasian continent is a big place, and the military power of the United States, though it is very great, has certain limitations which must be borne in mind if it is to be used effectively. We live on an island continent. We are separated from the theaters of conflict by the great oceans. We have a relatively small population, of which the greater proportion must in time of war be employed in producing, transporting and servicing the complex weapons and engines which constitute our military power. The United States has, as compared with the Russians, no adequate reserves of infantry. Our navy commands the oceans and we possess the major offensive weapons of war. But on the ground in the interior of the Eurasian continent, as we are learning in the Greek mountains, there may be many "individual sectors" where only infantry can be used as the "counterforce."

These considerations must determine American strategy in war and, therefore, also in diplomacy, whenever the task of diplomacy is to deal with a conflict and a contest of power. The planner of American diplomatic policy must use the kind of power we do have, not the kind we do not have. He must use that kind of power where it can be used. He must avoid engagements in those "individual sectors of the diplomatic front" where our opponents can use the weapons in which they have superiority. But the policy of firm containment as defined by Mr. X ignores these tactical considerations. It makes no distinction among sectors. It commits the United States to confront the Russians with counterforce "at every point" along the line, instead of at those points which we have selected because, there at those points, our kind of sea and air power can best be exerted.

American military power is peculiarly unsuited to a policy of containment which has to be enforced persistently and patiently for an indefinite period of time. If the Soviet Union were an island like Japan, such a policy could be enforced by American sea and air power. The United States could, without great difficulty, impose a blockade. But the Soviet Union has to be contained on land, and "holding the line" is therefore a form of trench warfare.

Yet the genius of American military power does not lie in holding positions indefinitely. That requires a massive patience by great hordes of docile people. American military power is distinguished by its mobility, its speed, its range and its offensive striking force. It is, therefore, not an efficient instrument for a diplomatic policy of containment. It can only be the instrument of a policy which has as its objective a decision and a settlement. It can and should be used to redress the balance of power which has been upset by the war. But it is not designed for, or adapted to, a strategy of containing, waiting, countering, blocking, with no more specific objective than the eventual "frustration" of the opponent.

The Americans would themselves probably be frustrated by Mr. X's policy long before the Russians were.

The policy of containment, which Mr. X recommends, demands the employment of American economic, political, and in the last analysis, American military power at "sectors" in the interior of Europe and Asia. This requires, as I have pointed out, ground forces, that is to say reserves of infantry, which we do not possess.

The United States cannot by its own military power contain the expansive pressure of the Russians "at every point where they show signs of encroaching." The United States cannot have ready "unalterable counterforce" consisting of American troops. Therefore, the counterforces which Mr. X requires have to be composed of Chinese, Afghans, Iranians, Turks, Kurds, Arabs, Greeks, Italians, Austrians, of anti-Soviet

Poles, Czechoslovaks, Bulgars, Yugoslavs, Albanians, Hungarians, Finns and Germans.

The policy can be implemented only by recruiting, subsidizing and supporting a heterogeneous array of satellites, clients, dependents and puppets. The instrument of the policy of containment is therefore a coalition of disorganized, disunited, feeble or disorderly nations, tribes and factions around the perimeter of the Soviet Union.

To organize a coalition among powerful modern states is, even in time of war and under dire necessity, an enormously difficult thing to do well. To organize a coalition of disunited, feeble and immature states, and to hold it together for a prolonged diplomatic siege, which might last for ten or fifteen years, is, I submit, impossibly difficult.

It would require, however much the real name for it were disavowed, continual and complicated intervention by the United States in the affairs of all the members of the coalition which we were proposing to organize, to protect, to lead and to use. Our diplomatic agents abroad would have to have an almost unerring capacity to judge correctly and quickly which men and which parties were reliable containers. Here at home Congress and the people would have to stand ready to back their judgments as to who should be nominated, who should be subsidized, who should be whitewashed, who should be seen through rose-colored spectacles, who should be made our clients and our allies.

Mr. X offers us the prospect of maintaining such a coalition indefinitely until—eventually—the Soviet power breaks up or mellows because it has been frustrated. It is not a good prospect. Even if we assume, which we ought not, that our diplomatic agents will know how to intervene shrewdly and skillfully all over Asia, the Middle East, and Europe, and even if we assume, which the Department of State cannot, that the American people will back them with a drawing account of blank checks both in money and in military power, still it is not a good prospect. For we must not forget that the Soviet Union, against which this coalition will be directed, will resist and react.

In the complicated contest over this great heterogeneous array of unstable states, the odds are heavily in favor of the Soviets. For if we are to succeed, we must organize our satellites as unified, orderly and reasonably contented nations. The Russians can defeat us by disorganizing states that are already disorganized, by disuniting peoples that are torn with civil strife, and by inciting their discontent which is already very great.

As a matter of fact this borderland in Europe and Asia around the perimeter of the Soviet Union is not a place where Mr. X's "unassailable barriers" can be erected. Satellite states and puppet governments are not good material out of which to construct unassailable barriers. A diplomatic war conducted as this policy demands, that is to say conducted indirectly, means that we must stake our own security and the peace of the world upon satellites, puppets, clients, agents about whom we can know very little. Frequently they will act for their own reasons, and on their own judgments, presenting us with accomplished facts that we did not intend, and with crises for which we are unready. The "unassailable barriers" will present us with an unending series of insoluble dilemmas. We shall have either to disown our puppets, which would be tantamount to appeasement and defeat and the loss of face, or must support them at an incalculable cost on an unintended, unforeseen and perhaps undesirable issue.

In his memoirs, Present at the Creation, *Truman's Secretary of State, Dean Acheson, recalled the premises behind the policy paper called National Security Council-68 (NSC-68). Acheson described the anticommunist programs which he began "preaching" at gatherings around the country and implicitly expressed his view of the relationship between foreign policy and public opinion. Acheson's speeches borrowed heavily from George Kennan's analysis, but in making his points "clearer than truth," Acheson went beyond Kennan to articulate a less flexible and more all-embracing Cold War world view.*

How accurate were the assumptions of NSC-68? Did Acheson feel he should respond to the wishes of public opinion? How did Acheson view domestic dissent? Is there any connection between the assumptions of the Truman-Acheson foreign policy and the later popularity of Joseph McCarthy?

Dean Acheson

Present at the Creation

NSC-68 has not been declassified and may not be quoted, but its contents have been widely discussed in print. Many of my own public statements were properly based upon the fundamental conclusions stated in this leading embodiment of Government policy.

The paper began with a statement of the conflicting aims and purposes of the two superpowers: the priority given by the Soviet rulers to the Kremlin design, world domination, contrasted with the American aim, an environment in which free societies could exist and flourish. Throughout 1950, the year my immolation in the Senate began, I went about the country preaching this premise of NSC-68.

The task of a public officer seeking to explain and gain support for a major policy is not that of the writer of a doctoral thesis. Qualification must give way to simplicity of statement, nicety and nuance to bluntness, almost brutality, in carrying home a point. It is better to carry the hearer or reader into the quadrant of one's thought than merely to make a noise or to mislead him utterly. In the State Department we used to discuss how much time that mythical "average American citizen" put in each day listening, reading, and arguing about the world outside his own country. Assuming a man or woman with a fair education, a family, and a job in or out of the house, it seemed to us that ten minutes a day would be a high average. If this were anywhere near right, points to be understandable had to be clear. If we made our points clearer than truth, we did not differ from most other educators and could hardly do otherwise.

So our analysis of the threat combined the ideology of communist doctrine and the power of the Russian state into an aggressive expansionist drive, which found its chief opponent and, therefore, target in the antithetic ideas and power of our own country. It was true and understandable to describe the Russian motivating concept as being that "no state is friendly which is not subservient," and ours that "no state is unfriendly which, in return for respect for its rights, respects the rights of other states." While our own society felt no compulsion to bring all societies into conformity with it, the Kremlin hierarchy was not content merely to entrench its regime but wished to expand its control directly and indirectly over other people within its reach. "It takes more," I said, "than bare hands and a desire for peace to turn back this threat."

Such an analysis was decried by some liberals and some Kremlinologists. The real threat, they said, lay in the weakness of the Western European social, economic, and political structure. Correct that and the Russian danger would disappear. This I did not believe. The threat to Western Europe seemed to be singularly like that which Islam had posed centuries before, with its combination of ideological zeal and fighting power. Then

Reprinted from *Present at the Creation: My Years in the State Department,* by Dean Acheson. By permission of W. W. Norton & Company, Inc. Copyright © 1969 by Dean Acheson, 375-380.

it had taken the same combination to meet it: Germanic power in the east and Frankish in Spain, both energized by a great outburst of military power and social organization in Europe. This time it would need the added power and energy of America, for the drama was now played on a world stage.

If these were the intentions of the Kremlin, what were its capabilities for realizing and ours for frustrating them? Ours was demonstrably the potentially stronger society, but did it have the strength now, and would it have it in the future, to frustrate the Kremlin design? At the end of the war we were the most powerful nation on earth, with the greatest army, navy, and air force, a monopoly of the most destructive weapon, and all supported by the most productive industry and agriculture. But now our army had been demobilized, our navy put in mothballs, and our air force no longer had a monopoly of atomic weapons. In three or four years at the most we could be threatened with devastating damage, against which no sure protection appeared. Surely we produced far more aluminum, for instance, than the Soviet Union; but while we splashed it over the front of automobiles, in Russia more went into military aircraft than here. On the other hand, our almost minute army cost many times what theirs did. A brief comparison of the pay, care, and equipment of private soldiers showed why. Half the total effort of their rival society went into creating military power, which in a short time at present rates could top ours. What relation did these facts have to foreign policy, national security, the existence of a spacious environment for free societies? How much of our national product would we need to divert, as sensible insurance, to an arms effort we loathed? The paper recommended specific measures for a large and immediate improvement of military forces and weapons, and of the economic and morale factors which underlay our own and our allies' ability to influence the conduct of other societies.

The Response Recommended. In explaining to the nation the course it recommended, I made clear, also—in an address in Dallas on June 13, 1950 —those it would not recommend. We should not pull down the blinds, I said, and sit in the parlor with a loaded shotgun, waiting. Isolation was not a realistic course of action. It did not work and it had not been cheap. Appeasement of Soviet ambitions was, in fact, only an alternative form of isolation. It would lead to a final struggle for survival with both our moral and military positions weakened. A third course, euphemistically called preventive war, adopted with disastrous results in other times by other types of people and governments than ours, would take the form of nuclear attack on the Soviet Union. It would not solve problems; it would multiply them. Then as now nothing seemed to be more depressing in the history of our own country than the speeches of the 1850s about "the irrepressible conflict." War is not inevitable. But talk of war's inevitability had, in the past, helped to make it occur.

While NSC-68 did not contain cost estimates, that did not mean we had not discussed them. To carry through the sort of rearmament and rehabilitation-of-forces program that we recommended, at the rate we thought necessary, for ourselves and with help for our allies, would require, our group estimated, a military budget of the magnitude of about fifty billion dollars per annum. This was a very rough guess, but, as the existing ceiling was thirteen and a half billion, the proposal—or rather the situation out of which it grew—required considerable readjustment of thinking. It seemed better to begin this process by facing the broad facts, trends, and probabilities before getting lost in budgetary intricacies. If that begins before an administration has decided what it *wants* to do, or made what diplomats used to call a decision "in principle"—in essence—the mice in the Budget Bureau will nibble to death the will to decide.

Furthermore, whatever the cost might be, some such program was essential and well within national economic capacity. It obviously would raise some difficult choices between this and other uses of production, but the national product was not static and might be increased—as, indeed, it was. Our duty was not to make these decisions but to press for decisions, combining persuasion with the most powerful statement of the case. Nor did our duty, as I saw it, stop there. It was not enough to give the President wise, though tough, advice and expect him to create acceptance in Congress and the country for the resulting action. We also had a duty to explain and persuade. An incident about this time illustrates my point. The Marquis of Salisbury, who had had long experience in the Foreign Office, coming into the main entrance of the State Department with me, saw posters announcing meetings with various groups then in session. When he asked about them, I suggested that we make a brief tour. In one room an officer was discussing with a group of schoolteachers our participation in the UN Educational, Scientific, and Cultural Organization; in another a foreign policy association was learning about a current crisis in the Middle East; in a third a Hispano-American group was talking about Latin American affairs. Lord Salisbury could not, he said, conceive of similar groups in the Foreign Office. "This is truly," he added, "democracy in action."

We Explain To the Country. The need to tell the country how we saw the situation created by the Soviet Union and the necessary response to it came soon after the President's announcement of his hydrogen bomb decision. Two friendly Democratic senators, Brien McMahon and Millard Tydings, made dramatic speeches in the Senate during February 1950. They reflected liberal criticism of Administration policy and a sort of guilt complex common among atomic scientists about the atomic bomb. McMahon urged the end of atomic armaments and an era of "world-wide atomic peace" and "atomic-created abundance for all men." This was to be achieved by a "moral crusade for peace" and a fifty-billion-dollar "global Marshall Plan" financed by the United States and augmented by an undertaking by all nations to put two-thirds of their armament expenditures to "constructive ends." Tydings, Chairman of the Armed Services Committee, proposed that the President convoke a world-disarmament committee to deal with all weapons. In one day's mail, I wrote our daughter, I had a letter from an old friend and leading liberal "which says that if I don't get up and lead, move, advance, radiate peace, etc., I shall be left watching an embattled country march by—where to, he says not. It is an interesting letter to one who is not inactive on a busy stage; but it is all meant well. I had the same from Mr. Trygve Lie, who is also more eager than aware."

At this time the Secretary General, preaching a ten-point program of negotiation with Moscow, was about to start off on a tour of United Nations capitals. This, he insisted, was not appeasement but "negotiation," which requires "honest give-and-take by both sides." "What we need," he said, "what the world needs, is a twenty year program to win peace through the United Nations." It was to start off with something that, despite Mr. Lie's protestations, sounded very much like appeasement to me, luring the Soviet Union back to the United Nations, from which Malik and his cohorts had withdrawn, by the majority's reversing itself and seating the Communists as the representatives of China. To me all this made little sense. I said that on Chinese representation we held to our expressed views but would "accept the decision of any organ of the United Nations made by the necessary majority, and we [would] not walk out." So far as negotiations were concerned we would consider anything put forward in the United Nations, but, meanwhile, "we can't afford to wait and merely hope that [Soviet] policies will change. We must carry forward in our own determination to create situations of strength in the free world, because this is the only basis on which lasting agreement with the Soviet Government is possible."

My long press conference on February 8, 1950, immediately after the two Senate speeches, began a continued discussion of our response to the Soviet threat. Four themes ran through it, beginning with the different conception in Soviet and Western thought of the purpose and role of negotiation in international relations and the consequences of this difference. In Western tradition negotiation was bargaining to achieve a mutually desired agreement. In communist doctrine it was war by political means to achieve an end unacceptable to the other side. In both cases it was a means to an end, but in the latter case the ends were, if understood, mutually exclusive. The second, related theme was that in dealing with the Soviet Union the most useful negotiation was by acts rather than words, and stability was better and more reliable than verbal agreement. From all this came insistence upon repairing weaknesses and creating "situations of strength" and, as a means to them, the NSC-68 program. Third came the transformation of our two former enemies into allies and their attachment by firm bonds of security and economic interest to the free nations in Europe and Asia. The fourth point was doubtless a futile one to make in view of existing political passions, but it had the small merit of being true. It was that continued quarreling within our own country regarding the proper mix of negotiation and strength in dealing with the Soviet threat created a major source of both weakness and the appearance of weakness.

I pointed out to the press that the speeches of the two senators dealt more with the goal toward which we were striving than with the way to get there; more with ends than means. If we could reach the ends on which we all agreed—peace, stability, and progress—by agreement on the means, that would be the simplest, easiest, and most desirable way to do it. Four years of trial had convinced us that agreement with the Kremlin was not then possible. Certain obstacles stood in the way that had to be removed. Among them was the existence in the non-Communist world of large areas of weakness, which by its very nature the Soviet system had to exploit. They presented irresistible invitations to fish in troubled waters. To urge them not to fish, to try to agree not to fish, was as futile as talking to a force of nature. One cannot argue with a river; it is going to flow. One can dam it or deflect it, but not argue with it. Therefore, we had been at work to create strength where there had been weakness, to turn our former enemies into allies, to replace the dams that once contained Russia to the east and to the west, to aid growth and progress in the undeveloped areas in the world.

The Need for National Unity. The next week I was talking to a group in the White House about the impediments to national unity that came from those who insisted upon the rightness and righteousness of their own paths to peace. There were those, I said, who believed that good will and negotiation would solve all problems, that if only the President and Stalin would "get their feet under the same table" they could iron out any and all international difficulties. The problem lay not in where the leaders' feet were but where their minds were. We had tried most earnestly to get Kremlin minds running toward cooperation and failed. Then there were those who frightened themselves and their fellow citizens into paralysis by apocalyptic warnings of the end to come through nuclear weapons. The dangers were great enough in all conscience, but the fact that war could be even more terrible in the future than in the past should increase rather than diminish action to eliminate situations that might lead to it.

Other fomenters of disunity declared that the time had come to "call the bluff" of our opponents and "have a showdown" with them. These resorts to the language of poker showed the recklessness of the gamble inherent in them. Finally, I said in concluding my talk, there were purists who would have no dealings with any but the fairest of democratic states, going from state to state with political litmus paper testing them for true-blue democracy. They were repelled by some of the practices reported in Greece, Turkey, and North and South Africa, among other places, but curiously hopeful about the Russian future. All these points of view represented escapism in dealing with the world as it was and escape from building with the materials at hand a strong, safer, and more stable position for free communities of which we were one.

My constant appeal to American liberals was to face the long, hard years and not to distract us with the offer of shortcuts and easy solutions begotten by good will out of the angels of man's better nature. "Until the Soviet leaders do genuinely accept a 'live and let live' philosophy . . . no approach from the free world . . . and no Trojan dove from the Communist movement will help to resolve our mutual problems," I said on one occasion; on another: "The road to freedom and to peace which I have pictured is a hard one. The times in which we live must be painted in the sombre values of Rembrandt. The background is dark, the shadows deep. Outlines are obscure. The central point, however, glows with light; and, though it often brings out the glint of steel, it touches colors of unimaginable beauty. For us, that central point is the growing unity of free men the world over. This is our shaft of light, our hope, and our promise."

These themes I repeated and elaborated from Massachusetts to Texas, on the Berkeley campus in California and at the United Nations in New York. What we expected to achieve by the creation of strength throughout the free world—military, economic, and political—to replace the inviting weak spots offered to Soviet probing was to diminish further the possibility of war, to prevent "settlements by default" to Soviet pressures, to show the Soviet leaders by successful containment that they could not hope to expand their influence throughout the world and must modify their policies. Then, and only then, could meaningful negotiation be possible on the larger issues that divided us. In the meantime the search for miracle cures for the earth's ills was a dangerous form of self-delusion, which only diverted us from the hard duties of our times.

In my speech at Berkeley in March 1950 I told my audience that even though important settlements through negotiation would be impossible for long years to come, there were some quite simple things the Soviet leaders could do to make coexistence a great deal more tolerable to everyone, while leaving much yet to do. For instance, for five years the Soviet Union had blocked all efforts to move toward ending the state of war and occupation in Germany, Austria, and Japan. Granted that peace treaties presented difficulties, some progress toward relaxation of tensions, return of prisoners, a peaceful settlement of Korea's problems would not seem impossible. Similarly, some relaxation of rule by Soviet force in Eastern Europe and lessening of Soviet obstruction in the United Nations or in continued discussion of atomic energy problems would be welcome. Perhaps on the most primitive level of international intercourse—the treatment of diplomatic representatives and the language of international communication—some improvement in debased Communist standards might be possible. "I must warn you not to raise your hopes," I told my listeners. "I see no evidence that the Soviet leaders will change their conduct until the progress of the free world convinces them that they cannot profit from a continuation of these tensions."

Richard J. Barnet's work, which questions the assumptions of cold war foreign policymaking, has helped stimulate a re-evaluation of America's role in the world. Drawing lessons from the Vietnamese war, critics of America's foreign policy such as Barnet have stressed Americans' preoccupation with international stability rather than with social justice and have analyzed the limitations of a world view which generally identified popular rebel movements as part of a vast communist conspiracy. But, according to Barnet, America's "national security managers" were not the only ones blinded by their own social backgrounds and the limits of ideology. Barnet scrutinizes the revolutionaries who guide foreign insurgent movements. Refusing to cast them as romantic rebels always fighting on the side of justice, Barnet shows how insurgency can build its own terrible spiral of violence and self-deception. Barnet is too sophisticated a scholar to ask which world view—that of the national security manager or that of the revolutionary—corresponds to "reality"; his concern is the escalation of misunderstanding and the violent consequences that occur when these "two worlds collide."

According to Barnet, what is the outlook of the "national security manager" and how does it differ from that of the revolutionary? Would it be possible to bridge the gap of misunderstanding between the two? What is the role of violence in the world view of both?

Richard J. Barnet

Two Worlds in Collision

The continuing American conflict with revolutionary movements arises from a fundamental clash of perspective on modern political history between those officials in the State Department, Pentagon, CIA, and the White House who manage U.S. foreign relations—the National-Security Managers—and the Revolutionaries, who guide insurgent movements. The conflict is fed by two fundamentally incompatible visions of world order. . . .

This clash of perspectives is dictated by radical differences in their education, theoretical and practical, and in their personal relationships to politics. The typical National-Security Manager during the last twenty years was trained in law, engineering, or banking. He entered government service in the war. Captivated by a chance to be a participant in great events, he stayed on or, more often, returned from time to time. If he has any firsthand knowledge at all of the Third World, it is likely to stem from a mining venture or the sugar business; or, perhaps, from wartime service in the OSS.

From his vantage point in the national-security bureaucracy, the National-Security Manager sees revolution in the underdeveloped world as a problem in the management of violence. Coming to power in the midst of World War II, he formed his view of international politics from his experience in the struggle with Hitler. The primary problem is aggression. The principal cause of aggression is weakness and instability. Unless aggressors are systematically opposed by "situations of strength," they will strike at their weaker neighbors. Nations act in accordance with Newtonian laws, rushing to fill up "power vacuums" wherever they find them. "Everything that happens in this world affects us," President Johnson told the troops in Vietnam in 1966, "because pretty soon it gets on our doorstep." Stripped of the intellectual counterpoint of the foreign-policy expert, the President voiced the most basic and primitive fears of the National-Security Manager. "There are 3 billion people in the world and we have only 200 million of them. We are outnumbered 15 to 1. If might did make right, they would sweep over the United States and take what we have. We have what they want." . . .

Communist intervention in the turmoil of revolution, decolonization, and civil strife threatens the security of the United States, for if the communists succeed in their bid "for sway over the destiny of man," the United States—as the National-Security Manager sees it—will be reduced to a vestigial enclave. Each revolutionary success, therefore, is seen as a Russian victory and an American defeat. This conviction is reason enough to mount a global campaign of containment, for National Security is its own justification.

But the National-Security Manager is also convinced that he has right as well as necessity on his side. Communist intervention is illegitimate because the communist is by definition a foreign agent. Ho Chi Minh's independence movement, Ambassador William C. Bullitt explained in 1947, was designed to "add another finger to the hand that Stalin is closing around China." Mao Tse-tung too was a Russian agent, according to Dean Rusk in a speech made two years after the Chinese Revolution, when he was in charge of Far East operations for the State Department. Mao's regime was "a colonial Russian government—a Slavic Manchukuo on a large scale—it is not the government of China. It does not pass the first test. It is not Chinese." The National-Security Manager has convinced himself that no people ever voluntarily choose communism, a system founded on a set of economic myths and made to work at all only by the systematic use of terror. Perhaps most of the protectorates of the Free World are not so free, the National-Security Manager concedes in the intimate atmosphere of a Task Force or a "backgrounder," but they are better off than if they had gone communist. And so are we.

Since the dawn of the sixties the National-Security Managers have taken it as an article of faith that the Third World is both the locus and the prize of the Cold War. "Today's struggle does not lie here," President Kennedy told Paul-Henri Spaak on a visit to Europe in the last year of his life, "but rather in Asia, Latin America and Africa." The less-developed lands, John J. McCloy wrote in 1960, "promise to be the principal battleground in which the forces of freedom and communism compete—a battleground in which the future shape of society may finally be tested and determined." The vision of Armageddon that had sustained the arms race of the fifties, the Nuclear War over Europe, had receded in the wake of a decade of tacit understandings between cautious adversaries and judicious crisis management on both sides of the Elbe. The prospect of the new Armageddon was more frightening, for its terrain was unfamiliar and its weapons unconventional. The clients to be assisted were volatile. They behaved brutally at home and ungratefully toward their benefactors. Yet the decolonizing world, known in the National-Security Manager's vernacular of the fifties as The Gray Areas, had become the major battleground.

For the National-Security bureaucrat, the Cold War conferred a manageable unity upon the landmass of Asia, Africa, and Latin America, with its two-thirds of the world's population, its staggering set of economic and social problems, and its confusing mosaic of race, culture, and politics. For all their differences, the politicians of the Third World shared a common role in the Great Power struggle, and whatever identity such "local" politicians were accorded in the State Department and the White House rested on that role.

The National-Security Manager still tends to look at the "Underdeveloped World" as a vast Gray Area in international politics. No part of it is of intrinsic interest, unless, of course, it supplies some vital commodity. Otherwise it can capture the official attention in Washington only if it symbolizes some struggle which transcends the minor turmoil of native politics. To the man of the West, Paris and Berlin are important places in their own right, for they symbolize his own historical heritage. But Danang, Santo Domingo, and Kinshasa penetrate his consciousness, if at all, only as battlefields, and then only if the fight is about something sufficiently important. He has almost no knowledge about such places, their people, or their politics, and little personal commitment to them. They represent either sources of strength, strategic or economic, or points of vulnerability. "Vietnam is not the issue," National-Security Managers have frequently confided to critics who question whether systematic bombardment is the best way to secure freedom for the Vietnamese people; "it is the testing ground for the Communist strategy of Wars of National Liberation. If they win here, they will strike elsewhere. If they lose, they will not be so ready to start another."

The National-Security Manager is a global thinker. In themselves, local problems of other countries are not worthy of his attention; it is the transcendent importance of local revolutionary struggles that warrants intervention. Interference in purely domestic matters is still unjustified as a matter of law and sound policy. Unfortunately, he hastens to add, the line between domestic and foreign matters has blurred. When political factions struggle with one another in far-off places, their conflict is an expression of a single world-wide struggle. The real contestants remain the same. Only the battlefield shifts. The battle, which takes the form of a series of guerrilla wars, is not about Vietnam or Greece or the Dominican Republic any more than World War II was about Iwo Jima or Sicily. Wherever men struggle for power, one can always find International Communism, the ubiquitous political scavenger, ready to use genuine local grievances as ammunition in a global holy war. Global strategy, more than local conditions, dictates the site of the next engagement between International Communism and the Free World. . . .

The National-Security Manager assumes that U.S. interests and those of the rest of humanity coincide. Governments and political movements which contest this idea have ulterior and illegitimate motives. Far from a simple cynic who mouths idealistic rhetoric to mask economic plundering, the Manager sincerely believes that in opposing Third World revolutions the United States is both pursuing its self-interest and promoting the ultimate welfare of the world community. The fight against insurgent movements is rationalized into a continuing crusade for a decent world, the latest episode in the battle to make the world safe for democracy. What gives plausibility to this characterization is that modern insurgent movements, so U.S. leaders have argued, can be lumped with the Kaiser's invasion of Belgium and Hitler's aggression against Europe, for they are all *violent* challenges to the status quo. If, as the National-Security Managers see it, the inevitable involvement of international communism is the key factor that makes U.S. intervention against revolutions ultimately necessary for national survival, the use of violence by the insurgents is the key factor that makes it legally justifiable and morally right.

Like everyone else, the National-Security Manager looks at the issue of violence from a highly personal perspective. He is selective in the violence he notices and inconsistent in the moral judgments he makes about it. On November 23, 1946, for example, at the very moment when the State Department was preparing a major U.S. intervention against Greek "terrorists," a French naval squadron turned its guns on the civilian population of Haiphong and killed more than six thousand in an afternoon. The United States did not protest, much less intervene. Violence in behalf of the established order is judged by one set of criteria, insurgent violence by another. When established institutions kill through their police or their armies, it is regrettable but, by hypothesis, necessary. When the weak rise up and kill, their violence threatens order everywhere. Sympathetic as U.S. bureaucrats were with the objectives of the Hungarian freedom fighters in 1956, they breathed a sigh of relief when they were disarmed.

The National-Security Manager is aware that violence in other countries has political causes, but he sees no other immediate way to handle it than suppression. Reform, modernization, greater political and social justice are all necessary, he knows, to assure stable regimes where the status quo will not be overturned by force. But how can you begin this process unless the snipers and assassins are first rounded up? Once the wretched of the earth and the cynical politicians who manipulate their misery for their own ends are made to see that violence will not work, they may come to cooperate in finding less dangerous ways to political change.

In the long run, political passions will be cooled by the slow process of opening up new doors of opportunity—a revolution from the top. In the short run, those who are impatient with this prolonged prospect will be taught patience by the army or the police. . . .

The National-Security Manager builds his model of political and economic development for the "less-developed nations," as he tactfully calls them, from his own picture of American political development. Too sophisticated to think that the American system of government or economy is the answer to the problems of the Third World or that, even if it were, it could be simply re-created in present societies, he nonetheless sees the process of change in American terms and believes that

American techniques offer the only real hope. Projecting his own conception of the dynamics of American life, he concludes that change is primarily a technical rather than a political problem, one that calls for a slow turn of the wheel rather than a sudden jerk. Under the American System man has gone far to transcend political conflict. The "consensus society," a national myth long before President Johnson made it a political slogan, consists of more open channels of opportunities than have ever been available before in human society. As he sees it, old class conflicts and animosities that have torn apart other societies play no role in the land of the Melting Pot. That there is great inequality in American society is clear, but the faith in equal opportunity is a source of personal contentment and national pride for all but a small minority that is very poor and nonwhite.

According to his vision of social change in America, the United States has escaped class conflict because of its economic system, which makes it possible for each man to contribute to the general welfare by looking after his own. The government, he knows, plays a larger role than we care to advertise. But its function is to prime the pump and to stimulate the general growth of the economy, not to make a radical redistribution of political and economic power. The economy continues to grow because the system has learned how to harness technology.

Looking at the underdeveloped world, the National-Security Manager assumes that what W. W. Rostow calls a "high-mass-consumption" society is the real ultimate goal of newly decolonized societies and a proper one. The best way to achieve the "takeoff" that can bring a modest version of the affluent society to poor nations is through a technological innovation and the education of an entrepreneurial class that can supply the energy for change. The economic system that stimulates entrepreneurship is private enterprise. Therefore, the developing nations' "greatest need," as Chester Bowles has put it, is "private investment to aid the free sectors of their economies."

Capital for the public sector of infant economies is likely to be wasted. It cannot be absorbed because the entrepreneurial classes who could invest it profitably do not yet exist. Corruption, waste, inefficiency, and political in-fighting all guarantee that grants of capital to new governments to be used to build planned economies would end up in Swiss bank accounts. The process of development is slow, but the attempt to speed it up through nationalization, confiscation, or other radical remedies would lead to the disasters of Stalinism. The National-Security Manager takes some comfort from the thought that the military of the Third World, the class that has most directly and handsomely benefited from U.S. aid around the world, are also the most promising entrepreneurs. In Latin America and parts of the Middle East the military have been "modernizing" influences. Furnished with U.S. training and equipment, they are the first in their societies to apply technology to public problems. They are now equipped for "civic action." The Department of Defense explains it this way: "As the interdependence of civil and military matters is increasingly recognized, the social and economic welfare of the people can no longer be considered a non-military concern."

There is hardly an assumption in this picture of change that the Revolutionary accepts. To him the military represent not a force for "nation-building" but a praetorian guard for the most reactionary elements of his society. For every company of soldiers sent out to build a bridge or repair a hospital there are, he is sure, five or more roaming the countryside looking for political unreliables or hounding the forces of dissent and reform in the city.

In place of the optimistic assumption of gradual economic growth put forward by the National-Security Managers and their experts on "modernization," he sees the harsh reality of peasant life. After ten or fifteen years of U.S. military and economic aid and technical assistance his country is still essentially a one-crop country with an average per-capita income under two hundred dollars, a place where starvation and disease, despite a few local relief and health programs, continue to rise. Like most politicians of the Third World, he accepts the analysis of Raoul Prebisch and most other non-American development economists that the gap between the poor nations and the rich is widening, not closing. He has seen country after country in Africa and Latin America fall before military coups. He notes that the professional, entrepreneurial classes on which the United States puts such faith carve out comfortable niches for themselves in the status quo rather than dedicate themselves to technological change. (In the early 1950's Brazilian universities turned out ten lawyers for every student of agriculture.) Private enterprise, as he sees it, finances extractive industries in which both the riches of the earth and the profits they produce wind up in someone else's country. In short, instead of the grim but improving picture of the Third World that hangs in the office of the National-Security Manager, the Revolutionary sees only accelerating misery.

He has some figures to support what he sees with his eyes. The World Conference on Trade and Development which met in Geneva in March, 1964, revealed that the share of the underdeveloped countries in world exports declined from almost one-third in 1950 to slightly more than one-fifth in 1962. At the same time, the prices of such primary products as coffee, cocoa, and tin, on which the economies of the underdeveloped world depend, have fallen drastically. Between 1959 and 1961 the price of coffee beans fell almost one-third. In 1965 Ghana could get only

371 dollars for a ton of cocoa. In 1954 the world price was 1,698 dollars. According to the United Nations Secretariat, these trends mean that by 1970 there will be an annual gap of twenty billion dollars a year between what the underdeveloped countries require merely to feed their expanding populations and what they can expect to earn from selling their products on the world market. To the Revolutionary the statistics of starvation are a cry for radical change.

The Revolutionary is a man who is passionately concerned with the degradation of his people and who believes that he understands its cause. For the National-Security Manager underdevelopment is a fact of the natural order. There are lucky nations and unlucky ones, energetic creative peoples, and peoples whom history has passed by. Stifling the Calvinist impulse to call wealth virtue, the American bureaucrat is convinced that the misery of the underdeveloped world is no one's fault except possibly its own. Perhaps they were exploited in the past by imperialist nations, but they received a little civilization in return. If they would work harder, spend the money they do get on the people rather than on bribes and showy buildings, try to keep appointments, and not make irresponsible statements, they would get along better.

To the Revolutionary the growing poverty and desperation of his people is not a natural calamity but the direct consequence of continuing human exploitation—external and internal. The rich nations are getting richer at the expense of the poor, not because history decrees it, but because the developed countries, particularly the United States, have the political power to impose terms upon the underdeveloped world which are profitable for the rich and impoverishing for the poor.

The Revolutionary is convinced that the very policies on which the United States banks its hopes of development actually destroy the possibilities of progress. He accuses the United States of using its foreign-aid funds to sponsor a small entrepreneurial elite who are able to pay for U.S.-manufactured imports, when, if it really wanted to encourage independent economies, it would finance local manufacturing facilities. (The trend is toward increased U.S. investment in factories, but local ownership is minimal.) The Revolutionary believes that his country is assigned a more or less permanent role in the world economy as the poor farmer and miner. Since the price of raw commodities can to a great extent be controlled by the powerful nations, this policy too ensures continued political dependence, with very little prospect of economic self-sufficiency. He is convinced that these policies are deliberate attempts to continue a pattern of exploitation. That the world's greatest capitalist nation should turn out to be the most imperialist merely confirms his deepest ideological prejudices. The performance of the United States at the World Conference on Trade and Development when it voted

—often alone among seventy-seven countries—against such propositions as "noninterference in the internal affairs of other countries," "the sovereign right freely to trade with other countries," and "to dispose of its natural resources in the interest of the economic development and well-being of its own people" provided additional evidence. The United States, he is convinced, has economic and political interests that are adverse to the political and economic independence of his country.

The Revolutionary ascribes the plight of his country not only to foreign enemies, of which the greatest is the United States, but also to local enemies, the handful of landowners who maintain a subsistence economy for the peasants and resist land reform, the businessmen who bank their profits abroad and block any increased political power or earning power for the worker, and the military. Every revolutionary movement spreads the myth that the removal of a man or a class is all that stands in the way of progress and justice. But the local targets are plausible enough. In Brazil about five percent of the population owns ninety-five percent of the cultivable land. In every other country in Latin America over fifty percent of the productive land is still in the hands of the top four percent of the population. The landowners resist land reform and are prepared to defend with the army and the police a land-tenure system surviving from the days of colonial land grants. Rebellious peasants, who have agitated for reform or have "squatted" on land, have, depending upon the character of the particular regime, been ignored, harassed, imprisoned, tortured, or murdered. "Each country is being occupied by its own army," the leader of the exiled Liberal party of Colombia declared in 1955. The Alliance for Progress, as President Kennedy put it, was to make the continent "a crucible of revolutionary ideas" and to "reverse the fatal policy of economic colonization, humiliation, and exploitation" which led to the Castro revolution. But the owners of the *latifundia* have shown themselves unwilling to give up their immense economic advantages voluntarily. Land-reform legislation has been adopted in several Latin-American countries, but where it has been implemented at all, it has not begun to touch the problem. Since only five percent of Latin America's land surface is actually cultivated, and all but a small fraction of the population depend on the land for survival—in Brazil forty million out of the seventy million population are outside the cash economy—in the Revolutionary's eyes the situation is clear. The physical survival of the poorest peasants demands a direct confrontation with the latifundists and the governments they control.

The concept of a revolution from above strikes him as a device for continuing the status quo, for in practice the burdens fall once again on the lowest classes. To accumulate capital necessary for an economic "takeoff," the government must be able to tax. But the landlord classes have been highly successful in resisting taxes in Asia, Africa, and Latin America. About three percent of the population pays taxes in Latin America and about one percent in Asia and Africa. So widespread is the refusal to pay that taxation produces only between five and ten percent of the Gross National Product in the Third World. As alternative sources of revenue, governments resort to indirect taxation and austerity programs, which depend upon wage freezes. The success of the rich in avoiding taxes goes a long way to explain why, in Brazil, for example, sixty-three percent of the income for 1957 went to seventeen percent of the population.

Thus the word "stability," which to the National-Security Manager evokes the image of a well-run town or a happy family, falls on the Revolutionary's ears like a death sentence. He is convinced that trying to work within the present political framework is hopeless, for the landowners and the generals who serve them will never voluntarily relax their grip on the scarce resources and undeveloped riches of their country.

The Revolutionary who becomes a guerrilla is a man who believes that all other avenues of political change are closed or the process of change is so controlled and slow as to be meaningless. Luis Taruc, the Philippine Huk leader, began a full-scale challenge of the government after he and other communists were denied the seats to parliament to which they had been legally elected. The Greek communists and members of the South Vietnamese National Liberation Front began terrorist activities when the constituted governments declared them ineligible to participate in the political process and hunted them down as outlaws. This is not to say that a revolutionary movement will not pursue a legal political struggle and a guerrilla war at the same time, if it can; but that violence, for the weak, is a weapon of last resort.

There is a strain in the revolutionary tradition that glorifies violence. In the nineteenth century some of the more romantic anarchists cherished the myth that a well-placed bomb could sweep away the tyrant and open the way to Utopia. In our day, Frantz Fanon, the West Indian psychiatrist who became an Algerian rebel, has struggled to shape an ideology of revolutionary violence. Acknowledging the fact that violence brings suffering to those who practice it, he declares that "decolonization is always a violent phenomenon." It is necessary for the Revolutionary, no matter how idealistic or civilized he is, to become a bomb-thrower and a sniper merely to defend himself against the state whose enemy he has become. The ruling elites will not give up their power and privilege without a fight.

But beyond these traditional explanations for the role of violence in revolution, Fanon offers another. The "wretched of the earth" cannot develop the sense of identity, self-esteem, and political consciousness necessary to challenge the established order without the therapeutic effect of violence. When an intimidated native discovers that the White Man dies when he is shot, he senses within himself a new power. Just as in the American West, the gun becomes "the great equalizer." Once having committed a violent act against the state, the rebel develops the confidence and the anger to repeat it. During the civil war following the Bolshevik Revolution, Lenin noted that those who served in the army became the most militant. Similarly, today the existential condition of becoming an outlaw with a price on his head turns a man into a political radical. A man may start fighting because of a local grievance. He may demand land. He may have been cheated by the authorities. Or he may become a guerrilla because of the vision of achieving national independence from a foreign nation. The commitment to violence, once made, binds him closer to the community of rebels, for he has burned the bridges back to his old life. The only emotional, political, and often financial support now open to him comes from his co-conspirators. Sharing moments of high danger for a great cause creates the intense feelings of camaraderie that warriors have always celebrated. Some professional revolutionaries, therefore, consciously use violence as a technique for whipping up their supporters and increasing their number.

But the Revolutionary uses violence primarily as a political weapon against his enemy, the state, and he uses the particular technique of violence out of necessity. He is not strong enough in the beginning to engage the armies of the state in open battle, nor does he have the political strength to execute a quick coup d'état, the most common and successful form of political violence. As Peter Paret and John Shy have pointed out in the *Marine Corps Gazette,* "Seldom if ever has anyone deliberately chosen a guerrilla strategy when other choices existed. If sufficient military strength is available, conventional organization and tactics produce a decision more quickly; if the goal is political, strength makes possible a coup d'état instead of a costly, protracted civil war."

The Revolutionary thus begins by using terrorism to make a political point. Harold Laswell has called political assassination "propaganda of the deed." He quotes the letter received by Lord Kimberly, the viceroy of Dublin. "My Lord, we intend to kill you at the corner of Kildare Street; but we would like you to know there is nothing personal in it." In the Huk rebellion, Taruc would arrange for a prominent citizen of a town to be murdered and his body displayed in the main street with a tag, "He resisted the Huks." The Vietcong assassinations in Vietnam, at least until the arrival of the American expeditionary force, were directed against the symbols of the state—teachers, village chiefs, and health officials. In many cases there *was* something personal behind it. The NFL often pinned a note to the shirt of a murdered official listing his crimes. It attempted to explain every killing.

Terror is sometimes used by guerrilla movements to encourage the cooperation of the surrounding population. In the official ideology of the National-Security Manager, this is a convenient explanation for the civilian support which guerrilla armies must have to survive. It disposes of the problem. Thus, according to Robert McNamara, guerrilla movements are gaining "for very simple reasons known as guns, bombs, fighters, and threats." But, as men who have been through a guerrilla war testify, terror has very definite limitations as a political instrument. Che Guevara, the theorist of the Cuban Revolution and adviser to many insurgent movements in Latin America, noted that terrorism "is a negative weapon which produces in no way the desired effects, which can turn a people against a given revolutionary movement. . . ." Actual enemies, particularly those who have defected, must be "justly punished," but supporters can be recruited only if they want to fight. An army that fights only out of fear of its own leaders cannot carry out a revolution.

For the Revolutionary, the ultimate and most important use of violence is to disrupt the power of the state, then to smash it. Mao Tse-tung and the more recent theorists of revolution insist that the revolutionary forces must eventually become an army capable of seizing the apparatus of the state. While the orthodox Marxist revolutionaries, including Mao, taught that the revolutionary army was an instrument of the political party, younger revolutionaries including Castro and Regis Debray now argue that the revolutionary army itself, the men who are daily risking their lives, is the nucleus of the revolutionary movement. "Who will make the revolution in Latin America?" Fidel Castro asks. "The people, the revolutionaries, with or without the party." For the modern generation of revolutionaries, violence has assumed the central role.

Fanon's encounters with patients who have committed acts of violence suggest that for the individual revolutionary, violence creates personal moral problems. At the ideological level, however, the Revolutionary disposes of the problem with the same psychological devices which the National-Security Manager uses to defend to himself and others his own use of violence. First, the violence is provoked. If the revolutionaries throw the first bomb, it must be understood as a reaction to the continuing institutionalized violence of the state. The authorities use the police and the army every day to keep the dispossessed peasant below the level of subsistence. His children starve. His crop is stolen. He is the victim of arbitrary arrest. Second, the people and not the authorities temporarily in control of the state have the legitimate claim to use violence. The state has forfeited it by becoming the private preserve of a small class. The National Front, the revolutionary coalition, represents popular aspirations, and the closest thing to a consensus in the society. Thus the revolutionaries lay claim to the basis of legitimacy for the use of political violence, which the state has lost through corruption or tyrannical behavior. If the revolutionaries look like bandits to the men in the palace, the high-living generals and politicians look like thieves and murderers to the men in the hills. Finally, the Revolutionary justifies violence with the familiar argument of expediency. It is a necessary means to a good end. Once the oppressors have been dislodged from power and the enemies of the revolution liquidated, then a good society free of terror and violence can come into being. If the state does not wither away, at least state repression will. In the end, liberation will mean that many violent deaths will have been avoided. Just as the National-Security Manager justifies the use of napalm, antipersonnel bombs, and crop destroyers as the necessary preparation for a peaceful society, so the Revolutionary shares the same guilt-assuaging illusion. Violence can be controlled. Once the objectives for which the killing is done are achieved, the killing will stop.

In the early 1950's Joseph McCarthy gained popularity (and notoriety) from his extravagant charges of communist influence in the government. The Wisconsin Senator did not create the anticommunist issue, but few people used it as effectively or ruthlessly. The following speech, given to a Republican Women's Club in Wheeling, West Virginia, catapulted him into the national headlines and provided an example of the kind of over-statement, innuendo, and guilt by association which McCarthy would regularly employ. McCarthy's charges against the State Department, though untrue, undoubtedly hampered foreign policy-making. They led to the dismissal of officials who favored detente or greater flexibility in foreign affairs and to the promotion of hardline anticommunist crusaders who tended to see world affairs in terms of conspiracies and simplistic categories. Until 1954, when the Senate reprimanded him, McCarthy and his followers increased Americans' fears of communist conspiracy and helped deepen the Cold War.

How did McCarthy characterize the upbringing of the people he claimed were supporting communism? Do you think this tactic contributed to or hurt McCarthy's popularity? What was McCarthy's opinion of Secretary of State Dean Acheson? After reading the past selection by Acheson, do you agree that he was "soft" on communism? How can you explain the fact that McCarthy could gain wide popularity for several years on the basis of unsubstantiated charges? In what way might government officials like Acheson, through their own statements about the communist menace, have contributed to McCarthyism?

Joseph McCarthy

Speech at Wheeling, West Virginia

Five years after a world war has been won, men's hearts should anticipate a long peace, and men's minds should be free from the heavy weight that comes with war. But this is not such a period—for this is not a period of peace. This is a time of the "cold war." This is a time when all the world is split into two vast, increasingly hostile armed camps—a time of a great armaments race. . . .

Today we are engaged in a final, all-out battle between communistic atheism and Christianity. The modern champions of communism have selected this as the time. And, ladies and gentlemen, the chips are down— they are truly down. . . .

Unless we face this fact, we shall pay the price that must be paid by those who wait too long.

Six years ago, at the time of the first conference to map out the peace— Dumbarton Oaks—there was within the Soviet orbit 180,000,000 people. Lined up on the antitotalitarian side there were in the world at that time roughly 1,625,000,000 people. Today, only 6 years later, there are 800,000,000 people under the absolute domination of Soviet Russia—an increase of over 400 percent. On our side, the figure has shrunk to around 500,000,000. In other words, in less than 6 years the odds have changed from 9 to 1 in our favor to 8 to 5 against us. This indicates the swiftness of the tempo of Communist victories and American defeats in the cold war. As one of our outstanding historical figures once said, "When a great democracy is destroyed, it will not be because of enemies from without, but rather because of enemies from within." . . .

The reason why we find ourselves in a position of impotency is not because our only powerful potential enemy has sent men to invade our shores, but rather because of the traitorous actions of those who have been treated so well by this Nation. It has not been the less fortunate or members of minority groups who have been selling this Nation out, but rather those who have had all the benefits that the wealthiest nation on earth has had to offer—the finest homes, the finest college education, and the finest jobs in Government we can give.

This is glaringly true in the State Department. There the bright young men who are born with silver spoons in their mouths are the ones who have been worst. . . .

When Chiang Kai-shek was fighting our war, the State Department had in China a young man named John S. Service. His task, obviously, was not to work for the communization of China. Strangely, however, he sent official reports back to the State Department urging that we torpedo our ally Chiang Kai-shek and stating, in effect, that communism was the best hope of China.

Later, this man—John Service—was picked up by the Federal Bureau of Investigation for turning over to the Communists secret State Depart-

Congressional Record, 81 Congress 2nd Session, 1954-1957.

ment information. Strangely, however, he was never prosecuted. However, Joseph Grew, the Under Secretary of State, who insisted on his prosecution, was forced to resign. Two days after Grew's successor, Dean Acheson, took over as Under Secretary of State, this man—John Service—who had been picked up by the FBI and who had previously urged that communism was the best hope of China, was not only reinstated in the State Department but promoted. And finally, under Acheson, placed in charge of all placements and promotions.

Today, ladies and gentlemen, this man Service is on his way to represent the State Department and Acheson in Calcutta—by far and away the most important listening post in the Far East. . . .

This, ladies and gentlemen, gives you somewhat of a picture of the type of individuals who have been helping to shape our foreign policy. In my opinion the State Department, which is one of the most important government departments, is thoroughly infested with Communists.

I have in my hand 57 cases of individuals who would appear to be either card carrying members or certainly loyal to the Communist Party, but who nevertheless are still helping to shape our foreign policy. . . .

I know that you are saying to yourself, "Well, why doesn't the Congress do something about it?" Actually, ladies and gentlemen, one of the important reasons for the graft, the corruption, the dishonesty, the disloyalty, the treason in high Government positions—one of the most important reasons why this continues is a lack of moral uprising on the part of the 140,000,000 American people. In the light of history, however, this is not hard to explain.

It is the result of an emotional hang-over and a temporary moral lapse which follows every war. It is the apathy to evil which people who have been subjected to the tremendous evils of war feel. As the people of the world see mass murder, the destruction of defenseless and innocent people, and all of the crime and lack of morals which go with war, they become numb and apathetic. It has always been thus after war.

However, the morals of our people have not been destroyed. They still exist. This cloak of numbness and apathy has only needed a spark to rekindle them. Happily, this spark has finally been supplied.

As you know, very recently the Secretary of State proclaimed his loyalty to a man guilty of what has always been considered as the most abominable of all crimes—of being a traitor to the people who gave him a position of great trust. The Secretary of State in attempting to justify his continued devotion to the man who sold out the Christian world to the atheistic world, referred to Christ's Sermon on the Mount as a justification and reason therefor, and the reaction of the American people to this would have made the heart of Abraham Lincoln happy.

When this pompous diplomat in striped pants, with a phony British accent, proclaimed to the American people that Christ on the Mount endorsed communism, high treason, and betrayal of a sacred trust, the blasphemy was so great that it awakened the dormant indignation of the American people.

He has lighted the spark which is resulting in a moral uprising and will end only when the whole sorry mess of twisted, warped thinkers are swept from the national scene so that we may have a new birth of national honesty and decency in government.

The anticommunist hysteria which Senator Joseph McCarthy rode to popularity in the early 1950's was a deadly serious matter to those whose lives were ruined by false charges or unfounded suspicion. The collection of government dossiers on private individuals and on government employees has likewise remained a subject of serious concern into the seventies. But satire has often proved an effective way of exposing injustice, and in this selection, former New Deal official Thurman Arnold employs wit against repression. In a light but earnest manner, Arnold attacks the kind of communist "witch-hunting" which grew so severe in the late 1940's and early 1950's.

Judging from McCarthy's speech, do you think that Arnold's "Ten Commandments" are exaggerated? Some people have claimed that the major danger of communism was that, in trying to fight it, Americans tended to become more like it. Do you agree? According to Thurman Arnold, how much freedom did a government employee have? How much should one have?

Thurman Arnold

How Not to Be Investigated

If you are planning at any future time to become a government employee, you would do well to obey the following Ten Commandments for Pure Conduct of Government Employees if you want to be safe. These commandments are in no way farcical or exaggerated. For in the effort to uncover the few men and women in government ranks whose loyalty is genuinely suspected, individual dossiers are now being collected on *all* federal employees—whether or not they work in areas of the government where secrets important to the national defense are guarded—and inevitably a large number of men and women are compelled to submit to formal hearings because of charges against them based on irrational gossip, hearsay, or rumor. As a lawyer practicing in Washington, I have come in contact with many government employees thus accused; and I can testify that each of the commandments set down here is based on actual cases either in my office or observed by me.

TEN COMMANDMENTS FOR PURE CONDUCT OF GOVERNMENT EMPLOYEES

1. Do not attend any social gathering, no matter how large, at which a "subversive" may also be present. This includes dances.

2. Never talk, even to your neighbors or at social gatherings, about controversial issues. If your views offend someone, they may show up in a report in a distorted fashion and you will never even know who gave the information.

3. Do not subscribe to the *New Republic* or the *Nation,* or any other liberal publication. Maybe it's communist and you don't know it. Don't read any books about Russia even out of curiosity, because you can never prove that it was only curiosity. You will be safer if you can honestly swear that you do not know where Russia is or what it is like.

4. If anyone sends you as a gift a publication of the sort described in the foregoing Commandment, cancel it at once, with an indignant letter. Otherwise it may be taken to mean you have communist friends.

5. Do not ever attend the large annual reception at the Russian Embassy. How can you prove that you merely wanted to see what the Russians look like and to eat caviar? I recently advised a friend of mine not to attend a party at the Polish consulate in New York City.

6. Do not contribute any money for the legal defense of some old acquaintance or college classmate charged with disloyalty, for even if he is found innocent, you may be charged because of your contribution.

7. Do not marry anyone who, however many years before, had radical associations in college. Avoid, if you can, marriage with anyone who has ever visited Russia, read Karl Marx, or contributed to war relief drives for the Spanish Loyalists.

8. Be particularly careful never to ride in an automobile in which a "subversive" may be another rider. The car pool is a favorite object of suspicion.

9. Do not yourself be unduly critical of Fascists or Nazis, and carefully avoid the company of those who have been outspoken on these subjects.

10. If any relative of yours, no matter how distant and no matter how much you disagree with him, has ever been a "radical," do not take a government position at all. The salary can't possibly be worth the effort it may take to defend yourself.

The conduct required by the above Commandments will not, by itself, keep you out of trouble. There are cases pending before loyalty boards in which, for example, a person is charged with an association which may lead to divulging secrets, where the alleged associate is dead; or where a person has been charged with activities sympathetic to communism in a certain year and in a certain city in which he never set foot in the year in question; or where a person is charged with desertion from the Army during World War I at a time when he was nine years old. So nothing will keep you entirely in the clear, but these Ten Commandments will help.

Such pressures paralyze independent thought and action in government today. Walter Lippmann may safely argue that owing to blunders in connection with the Berlin crisis, Russia today has much logic on her side and we must beat a diplomatic retreat. But if an employee of the State Department presented the same sort of a memorandum for consideration he would in my opinion be undergoing a serious risk. True, most of those charged in my Ten Commandment cases were cleared, but only after worry and strain exceedingly unpleasant for sensitive people.

Twelve million dollars is being spent on collecting gossip as to the thoughts, private lives, associations, reading, political opinion, and social views of government employees. Everyone expects sooner or later to be investigated. Given the assurance of secrecy and complete anonymity, your enemies may fill your file with gossip and innuendo. You will never see the evidence against you, or know who your accuser is. It will be your word against an unknown. If that unknown is believed, your job will be lost, your career ruined, and your chance of finding a good job elsewhere scant.

Most of the people charged can't afford a lawyer. Preparation of the cases is long and difficult, particularly because the charges are hopelessly vague. The hearings are long, the appeals endless. The result is humiliation and mental torture. The public and the press do not seem to care. They assume, as in all witch-hunts, that an accused employee must be guilty or he wouldn't be accused. And why should anybody object to proving his innocence?

This attack on government employees is a poor way of fighting a cold war against Russia, and as counterespionage it is sheer nonsense. Secret investigations of private lives, opinions, and associations, can never strengthen a democracy. Instead, they bleed it white of those corpuscles of independent thought which are essential to the character of democratic government. In independence of thought and action is the safety of our country. It is not difficult to drive such independence out of government.

True, not many are hit by the lightning that flashes over the heads of government servants today. But only the most hardy spirits can avoid fright from the thunder, and they are usually those who will not choose to serve a government that subjects them to wild suspicions. They are the kind who can get jobs elsewhere, and they are leaving. The trouble with government service is its tendency to develop a type usually called "bureaucrats." These are timid people, afraid to take a chance, relying on the most absurd technicalities because inaction is always safer than action. They want their pension at the end. Their chief purpose in life is not to do anything to disturb security. The Thomas Committee is turning the government over to that kind of bureaucrat.

In the sixteenth century, Elizabeth of England was conducting a cold war against Philip of Spain, not entirely unlike the cold war that Stalin is conducting against us. Elizabeth used every art of deception. Like Stalin, she was too weak to precipitate a war. She commissioned men like Drake and Hawkins to capture Philip's ships and sack his towns in the new world, all the while denying responsibility for these acts. Philip thought he knew the answer. The English were heretics. The real danger, therefore, was that heresy would sap the foundations of the Church that was the cornerstone of the Spanish way of life. And so when Elizabeth sank ships, Philip investigated heresy in Spain and burned Spaniards whose thoughts and associations were suspected. He succeeded in bleeding Spain white. He destroyed independence and initiative in his empire.

Today many Americans think that the same sort of purge, conducted of course on more civilized lines, is useful to protect our own government. And many others who consider such an undertaking suicidal nonsense are afraid to speak out lest they themselves be accused.

It might be well also to remember what our blind preoccupation with the problem of spies and internal sabotage at the expense of examination of the real danger cost us at Pearl Harbor. We had broken the Japanese code. We might have deduced from that information where the Japanese fleet was, and what it was doing. Instead, generals in the War Department cabled Kimmel and Short to take measures against internal sabotage. The planes at Pearl Harbor were bunched together in response to that fear. They never got off the ground. If we had given Japanese spies free passports they could not have served their country as well as did this obsession that the real danger was from within and not from without.

2

postwar america, 1945-1960

From World War II on, an ever closer connection developed between government funds and scientific advance. Scientist Vannevar Bush set forth the rationale for government spending to advance science in this 1945 Report to the President, *and his arguments contributed to creation of the National Science Foundation in 1950. Bush claimed that advancement of science would contribute to better health for Americans and serve as a stimulus to industrial growth and job expansion. He placed major emphasis on the need for continuous peacetime military research financed by the government, an idea which sharply departed from past American practice.*

Why did Bush advocate government-financed scientific research programs? How has the close connection between government and science and industry since World War II affected American life? What are the advantages and disadvantages of having research development funds come primarily from government, as opposed to private, sources?

Vannevar Bush

Science—The Endless Frontier

Science can be effective in the national welfare only as a member of a team, whether the conditions be peace or war. But without scientific progress no amount of achievement in other directions can insure our health, prosperity, and security as a nation in the modern world.

For the War Against Disease

We have taken great strides in the war against disease. The death rate for all diseases in the Army, including overseas forces, has been reduced from 14.1 per thousand in the last war to 0.6 per thousand in this war. In the last 40 years life expectancy has increased from 49 to 65 years, largely as a consequence of the reduction in the death rates of infants and children. But we are far from the goal. The annual deaths from one or two diseases far exceed the total number of American lives lost in battle during this war. A large fraction of these deaths in our civilian population cut short the useful lives of our citizens. Approximately 7,000,000 persons in the United States are mentally ill and their care costs the public over $175,000,000 a year. Clearly much illness remains for which adequate means of prevention and cure are not yet known.

The responsibility for basic research in medicine and the underlying sciences, so essential to progress in the war against disease, falls primarily upon the medical schools and universities. Yet we find that the traditional sources of support for medical research in the medical schools and universities, largely endowment income, foundation grants, and private donations, are diminishing and there is no immediate prospect of a change in this trend. Meanwhile, the cost of medical research has been rising. If we are to maintain the progress in medicine which has marked the last 25 years, the Government should extend financial support to basic medical research in the medical schools and in universities.

For Our National Security

The bitter and dangerous battle against the U-boat was a battle of scientific techniques—and our margin of success was dangerously small. The new eyes which radar has supplied can sometimes be blinded by new scientific developments. V-2 was countered only by capture of the launching sites.

We cannot again rely on our allies to hold off the enemy while we struggle to catch up. There must be more—and more adequate—military research in peacetime. It is essential that the civilian scientists continue in peacetime some portion of those contributions to national security which they have made so effectively during the war. This can best be

Vannevar Bush, *Science—The Endless Frontier: A Report to the President* (Washington, D.C., 1945), 1-30.

done through a civilian-controlled organization with close liaison with the Army and Navy, but with funds direct from Congress, and the clear power to initiate military research which will supplement and strengthen that carried on directly under the control of the Army and Navy.

And for the Public Welfare

One of our hopes is that after the war there will be full employment. To reach that goal the full creative and productive energies of the American people must be released. To create more jobs we must make new and better and cheaper products. We want plenty of new, vigorous enterprises. But new products and processes are not born fullgrown. They are founded on new principles and new conceptions which in turn result from basic scientific research. Basic scientific research is scientific capital. Moreover, we cannot any longer depend upon Europe as a major source of this scientific capital. Clearly, more and better scientific research is one essential to the achievement of our goal of full employment.

How do we increase this scientific capital? First, we must have plenty of men and women trained in science, for upon them depends both the creation of new knowledge and its application to practical purposes. Second, we must strengthen the centers of basic research which are principally the colleges, universities, and research institutes. These institutions provide the environment which is most conducive to the creation of new scientific knowledge and least under pressure for immediate, tangible results. With some notable exceptions, most research in industry and in Government involves application of existing scientific knowledge to practical problems. It is only the colleges, universities, and a few research institutes that devote most of their research efforts to expanding the frontiers of knowledge . . .

For science to serve as a powerful factor in our national welfare, applied research both in Government and in industry must be vigorous. To improve the quality of scientific research within the Government, steps should be taken to modify the procedures for recruiting, classifying, and compensating scientific personnel in order to reduce the present handicap of governmental scientific bureaus in competing with industry and the universities for top-grade scientific talent. To provide coordination of the common scientific activities of these governmental agencies as to policies and budgets, a permanent Science Advisory Board should be created to advise the executive and legislative branches of Government on these matters.

The most important ways in which the Government can promote industrial research are to increase the flow of new scientific knowledge through support of basic research, and to aid in the development of scientific talent. In addition, the Government should provide suitable incentives to industry to conduct research, (a) by clarification of present uncertainties in the Internal Revenue Code in regard to the deductibility of research and development expenditures as current charges against net income, and (b) by strengthening the patent system so as to eliminate uncertainties which now bear heavily on small industries and so as to prevent abuses which reflect discredit upon a basically sound system. In addition, ways should be found to cause the benefits of basic research to reach industries which do not now utilize new scientific knowledge.

WE MUST RENEW OUR SCIENTIFIC TALENT

The responsibility for the creation of new scientific knowledge—and for most of its application—rests on that small body of men and women who understand the fundamental laws of nature and are skilled in the techniques of scientific research. We shall have rapid or slow advance on any scientific frontier depending on the number of highly qualified and trained scientists exploring it.

The deficit of science and technology students who, but for the war, would have received bachelor's degrees is about 150,000. It is estimated that the deficit of those obtaining advanced degrees in these fields will amount in 1955 to about 17,000—for it takes at least 6 years from college entry to achieve a doctor's degree or its equivalent in science or engineering. The real ceiling on our productivity of new scientific knowledge and its application in the war against disease, and the development of new products and new industries, is the number of trained scientists available.

The training of a scientist is a long and expensive process. Studies clearly show that there are talented individuals in every part of the population, but with few exceptions, those without the means of buying higher education go without it. If ability, and not the circumstance of family fortune, determines who shall receive higher education in science, then we shall be assured of constantly improving quality at every level of scientific activity. The Government should provide a reasonable number of undergraduate scholarships and graduate fellowships in order to develop scientific talent in American youth. . . .

A PROGRAM FOR ACTION

. . . Therefore I recommend that a new agency for these purposes be established. Such an agency should be composed of persons of broad interest and experience, having an understanding of the peculiarities of scientific research and scientific education. It should have stability of funds so that long-range programs may be undertaken. It should recognize that freedom of inquiry must be preserved and should leave internal control of policy, personnel, and the method and scope of research to the institutions in which it is carried on. It should be fully responsible to the President and through him to the Congress for its program.

Early action on these recommendations is imperative if this nation is to meet the challenge of science in the crucial years ahead. On the wisdom with which we bring science to bear in the war against disease, in the creation of new industries, and in the strengthening of our Armed Forces depends in large measure our future as a nation. . . .

. . . Nowhere in the Governmental structure receiving its funds from Congress is there an agency adapted to supplementing the support of basic research in the universities, in both medicine and the natural sciences; adapted to supporting research on new weapons for both Services; or adapted to administering a program of science scholarships and fellowships.

A new agency should be established, therefore, by the Congress for the purpose. Such an agency, moreover, should be an independent agency devoted to the support of scientific research and the advanced scientific education alone. Industry learned many years ago that basic research cannot often be fruitfully conducted as an adjunct to or a subdivision of an operating agency or department. Operating agencies have immediate operating goals and are under constant pressure to produce in a tangible way, for that is the test of their value. None of these conditions is favorable to basic research. Research is the exploration of the unknown and is necessarily speculative. It is inhibited by conventional approaches, traditions, and standards. It cannot be satisfactorily conducted in an atmosphere where it is gauged and tested by operating or production standard. Basic scientific research should not, therefore, be placed under an operating agency whose paramount concern is anything other than research. Research will always suffer when put in competition with operations. The decision that there should be a new and independent agency was reached by each of the committees advising in these matters.

I am convinced that these new functions should be centered in one agency. Science is fundamentally a unitary thing. The number of independent agencies should be kept to a minimum. Much medical progress, for example, will come from fundamental advances in chemistry. Separation of the sciences in tight compartments, as would occur if more than one agency were involved, would retard and not advance scientific knowledge as a whole.

Five Fundamentals

There are certain basic principles which must underlie the program of Government support for scientific research and education if such support is to be effective and if it is to avoid impairing the very things we seek to foster. These principles are as follows:

1. Whatever the extent of support may be, there must be stability of funds over a period of years so that long-range programs may be undertaken.

2. The agency to administer such funds should be composed of citizens selected only on the basis of their interest in and capacity to promote the work of the agency. They should be persons of broad interest in and understanding of the peculiarities of scientific research and education.

3. The agency should promote research through contracts or grants to organizations outside the Federal Government. It should not operate any laboratories of its own.

4. Support of basic research in the public and private colleges, universities, and research institutes must leave the internal control of policy, personnel, and the method and scope of the research to the institutions themselves. This is of the utmost importance.

5. While assuring complete independence and freedom for the nature, scope, and methodology of research carried on in the institution receiving public funds, and while retaining discretion in the allocation of funds among such institutions, the Foundation proposed herein must be responsible to the President and the Congress. Only through such responsibility can we maintain the proper relationship between science and other aspects of a democratic system. The usual controls of audits, reports, budgeting, and the like, should, of course, apply to the administrative and fiscal operations of the Foundation, subject, however, to such adjustments in procedure as are necessary to meet the special requirements of research.

Basic research is a long-term process—it ceases to be basic if immediate results are expected on short-term support. Methods should therefore be found which will permit the agency to make commitments of funds from current appropriations for programs of five years duration or longer. Continuity and stability of the program and its support may be expected (a) from the growing realization by the Congress of the benefits to the public from scientific research, and, (*b*) from the conviction which will grow among those who conduct research under the auspices of the agency that good quality work will be followed by continuing support.

Military Research

As stated earlier in this report, military preparedness requires a permanent, independent, civilian-controlled organization, having close liaison with the Army and Navy, but with funds direct from Congress and the clear power to initiate research which will supplement and strengthen that carried on directly under the control of the Army and Navy. As a temporary measure the National Academy of Sciences has established the Research Board for National Security at the request of the Secretary of War and the Secretary of the Navy. This is highly desirable in order that there may be no interruption in the relations between scientists and military men after the emergency wartime Office of Scientific Research and Development goes out of existence. The Congress is now considering legislation to provide funds for the Board by direct appropriation.

I believe that, as a permanent measure, it would be appropriate to add to the agency those needed to perform the other functions recommended in this report such as the responsibilities for civilian-initiated and civilian-controlled military research. The function of such a civilian group would be primarily to conduct long-range scientific research on military problems—leaving to the Services research on the improvement of existing weapons.

Some research on military problems should be conducted, in time of peace as well as in war, by civilians independently of the military establishment. It is the primary responsibility of the Army and Navy to train the men, make available the weapons, and employ the strategy that will bring victory in combat. The Armed Services cannot be expected to be experts in all of the complicated fields which make it possible for a great nation to fight successfully in total war. There are certain kinds of research—such as research on the improvement of existing weapons—which can best be done within the military establishment. However, the job of long-range research involving application of the newest scientific discoveries to military needs should be the responsibility of those civilian scientists in the universities and in industry who are best trained to discharge it thoroughly and successfully. It is essential that both kinds of research go forward and that there be the closest liaison between the two groups.

Placing the civilian military research function in the proposed agency would bring it into close relationship with a broad program of basic research in both the natural sciences and medicine. A balance between military and other research could thus readily be maintained.

The establishment of the new agency, including a civilian military research group, should not be delayed by the existence of the Research Board for National Security, which is a temporary measure. Nor should the creation of the new agency be delayed by uncertainties in regard to the postwar organization of our military departments themselves. Clearly, the new agency, including a civilian military research group within it, can remain sufficiently flexible to adapt its operations to whatever may be the final organization of the military departments.

Leon H. Keyserling, a member of President Truman's Council of Economic Advisers, was an important advocate of governmental economic planning, and his view that Washington should make a major commitment to full employment became law in the Employment Act of 1946. Keyserling's propositions reflect many economists' postwar optimism, their faith that they could master the mysteries of the business cycle and prevent serious recessions. Keyserling held forth the promise of full employment without unmanageable inflation, a situation considered impossible by most other economic theorists. Judicious governmental policies, Keyserling believed, could eradicate America's "economic problem" and release its energies for other creative endeavors.

What role would be left to private enterprise in Keyserling's scheme? Why did he consider his ideas an alternative to communism or fascism? Why did Keyserling become a persistent critic of government economic policies as developed by both Republicans and Democrats after 1950?

Leon H. Keyserling

A Policy for Full Employment

In the employment act of 1946, the people of the United States pledged themselves to the objective of maintaining "maximum" employment, which for all practical purposes is the same as "full" employment. The Act was in essence much stronger than the original "Full Employment Bill." For while that bill concentrated mainly upon using one device (compensatory public spending), the final law provided that *all* the resources and policies available to a free people should be utilized in combination to promote "maximum employment, production, and purchasing power."

Today, when we are substantially short of a condition of full employment, it is more important to regain that condition than to dispose of all the tendentious arguments that stand in the way. But it is essential to dispose of the proposition advanced in some quarters that full employment is undesirable because it is "inflationary." The undesirable element in the inflationary prosperity of 1947-48 was not that employment and production were at very high levels; that was all to the good, as witness those who said that the cure for inflation was "still more production." The dangerous element was rather that a commendably high level of business activity, employment and production did not generate the kind of price-income and other economic relationships required to maintain these levels and lift them still higher from year to year with a growing labor force and improved industrial techniques.

Consequently, the full-employment period has been succeeded by a recession thus far of quite moderate proportions, but initiated, clearly, by an insufficiency of consumer demand relative to output at full employment. This has been coupled with some uncertainty in the business-investment outlook, primarily in response to a perception of insufficient demand. We are still vulnerable to the business cycle; and saying that full employment is "inflationary" is merely another way of noting a recent demonstration that American prosperity periods have had a way of generating their own undoing.

We should all admit that to achieve fairly continuous full employment we shall need much more knowledge, experience, effort and coöperation than we have thus far marshaled. But I believe that in setting so high a goal and striving to reach it, our analysis will be clearer, our policies sounder and our achievements greater than if we set our sights lower—even though we might fall somewhat short of the mark.

Besides, no lower goal is any safer or easier to attain. It is not really true that a downward "correction" every now and then leaves our economy in a healthier state, or that the valleys will not be so deep if the

Leon H. Keyserling, "A Policy for Full Employment." Reprinted by permission of *The New Republic,* © 1949, The New Republic, Inc., 13-15.

peaks are not so high, or that any economy with four million unemployed is "safer" or more "sustainable" than a full economy. For example, during the last year unemployment has increased by about 1.5 million and the industrial-production index has declined by about 10 percent. Has this downward "correction" made our economic problems less difficult? Has it become easier to manage the huge national debt, to achieve a budget surplus or to apply correct tax policies? Easier to execute our international programs? Will it be easier now to stimulate a high enough level of business investment and to avoid the undue "pessimism" which could exercise an unfavorable "psychological" influence, than it would have been a year ago to dampen the excessive ebullience? Is it going to be easier to reach a sound wage conclusion in the steel industry, or in other industries, than it would have been to reach sound price or wage adjustments a year or two ago? Have we any greater assurance now than a year ago that the current situation will generate patterns of investment, saving and spending, of prices and profits and wages and other incomes, which will carry production and employment further upward instead of downward?

If we recover from the recent setback without too much damage—which I expect we probably shall—it will not be because the setback proved to be a desirable and unavoidable corrective, any more than a man gets influenza because it is inevitable or recovers because the disease produces the cure. Complete recovery, if it comes quickly, will be because the scare has prompted us to make careful price-income adjustments where we were previously neglectful, or because our economic system is already braced with a variety of measures which make full employment harder to lose and easier to regain than in previous eras. Examples are farm-price supports, social-security cushions, improved banking and financial practices, sounder pricing and inventory policies on the part of business, and a wage structure less vulnerable to deflation. We are strong because of the portions of a full-employment program that we have already adopted, and not as strong as we should be because of the portions that we have thus far neglected to adopt.

We should not confuse the classical rationalization of *why* business recessions or depressions occur with the notion that they are helpful or unavoidable. If the current "process of adjustment" restores higher levels of employment and production even *without* price inflation, we shall still not be in a zone of safety. Prices were practically stable during the prosperity period of 1927-29, but that did not prevent what followed. *It is an axiom from experience that any level of business activity high enough to be called "prosperity" generates in the absence of an affirmative program the conditions which defeat stability.* And a return to reasonably full employment even if without inflationary price trends would face us again with the problem of its maintenance, perhaps in even more acute form than in the 1947-48 period. War-created supports for the economy are still massive, and it is when these begin to dwindle that we shall be confronted with a far greater problem than that of 1949.

In a democracy, we can make progress only by broadening the areas of general agreement; toward this end I suggest the following major elements in a full-employment policy.

First, the problem of maintaining full employment is neither insoluble nor beyond our organizational skills. Technically, our economic achievements in wartime were far more difficult. Those who say, "Oh, yes, but in wartime we did things that the people would not accept in peacetime," miss the point that a peacetime full-employment program, if undertaken before it is too late, would involve much more moderate measures. They also miss the equally important point that the most powerful democratic symbol of man's hope in the twentieth century—the United States—cannot afford to concede that under our institutions nothing but war can produce unity and purpose.

Second, while "forecasting" is useful, we have overdone attempting to forecast when or how a recession or a depression was coming, when and how much unemployment would increase, when and how much businessmen would start to cut down their investments. Instead, we should concentrate more attention upon what we *want* to have happen and utilize our resources toward that end.

Third, a full-employment program should look a few years ahead. True, emergency action has been inevitable when we have waited until crisis was upon us. But the economic situation now is comfortable enough to permit us to forge and apply longer-range policies. A family or business looks years ahead; the progress of a great nation is measured not in months but in decades.

Fourth, a full-employment program should be rounded, embracing a wide variety of measures in skillful combination. We should reject those panacea schools which, in accord with changing fashion, tell us at one time that the whole task can be accomplished through wage-price policy, at another time that the whole task can be accomplished through compensatory fiscal policy, and at still another time that the whole solution is to expand our foreign markets to help absorb our domestic "over-production."

Fifth, we should recognize that price-wage-profit policy in the private and voluntary sectors of the economy is of basic importance, because it most powerfully conditions the levels and trends of both production and consumption. We are moving, whether we like it or not, toward "patterns" of action in prices and wages. No field of action is more essential than the exploration of conference techniques whereby industry, labor, agriculture and government can together examine problems of prices and wages. This, of course, does not negate the need for minimum-wage legislation and other supplementary programs affecting the income structure.

Sixth, while general tax policy can be varied to "compensate" for minor ups and downs in private business activity, any effort to promote a stable and expanding economy through tax policy alone—on the ground that it is "simple"—would be only a grandiose illusion. We should aim toward a reasonably stable tax policy based upon careful analysis of its impact upon the investment and consumption patterns required for full employment while providing a surplus for debt retirement.

Seventh, we should guard against overemphasizing the idea that compensatory public spending can itself stabilize the economy, even if used on a grand scale. This device can achieve considerable stabilizing effect, and it should be used where needed. But the expansion of public spending in a serious depression, while necessary, could not alone restore full employment even if it were so extensive as to include projects of secondary long-range utility. Conversely, too severe limitation of public spending in times of full employment sacrifices national objectives which we should not forego merely because we are prosperous. More attention should be focused upon the relative utility of various types of public investment in stabilizing and encouraging private expansion. Moreover, the magnitudes of our resources development, educational and health activities, social security, etc., should be determined increasingly by the amounts that a stable and expanding economy can afford.

Eighth, neither private price-wage policy nor public policy can achieve maximum effectiveness unless set in the context of at least a few general goals for the economy at large. The surest way to evaluate price-profit policy, wage policy and government policy is by measuring each specific in terms of the investment and consumption requirements and the social desiderata relevant to a full economy. To give meaning and direction to President Truman's goal of a $300 billion economy within a very few years, it is necessary to contemplate these specific objectives:

First, the end objective of our economy is to improve standards of living and to spread these improvements more widely over the whole population. As one aspect of the goal of a $300 billion economy, we should inquire what minimum standard of living this implies for the industrious American family.

Second, we need to examine further what agricultural output, in the context of a $300 billion economy, will maintain and increase farm income, and furnish enough farm products both for industrial needs and for an adequate national diet.

Third, we need to appraise the capital requirements and incentives for the amount of expansion in our basic industries, and in our transportation systems, that will support and nourish a $300 billion economy.

Fourth, we need further to integrate our foreign economic policy with our domestic economic policy so that each complements the other at expanding levels of output and income.

The underscoring of these basic elements in the effort to achieve a $300 billion economy should not be misinterpreted to imply vast new efforts in central planning or direction from the top. We have long been wrestling with these problems (and others) in isolation. But better perception of the relationship of each of them to the general purpose of a steadily expanding economy will bring to our farm policy, our fiscal policy, our wage-price policy—to mention a few of many—a keener perception of their significance and a better judgment of their consequences. Such unified consideration of our fundamental situation will give all of us a better understanding of our common aims and special group problems.

The challenge we now face is less how to avert a depression than how affirmatively to advance prosperity. This poses a great moral test, because it is not so difficult to act in the face of a disaster as it is to reach out for higher goals when the going is not particularly bad. Yet the latter obligation is forced upon us by the imperatives of the world situation and by the needs and desires of our own people. We can afford to do no less than our best, and if we do our best the next decade can witness the virtual liquidation of the "economic problem" in America, and the turning of more of our energies to those attributes of civilization for which material sufficiency is only the foundation.

After World War II Senator Robert A. Taft of Ohio gained the title "Mr. Republican." Son of a former president and doyen of middle western conservatism, Taft became one of the most respected critics of liberal Democratic proposals, such as those offered by Leon Keyserling. Taft made several unsuccessful attempts to secure the Republican nomination for president; in his last try in 1952 he lost out to General Dwight D. Eisenhower, a political newcomer who enjoyed the backing of the more "liberal" eastern wing of the GOP. Nevertheless, Taft campaigned vigorously for the Eisenhower-Nixon ticket, and in this 1952 speech he still linked the Republican party to his own conservative view of national political issues.

Why, according to Taft, was "liberty" versus "socialism" the major issue of the 1952 campaign? How does he define "liberty?" "socialism?" Would liberal Democrats such as Leon Keyserling have agreed with Taft's definitions? What social and economic groups would stand to benefit from implementation of Taft's views? What groups would stand to lose?

Robert A. Taft

Restore Government
Based on American Principles

During this campaign I expect to speak on all the issues—corruption and degradation in Washington, Communist influences in the State Department, the surrender of China to the Communists, the Korean war and Acheson foreign policy.

But to my mind there is one great fundamental issue before the American people in this election of 1952. It is the resumption and continuation of progress under a free American way of life, as opposed to the alleged advances to be obtained by surrendering our money and our freedom to the tender mercies of an all-powerful and arbitrary government.

Socialism is a relative term, but if and when Government power threatens to direct all the lives of its people and absorb the greater part of the activities of the nation, it is fair to say that socialization reaches the goal of socialism itself. Basically the issue is one of liberty against socialism and we must decide it in 1952. This nation was conceived in liberty. Liberty has been the basis of its tremendous progress in the past. It is the cause of the great production and productivity per worker which have made us the greatest country in the history of the world and given our people the highest standards of living.

There is no reason why that progress should not continue to heights undreamed of today, but only if we follow the same principles and the same kind of Government which we have enjoyed during the past 165 years. There is no assurance that progress can continue if we turn from American principles to adopt the European philosophy of today that only more Government operation and control can improve the condition of the people.

Today we are at the crossroads because our liberty is threatened by big government, government which has already grown in spending power to a point where it threatens to dominate the lives of all of us. The New Deal-Fair Deal is the party of big government.

14 YEARS IN WASHINGTON

I have spent fourteen years in Washington and have fought against that steady growth. Congress has blocked much of it, but it has reached a point where it can go no farther without destroying for all practical purposes our individual freedom and the whole strength of our free economy.

The thousands of influential men who make up the Fair Deal Administration built up during these past twenty years are bound to dominate the thinking of Governor Stevenson [Adlai Stevenson, the Democratic candidate for president in 1952], or any other man suddenly brought in

Robert A. Taft, "Restore Government Based on American Principles," *Vital Speeches of the Day*, Vol. 18, October 1, 1952, 743-746.

to head the Government, unless he has a free hand to clean up the mess, as no one elected by the Democratic organization can have.

No one man today can know more than a small part of what goes on in hundreds of bureaus. One Government project after another is presented in attractive guise and with the claim that is only a slight change or improvement in our present system.

We in Congress have learned to be constantly on our guard; and yet we are often fooled on minor proposals. Every department in Washington is dominated by the philosophy of Government spending and increased Government power.

We have succeeded in blocking many attempts to increase this power, but in the field of spending Congress has been exceedingly ineffective, until through lavish spending out of the Treasury, every one of you feels the power of the bureaucracy on the banks of the Potomac.

The increase of Government can be best judged by the percentage of the people's income taken by Government for its activities. Twenty years ago the last Republican Administration took 6 per cent of the people's income for the Federal Government. Today Mr. Truman is taking 25 per cent to which must be added about 8 per cent for state and local government, or a total burden of 33 per cent.

An attempt is made to impose this tax burden with special force on corporations and on the wealthy, but this effort can only be partially successful. It is fair to say that the average workman in this country today pays to Government directly and indirectly 25 per cent of his income.

Our Democratic friends like to ask the question, has your liberty been reduced? Apart from all kinds of business and farm and labor regulations, apart from the drafting of yourself or your sons for two years' military service in Korea or Germany, you are losing at least a fourth of your liberty because you have lost the right to spend a fourth of the money which you have earned by the sweat of your brow.

The Government takes your earnings and decides for you how that money shall be spent—for services you probably will not receive and for services which you may not desire.

After all, what is liberty? I never have liked the term "free enterprise" because it seems to refer only to business liberty and we are interested in something much broader than that.

LIBERTY DEFINED

Liberty is the right of man to live his own life and choose his own job; the right of every family to spend its earnings on those things which it desires and not have them spent for it by a benevolent government;

liberty of the farmer to run his own farm; liberty of the workman to work at his chosen occupation in life; liberty of speech and of the press; liberty to express ideas and to have those ideas taught if anyone is interested enough to teach them; liberty of every community to decide how its children shall be educated and its health and welfare activities and local government be conducted; liberty of the business man to run his own business the way he thinks it ought to be run without interference and limitation by Government, or discouragement by excessive taxes.

It is this general liberty which has given the reward and incentive to men to spend their own time and their own money on new ideas—new ideas in education, in science and in industry.

In particular, the free competition of new ideas and new methods and new products has steadily increased the productivity of the American workman until today he makes two-and-a-half times as much product on the average as the British workman, who is probably better than most others in the world.

We produce more per person, not only in the factory but on the farm and so there is more to divide up per person. Therefore, the American standard of living is about two-and-a-half times that of the British—better homes, more home equipment, more automobiles, radios, television, better education, better recreation and more of all the things that make life worth while.

This steady gain hasn't happened in the last twenty years either. It has been a steady progress since this country was founded. In fact, the increase in the standard of living of Americans for the fifty years from 1869 to 1919 was about 150 per cent, or 3 per cent a year, while the increase in the twenty years from 1929 to 1949 was 50 per cent, or 2½ per cent a year on the average.

In the last two years, there has been a general decrease in the standard of living and quite a deficit in most family budgets. Real wages in industry have been practically stationary during these two years and the steady increase in taxes has reduced the take-home pay to a point where most families are worse off than they were before the Korean war.

But the industrial workman is comparatively well off because his unions have done their best to increase their wage rates in accord with the cost of living. Millions of other workers have had no increase in wage rates and have had to pay more for all the necessities of life. Millions of families living on their savings or fixed allowances are much worse off than they were two years ago.

Some of the increase in taxes from big government appears in direct reductions from take-home pay and income tax payments, but even more in the increased prices on every article, food, clothing, furnishings that you buy at the stores. Excise taxes admittedly are passed on to the consumer.

Generally speaking, corporation taxes and even individual income taxes get into the cost of production and are reflected in the prices that you pay. When the Government fails to balance the budget as last year and this year, prices are further increased by inflation. Some taxes are passed back from the central market to the farmer, so that he gets less for produce than he sells.

Once taxes get to a point where they are really burdensome, they become inflationary.

The prosperity of which the Democrats boast is a false illusion. Whatever increased wages you get you pay out in higher prices. Inflation if long continued means first a boom and then a bust.

High taxes also block the progress we have made in new jobs and more efficient production. Today they are so high it is almost impossible to start a new business. Only the big companies can get the capital to expand further and thus they acquire a more and more dominating influence in the industrial field.

We have always progressed in the past because men with new ideas, new products, new methods had an incentive to start their own little business and then build it up from their own earnings. That is the way most of the big companies began.

Today the whole process is choked down by the tremendous tax on earnings which used to be plowed back into the business. I doubt if Henry Ford could ever have developed his new ideas of high wages and cheap automobiles under our present system of tax laws.

When I was young, young couples were able to save to protect their families in their old age. Today I know very few people, young or old, who don't have to spend every cent of their income to support and educate their children. Big government is not only destroying liberty, but also self-reliance and initiative.

General Eisenhower has spoken unequivocally of his determination to reduce drastically the over-all expenses of the Government. Mr. Truman proposed to spend $85,000,000,000 in this fiscal year and $85,000,000,000 next year. The only reason he isn't doing it is because his organization is so inefficient it can't manage to get it spent.

General Eisenhower's goal is $70,000,000,000 next year and $60,-000,000 in the fiscal year of 1955.

Certainly no one knows as well as he how the tremendous expenditures for armament can be cut. His organizing ability was proved in Europe during the war and in his NATO command. We have just had one example of unnecessary expense from the report of the Democratic subcommittee of the Senate Committee on Armed Services which vividly portrays the tremendous waste and corruption in the building of military airports in Morocco. A reduction of Government expense to $60,-000,000 in fiscal 1955 would mean a tax reduction of 13 per cent in 1954.

THREATS CITED

Our freedom is threatened not only by spending and the power which it gives, but by the increased power directly sought in project after project designed to carry out the economic plans of the long-haired brain trusters.

Economic planning itself may show us the goals we are trying to reach. But the New Deal or the Fair Deal or the Stevenson Deal is imbued with the thought that the goals of such plans can only be reached by Government control, regulations and direction. Their only remedy for every problem is to create a new Federal bureau and give it unlimited power and money to find a solution. . . .

In business, the Philosophy of the New Deal calls for the fixing of prices and wages and the allocation of materials, under O. P. A. or O. P. S. Except in the greatest emergency, Government control in this field not only interferes with liberty, but it is ultimately without effect, or even defeats its own purposes.

The philosophy of the New Deal has threatened to take over the whole welfare field from state and local control. In the last fifty years we have steadily improved our handling of welfare matters—education, welfare, health and social relief, but these improvements have been primarily made by the communities themselves.

These are the fields in which each community should determine exactly what it wishes and certainly should have full control of every program. The place of the Federal Government is one of research, advice, and assistance where that assistance is vitally needed to achieve adequate service.

Unfortunately, the men who run the bureaus in Washington have been determined to Federalize these services. This is the basis of the national health insurance program repeatedly recommended by President Truman and ambiguously endorsed by Governor Stevenson. . . .

In my opinion, we cannot have freedom in a country the size of the United States unless we do maintain in all possible strength the power of communities to decide their own affairs to the extent of their ability.

No Federal bureau is responsive to public opinion; nor is it able to adjust its global plans to the needs of each special locality. It is necessarily arbitrary and tyrannical in its dealings with millions of unfortunate families who may need these services.

This same philosophy of Federal power does not stop today at constitutional restraint. President Truman seized the steel mills without statutory authority, and fortunately was rebuked by the Supreme Court. He and Secretary Acheson assert the right to send American troops to any point in the world, even though it involves us necessarily in war, though the Constitution says that only Congress can declare war.

The only reason that we have any real liberty left in the United States is the independence of Congress shown during the past fourteen years. There isn't any doubt in my mind that we have represented the attitude of the people of this country against a Government-planned economy, power and bureaucracy.

It is said that Governor Stevenson is a nice guy and wouldn't think of violating anybody's rights. I can tell you that if he is elected on the Democratic ticket with the support of the same people who supported President Truman, he is going to be engulfed in the same totalitarian philosophy that dominates four-fifths of those who are influential in the present Administration.

He cannot clean up the mess of false philosophy of spending and power any more then he can clean up the mess of corruption. He is a captive candidate. He would be a captive President.

General Eisenhower has stated without qualification his belief in the philosophy of liberty. He stated it long before I met him last week, and only reaffirmed at that time what he has frequently said in the past. He believes strongly in our system of constitutional limitations and Government power.

He abhors the left wing theory that the Executive has unlimited powers. There is only one way to change the philosophy of Government spending and power, and that is to elect General Eisenhower and let him create a new administration, with new faces and new thought.

Governor Stevenson apparently is disappointed to find that General Eisenhower and I agree that liberty is the basis of all future progress, that there isn't any basic difference in the Republican party on that belief, and that government spending and power must be reduced. . . .

The Republican party is a party of progress. It rejects the whole theory of socialism and big government as reactionary and destructive of human liberty. It proposes to resume progress, stimulated and assisted by Government, without Government control and regulation. It promises to reduce expenses and to cut taxes.

Robert Taft saw a clear ideological cleavage between the two national parties and claimed that the election of Dwight Eisenhower would advance basic Republican principles. Compare Taft's analysis of the issues during the early 1950's to the following interpretation by political analyst Samuel Lubell. Writing in 1956, Lubell sought to explain President Eisenhower's popularity and the Republicans' political resurgence. Resisting the temptation to stress Eisenhower's personal popularity to the exclusion of other factors, Lubell tried to frame a broader explanation for the political climate of the 1950's.

Where, according to Lubell, was the best place to seek the "true" meaning of national politics during the early 1950's? Are there problems with such a perspective? How accurate was Lubell's assessment of the future course of national politics?

Samuel Lubell

The Revolt of the Moderates

Rarely in American history has the craving for tranquility and moderation commanded more general public support. In foreign affairs the gossipy myth that ours is a mercurial, impatient temperament has been belied by how steadfastly we have plugged away at the role of global philanthropic policeman, trying now with dollars and now with guns to stabilize governments in lands many of us could not locate on a map.

At home, the New Deal generation, once so zealous to make America over, devotes its evenings to wrestling with mortgage payments and inculcating a respect for tradition and discipline in overly progressive children.

Even among the "younger" generation there is hardly a flutter of iconoclastic revolt. No collegians are swallowing goldfish or eating phonograph records; marriage has become a campus vogue, while the boldest collegiate exhibitionists can conceive of little that is more daring than growing a beard. Not too long ago a friend was interviewing a college graduate for a prospective job. Asked the youthful graduate in his first question, "What kind of pension plan does your company have?"

Why then, if this yearning for conservatism seems virtually unchallenged in the country, is it proving so difficult to give it effective reality?

Part of the answer is that intellectually all of us believe in ghosts, that our minds cling tenaciously to symbols forged by a past that is dead. Our political parties, in particular, are like haunted houses. To the extent that they have meaning to the voters it is mainly in terms of the animosities and loyalties, the medals and scars, of the political wars of Franklin D. Roosevelt. Yet the election returns show that neither the Democrats nor the Republicans can sustain a clean-cut majority in the country in terms of these ghostly mementos.

Before a decisive majority can be brought into being one—or both—of the major parties must come to mean something different from what it stood for during the age of Roosevelt.

Partly because of the illusion that conservatism and wealth are synonymous, many people still picture the politics of our time as a clash between "right" and "left." But the truly crucial struggle is being waged between the past and the future, between those who would continue to fight the battles of the 1920's and 1930's and those who would empty the parties of their old symbolism so they can meet the issues of what President Eisenhower once termed "not a moment but an age of danger."

Still, if the stakes were little more than party supremacy, the striving for conservatism could hardly be considered an epochal affair. The current state of American politics could then be summarized as a race between the two parties as to which can free itself first of the dividing distrusts of the Roosevelt period.

Samuel Lubell, *The Revolt of the Moderates,* Harper & Row Publishing Co., 1956, 4-7, 119-120.

In this race the role assigned Eisenhower was that of a substitute for the realignment the parties have not been able to manage. His has been the mediating task of transition, reflecting the fact that the balance of political power rests with those moderate voting elements who are in restless revolt against both parties.

But what lifts this "revolt of the moderates" to world-shaping importance is the fact that the contest for domestic political power is being fought against the backdrop of a world in upheaval. The effort to re-fashion a new political majority at home comes at the same time that the United States, no longer able to wield a free hand in foreign affairs, has been striving to build a coalition of peace and order abroad. Only too often and too violently do the needs of these two coalitions clash.

When Eisenhower was inaugurated some commentators referred to him as "the President of the free world," without perhaps realizing the full implications of the phrase. The test that must be applied to the Eisenhower administration is its success—or failure—in striking a double balance, both at home and abroad.

Examined by this standard, the drama of the Eisenhower Presidency becomes transformed. Its true hero has been not the man in the White House but the American people. As this struggle to reconcile the needs of domestic and world balance has unfolded, it has become a testing of the entire American nation, at perhaps the most critical juncture in its history.

This was true even before Eisenhower's illness. The heart attack he suffered in Denver was but a reminder of what we should have known, that in any circumstances it is the American people who will have to finish what President Eisenhower started . . . the essential quality of his leadership has lain in the skill and faithfulness with which he has followed the public temper. Throughout his Presidency, Eisenhower has been the understudy for the people themselves. . . .

What the decisive margin of voters wanted was clear enough. They wanted to stay squarely in the "middle," avoiding depression and war, deflation and inflation, too much or too little government, too heavy a preponderance of influence for either business or labor.

This, of course, adds up to the same goal of "moderate government" which Eisenhower professed during the 1954 campaign. But where Eisen-however sought to convince the public that moderation could best be attained through the Republican party, the people preferred to seek it by using each party as a check upon the other.

Near McLeansboro, in southern Illinois, to give one example, Carroll Phillips, who combines preaching in a Baptist church with farming, felt Eisenhower was doing a "fine job" and deserved re-election. But when I asked about Eisenhower's campaign arguments that a President should have a Congress of the same party, Phillips replied, "It's better to have it split up so neither party has too much say."

This widespread distrust of both parties, I suspect, explains why so many people have talked of Eisenhower as being "above both parties," despite his strenuous activity on behalf of the G.O.P. It is not that the people are being fooled but that they want a President before whom they can deposit their mistrusts of both parties.

That this feeling does not reflect Eisenhower's personal charm is indicated by the popularity of many other politicians who are "liberal" on some issues and "conservative" on others, like Senators Paul Douglas, Stuart Symington, Irving Ives or Governor Frank Lausche. Through such "hybrid" candidates the voters pick what they like about both parties.

Since 1954 this desire for two evenly balanced parties has grown stronger in the farm belt, as will be seen in a later chapter. In the urban areas the conservative yearning to "hold on to what we have" can be expected to help the party in power as long as economic conditions are good. Still, booming prosperity does not seem to have overcome the desire to hedge one's fears of the uncertain future by balancing one party against the other.

This mistrust of both parties helps explain why the realignment now under way differs so markedly from that which followed Roosevelt's rise to power.

The reshuffling of party loyalties precipitated by the New Deal was a mass affair, with whole groups of voters swinging virtually en masse. Basically this was made possible by the fact that when Roosevelt came into office he quickly transformed what the Democratic party meant to people.

Negroes, for example, had remained loyal to the party of Abraham Lincoln in 1932, despite all their depression hardships. By 1936, however, they had swung with equal solidarity to the party which had introduced WPA and given every Negro a minimum standard below which his wages could not be cut since he could then go on relief.

Similarly, the bulk of workers, who had never felt there was too much choice between the parties during the 1920's, marched virtually as a bloc into what many termed the new "labor party."

In contrast the Republican gains of recent years have come through a shifting of individuals, not groups. At every income level and among all social classes one finds some families who have turned Republican, but there has not yet been any dramatic conversion of whole blocs of voters.

This slow tempo of realignment can be attributed largely to the curious paradox that both the voters and the country have changed so much more than have the symbols attached to the parties.

To sum up, the usual agitation for a "real two-party politics" has come from those who wanted to draw a sharp line of cleavage which would force all "conservatives" into one party and all "liberals" into the other. But the reappearance of a two-party politics at this perilous point in our history has virtually nothing in common with any such motive. Instead of seeking to sharpen the party cleavage, it is aimed at moderating both parties and using them to preserve the gains of the last two decades.

What has happened, in short, is that the moderate elements, by refusing to cast their lot with either party, have forced both the Democrats and Republicans to turn their backs on the extremists in their ranks and to fight for the middle ground where the balance of victory lies.

To the many Americans who experienced rising incomes and favorable job opportunities during the 1950's, poverty seemed to be a thing of the past. According to socialist Michael Harrington, however, a "new poverty" had developed—one which was easily overlooked because it was nearly invisible. Harrington's influential study of this "hard core" poverty, which persisted generation after generation in certain segments of the population, became the rallying point for antipoverty activists during the 1960's. It also provided an intellectual foundation for Lyndon Johnson's Great Society Programs, the ambitious governmental effort to break through the so-called culture of poverty.

What was the "new poverty" and how did it differ from the old? Who did Harrington believe were the victims of the "new poverty"? Why was Harrington's book so influential? Did it stimulate much meaningful change? Does Harrington see poverty primarily as an economic or a cultural problem?

Michael Harrington

The Other America

Out of the thirties came the welfare state. Its creation had been stimulated by mass impoverishment and misery, yet it helped the poor least of all. Laws like unemployment compensation, the Wagner Act, the various farm programs, all these were designed for the middle third in the cities, for the organized workers, and for the upper third in the country, for the big market farmers. If a man works in an extremely low paying job, he may not even be covered by social security or other welfare programs. If he receives unemployment compensation, the payment is scaled down according to his low earnings.

One of the major laws that was designed to cover everyone, rich and poor, was social security. But even here the other Americans suffered discrimination. Over the years social security payments have not even provided a subsistence level of life. The middle third have been able to supplement the Federal pension through private plans negotiated by unions, through joining medical insurance schemes like Blue Cross, and so on. The poor have not been able to do so. They lead a bitter life, and then have to pay for that fact in old age.

Indeed, the paradox that the welfare state benefits those least who need help most is but a single instance of a persistent irony in the other America. Even when the money finally trickles down, even when a school is built in a poor neighborhood, for instance, the poor are still deprived. Their entire environment, their life, their values, do not prepare them to take advantage of the new opportunity. The parents are anxious for the children to go to work; the pupils are pent up, waiting for the moment when their education has complied with the law.

Today's poor, in short, missed the political and social gains of the thirties. They are, as Galbraith rightly points out, the first minority poor in history, the first poor not to be seen, the first poor whom the politicians could leave alone.

The first step toward the new poverty was taken when millions of people proved immune to progress. When that happened, the failure was not individual and personal, but a social product. But once the historic accident takes place, it begins to become a personal fate.

The new poor of the other America saw the rest of society move ahead. They went on living in depressed areas, and often they tended to become depressed human beings. In some of the West Virginia towns, for instance, an entire community will become shabby and defeated. The young and the adventurous go to the city, leaving behind those who cannot move and those who lack the will to do so. The entire area becomes permeated with failure, and that is one more reason the big corporations shy away.

Indeed, one of the most important things about the new poverty is that it cannot be defined in simple, statistical terms. Throughout this

Abridged with permission of Macmillan Publishing Co., Inc., from *The Other America* by Michael Harrington. Copyright © Michael Harrington, 1962, 1969, 9-26.

book a crucial term is used: aspiration. If a group has internal vitality, a will—if it has aspiration—it may live in dilapidated housing, it may eat an inadequate diet, and it may suffer poverty, but it is not impoverished. So it was in those ethnic slums of the immigrants that played such a dramatic role in the unfolding of the American dream. The people found themselves in slums, but they were not slum dwellers.

But the new poverty is constructed so as to destroy aspiration; it is a system designed to be impervious to hope. The other America does not contain the adventurous seeking a new life and land. It is populated by the failures, by those driven from the land and bewildered by the city, by old people suddenly confronted with the torments of loneliness and poverty, and by minorities facing a wall of prejudice. . . .

One might summarize the newness of contemporary poverty by saying: These are the people who are immune to progress. But then the facts are even more cruel. The other Americans are the victims of the very inventions and machines that have provided a higher living standard for the rest of the society. They are upside-down in the economy, and for them greater productivity often means worse jobs; agricultural advance becomes hunger.

In the optimistic theory, technology is an undisguised blessing. A general increase in productivity, the argument goes, generates a higher standard of living for the whole people. And indeed, this has been true for the middle and upper thirds of American society, the people who made such striking gains in the last two decades. It tends to overstate the automatic character of the process, to omit the role of human struggle. (The CIO was organized by men in conflict, not by economic trends.) Yet it states a certain truth—for those who are lucky enough to participate in it.

But the poor, if they were given to theory, might argue the exact opposite. They might say: Progress is misery.

As the society became more technological, more skilled, those who learn to work the machines, who get the expanding education, move up. Those who miss out at the very start find themselves at a new disadvantage. A generation ago in American life, the majority of the working people did not have high-school educations. But at that time industry was organized on a lower level of skill and competence. And there was a sort of continuum in the shop: the youth who left school at sixteen could begin as a laborer, and gradually pick up skill as he went along.

Today the situation is quite different. The good jobs require much more academic preparation, much more skill from the very outset. Those who lack a high-school education tend to be condemned to the economic underworld—to low-paying service industries, to backward factories, to sweeping and janitorial duties. If the fathers and mothers of the contemporary poor were penalized a generation ago for their lack of schooling, their children will suffer all the more. The very rise in productivity that created more money and better working conditions for the rest of the society can be a menace to the poor. . . .

Poverty in the 1960's is invisible and it is new, and both these factors make it more tenacious. It is more isolated and politically powerless than ever before. It is laced with ironies, not the least of which is that many of the poor view progress upside-down, as a menace and a threat to their lives. And if the nation does not measure up to the challenge of automation, poverty in the 1960's might be on the increase.

There are mighty historical and economic forces that keep the poor down; and there are human beings who help out in this grim business, many of them unwittingly. There are sociological and political reasons why poverty is not seen; and there are misconceptions and prejudices that literally blind the eyes. The latter must be understood if anyone is to make the necessary act of intellect and will so that the poor can be noticed.

Here is the most familiar version of social blindness: "The poor are that way because they are afraid of work. And anyway they all have big cars. If they were like me (or my father or my grandfather), they could pay their own way. But they prefer to live on the dole and cheat the taxpayers."

This theory, usually thought of as a virtuous and moral statement, is one of the means of making it impossible for the poor ever to pay their way. There are, one must assume, citizens of the other America who choose impoverishment out of fear of work (though, writing it down, I really do not believe it). But the real explanation of why the poor are where they are is that they made the mistake of being born to the wrong parents, in the wrong section of the country, in the wrong industry, or in the wrong racial or ethnic group. Once that mistake has been made, they could have been paragons of will and morality, but most of them would have never even have had a chance to get out of the other America.

There are two important ways of saying this: The poor are caught in a vicious circle; or, The poor live in a culture of poverty.

In a sense, one might define the contemporary poor in the United States as those who, for reasons beyond their control, cannot help themselves. All the most decisive factors making for opportunity and advance are against them. They are born going downward, and most of them stay down. They are victims whose lives are endlessly blown round and round the other America.

Here is one of the most familiar forms of the vicious circle of poverty. The poor get sick more than anyone else in the society. That is because they live in slums, jammed together under unhygienic conditions; they have inadequate diets, and cannot get decent medical care. When they become sick, they are sick longer than any other group in the society. Because they are sick more often and longer than anyone else, they lose wages and work, and find it difficult to hold a steady job. And because of this, they cannot pay for good housing, for a nutritious diet, for doctors. At any given point in the circle, particularly when there is a major illness, their prospect is to move to an even lower level and to begin the cycle, round and round, toward even more suffering.

This is only one example of the vicious circle. Each group in the other America has its own particular version of the experience, and these will be detailed throughout this book. But the pattern, whatever its variations, is basic to the other America.

The individual cannot usually break out of this vicious circle. Neither can the group, for it lacks the social energy and political strength to turn its misery into a cause. Only the larger society, with its help and resources, can really make it possible for these people to help themselves. Yet those who could make the difference too often refuse to act because of their ignorant, smug moralisms. They view the effects of poverty—above all, the warping of the will and spirit that is a consequence of being poor—as choices. Understanding the vicious circle is an important step in breaking down this prejudice.

There is an even richer way of describing this same, general idea: Poverty in the United States is a culture, an institution, a way of life.

There is a famous anecdote about Ernest Hemingway and F. Scott Fitzgerald. Fitzgerald is reported to have remarked to Hemingway, "The rich are different." And Hemingway replied, "Yes, they have money." Fitzgerald had much the better of the exchange. He understood that being rich was not a simple fact, like a large bank account, but a way of looking at reality, a series of attitudes, a special type of life. If this is true of the rich, it is ten times truer of the poor. Everything about them, from the condition of their teeth to the way in which they love, is suffused and permeated by the fact of their poverty. And this is sometimes a hard idea for a Hemingway-like middle-class America to comprehend.

The family structure of the poor, for instance, is different from that of the rest of the society. There are more homes without a father, there are less marriages, more early pregnancy and, if Kinsey's statistical findings can be used, markedly different attitudes toward sex. As a result of this, to take but one consequence of the fact, hundreds of thousands, and perhaps millions, of children in the other America never know stability and "normal" affection.

Or perhaps the policeman is an even better example. For the middle class, the police protect property, give directions, and help old ladies. For the urban poor, the police are those who arrest you. In almost any slum there is a vast conspiracy against the forces of law and order. If someone approaches asking for a person, no one there will have heard of him, even if he lives next door. The outsider is "cop," bill collector, investigator (and, in the Negro ghetto, most dramatically, he is "the Man").

While writing this book, I was arrested for participation in a civil-rights demonstration. A brief experience of a night in a cell made an abstraction personal and immediate: the city jail is one of the basic institutions of the other America. Almost everyone whom I encountered in the "tank" was poor: skid-row whites, Negroes, Puerto Ricans. Their poverty was an incitement to arrest in the first place. (A policeman will be much more careful with a well-dressed, obviously educated man who might have political connections than he will with someone who is poor.) They did not have money for bail or for lawyers. And, perhaps most important, they waited their arraignment with stolidity, in a mood of passive acceptance. They expected the worst, and they probably got it.

There is, in short, a language of the poor, a psychology of the poor, a world view of the poor. To be impoverished is to be an internal alien, to grow up in a culture that is radically different from the one that dominates the society.

3

foreign policy
since 1960

Throughout the 1950's a vocal group of conservative critics assailed American foreign policy, charging that the goal of merely containing communism represented a "no-win" strategy. During the early sixties, Republican Senator Barry Goldwater of Arizona became the most popular political figure associated with this point of view, and in 1964 he captured the Republican presidential nomination. In the words of one of his right-wing supporters, Goldwater offered both the GOP and the nation "a choice, not an echo." In the area of foreign policy this meant a tough, sometimes saber-rattling approach to the "menace" of "worldwide communism."

According to Goldwater, why must victory over "communism" become the primary goal of United States foreign policy? How does Goldwater use the term "communism?" What room does his view of world affairs leave for the traditional methods of diplomacy?

Barry Goldwater

Why Not Victory?

If our foreign policy has had a hallmark since the end of World War II, it has been inconsistency. We have marched resolutely up the hill of power and then timidly allowed ourselves to be maneuvered onto a toboggan back down that slope. We have made strong pronouncements of intention based on our power, then refused to use that might to augment the words. When we have spoken strongly and acted in character with the words, we have been successful.

At those moments, we experienced the respect due the greatest power on earth beginning to manifest itself, only to see it smitten down with a subsequent act of weakness inspired by indecision, doubt, and confusion.

On the whole, no one can say convincingly that our foreign policy since the Second World War has consistently gained our ends, even when those ends were clearly defined. We have lived in an almost perpetual state of crisis with the determined Communists, who never for a second have doubted or questioned their aims. We have watched them as one watches the weaving head of a cobra while they have subverted, betrayed, and manipulated wherever the opportunity presented itself and, being awed, we have been confused.

What course, then, should we take if we are determined to stop communism and eventually replace the whole destructive idea of communism with our free and productive one?

To answer this question, I must begin by setting down some assumptions with regard to our national objectives. I do not mean to suggest that everyone will agree with them. I mean, however, that I do take them as valid and that everything I say on this subject is set against their background.

Assumption 1. The objective of American policy must be to protect the security and integrity of Americans and thereby help establish a world in which there is the largest possible measure of freedom and justice and peace and material prosperity. I speak of "the largest possible measure" because any person who supposes that these conditions can be universally and perfectly achieved—ever—reckons without the inherent imperfectability of himself and his fellow human beings.

Assumption 2. Attainment of the largest possible measure of freedom, justice, peace, and prosperity is impossible without the prior defeat of world communism. This is true for two reasons: (1) because communism is both doctrinally and in practice antithetical to these conditions and (2) because Communists have the will and, so long as their power remains intact, the capacity to prevent their realization. Moreover, as Communist power increases, the enjoyment of these conditions throughout the world diminishes by that much and the possibility of their restoration becomes increasingly remote—becomes, at the end of the road, a cause that is absolutely and tragically and irretrievably lost.

Assumption 3. It follows that victory over communism must be the dominant, proximate goal of American policy. Proximate because there are more distant, more "positive" ends we seek, goals to which victory over communism is but a means. But victory is dominant in the sense that every other objective, no matter how worthy intrinsically, depends on it and thus must defer to it. Peace is a worthy objective but if we must choose between peace and keeping the Communists out of West Berlin, then we must fight. Freedom, in the sense of self-determination, is a worthy objective, but if granting self-determination to the Algerian rebels entails sweeping that area into the Sino-Soviet orbit, then Algerian freedom must be postponed. Justice is a worthy objective but if justice for Bantus entails driving the government of the Union of South Africa away from the West, then the Bantus must be prepared to carry their identification cards yet a while longer. Prosperity is a worthy objective, but if providing higher living standards gets in the way of producing sufficient weapons to be able to resist possible Communist aggression, then material sacrifices and denials will have to be made. It may be, of course, that we can safely seek such objectives and at the same time assure a policy designed to overthrow communism; the important point here is that when conflicts arise they must always be resolved in favor of achieving the indispensable condition for a tolerable world—the absense of Soviet-Communist power.

The question now remains whether we have the resources for the job we have to do—defeat communism—and, if so, how those resources ought to be used. This brings us squarely to the problem of *power* and the uses a nation makes of power. This is the key problem in international relations; it always has been, it always will be. Further, the main cause of the trouble we are in today has been the failure of American policy-makers, ever since we assumed free-world leadership in 1945, to deal with this problem of power realistically and seriously.

During the Presidential campaign of 1960 the absurd charge was made by Mr. Kennedy and others that America had become—or was in danger of becoming—a second-rate military power. Any comparison of over-all American strength with over-all Soviet strength reveals the United States not only superior, but so superior both in present weapons and in the development of new ones that our advantage promises to be a permanent feature of the United States–Soviet relations for the foreseeable future. . . .

What of the uses we are to make of our power? History shows powerful nations that have used their strength to preserve the peace and to preserve a climate in which their ideals and their concepts of government have flourished. Have we followed this wise and valid course?

No, we have not.

Laos and Cuba are the tragic results of weakness in our dealings with the Communist leaders, a softness that has resulted in a constant acquiescence to their gruff freedom-killing demands. This is the result of an attempt to buy the world for our side rather than to gain its respect by strong action for freedom.

The loss of Laos and Cuba to communism, if that be their fate, is not simply the tragedy of people going into slavery; it will also be the disaster of losing friends at a time when friends are needed.

Strong words alone do not wave off the Russian leaders. They understand and they respect strength and strength alone. The sadness is not that we are weak militarily or economically. The sadness lies in our consistent refusal to orient our foreign policy to our true strengths.

I suggest that the United States and her allies go on the offensive. We can't win merely by trying to hold our own. In other words, in all our dealings with Communist or neutralist nations, we *must not* be on the defensive. We must go on the offensive with what we have, knowing that what we have in America now is better than man has ever devised before in the history of the world.

We have had opportunities—clear invitations to plant our influence on the other side of the Iron Curtain. There was the Hungarian Revolution in October of 1956, which we praised and mourned but did nothing about. There was the spectacle of Korea, where, with victory in our hands, we chose instead the bitterness of stalemate. Only in one instance have we moved truly purposively and effectively to dislodge existing Communist power: in Guatemala, in July, 1954. We moved decisively to effect an anti-Communist *coup d'état,* and there is no need to apologize for what we did. We served our national interests, and, in so doing, we saved the Guatemalan people the ultimate misery. If there are doubts, ask the Hungarians. Or the Cubans.

Think long on Guatemala, for this is our single full-fledged triumph. We have held the line in some places—in Lebanon, in Berlin, in the Formosa Straits—but nowhere else in the far-flung battle for the world have we *extended* the influence of the United States and *advanced* the cause of freedom.

Last December in Berlin, I saw with my own eyes the latest result of our hesitation and weakness—the notorious wall between East and West. I know that hindsight is easier than foresight but I have yet to talk with a Berliner or an American commentator who was on the spot or a knowledgeable military man who has not expressed the opinion that had the West destroyed this wall brick by brick as it was being constructed, the

East Germans would have retired from the border and today there would be no wall. The wall is not so important as a physical barrier as it is as a great propaganda victory for the Communists. They wanted to seal off East Berlin—so they did it. The West did not raise a hand. The rest of Europe stands by and shrugs resignedly. They have seen another show of Communist strength.

We may take it, then, that unless radical changes are made on our side, the situation will progressively worsen until the United States is at bay—isolated and besieged by an entirely hostile world. What changes? One thing, but it is everything: We are going to have to shed the attitudes and strategies of weakness and start behaving once again like a great power. We must act from strength to gain respect not prestige.

In this we must recognize that the affairs of nations are not determined by good-will tours, alms-giving, gestures of self-denial, rehabilitation projects, and discussion programs. The affairs of nations are determined —for good or for evil—by *power.*

On July 15, 1953, the United States, at the request of President Carmille Chamoun, landed a brigade of Marines in Lebanon to help prevent a revolt inspired by the United Arab Republic intent on overthrowing Chamoun's democratic government. President Eisenhower complied immediately with President Chamoun's request on the theory that Lebanon in revolt would certainly fall victim to Communist infiltration. He acted wisely. Three months later, Chamoun's control having been stabilized, the Marines withdrew without ever firing a shot in anger. American power, in this situation, was used promptly and to excellent effect as it has been so seldom since the end of World War II.

The Soviet Union has not gotten where it is today through the attractiveness of its doctrines and practices. It has set its sights on distinct targets—geographical areas or power centers which it means to infiltrate and eventually conquer—and then turned the full weight of its national power, plus the power of the international apparatus it controls, on these particular targets. The United States has never viewed the world struggle in quite this way—as essentially a military campaign in which a commander isolates his objective, marshals his forces, and takes it!

We have rather proceeded on the assumption that virtue was its own reward and that our real goal is to make the world love us and perceive our virtue.

Moreover, we entered this supposed contest for world approval with a kind of guilt complex. Perhaps the dropping of the atom bomb on Hiroshima had something to do with it. But more probably the cause lies deep in America's past, in our traditional attitude toward power politics. Having been brought up on childish myths about the evils of European power politics, Americans felt uneasy when the rights and duties of being the greatest power on earth suddenly fell upon them at the end of the Second World War. In order to prove that we were not selfish, ambitious, warlike, as our predecessors in power were, we began to lean over backward and to gear our policies to the opinions of others. There are notable exceptions—as when, for example, we have submitted to the imperatives of self-defense: in Greece, in Korea, in the Formosa Straits, in Berlin. But in theme and thrust and motive American foreign policy has been primarily an exercise in self-ingratiation.

I am, of course, oversimplifying the case but not exaggerating it. Call into question any aspect of American policy, and the argument you will hear after the others have been laid to rest is some variation of the world-opinion theme. Foreign aid, deference to the United Nations, and cultural exchange programs, exchange visits of American and Soviet functionaries, summit conferences, the nuclear-test ban, advocacy of general disarmament, anti-colonialism, the refusal to intervene early enough in Cuba, the establishment of world government—all of these programs and postures have a single common denominator: an effort to please world opinion. Indeed, many of these policies are frankly acknowledged by their proponents to be contrary to the immediate interest of the United States; yet they must be pursued, we are told, because of the overriding importance of having the world think well of us. This sluggish sentimentality, this obsession for pleasing people, has now become a matter of grand strategy; it has become no less than the guiding principle of American policy, leading us—for all the good intentions it implies —to national and international disaster.

And what does the world admire anyway? Strength, courage, and ingenuity! When was the United States more admired than during the Berlin Airlift? After the Russians blocked our road access to Berlin on April 1, 1948, we and the British started the air shuttle which was to last eighteen months until September 30, 1949, and which was to bring to West Berlin the staggering sum of 2,343,301 tons of food and coal. In almost 300,000 flights seventy airmen lost their lives—but the blockade was broken and the free world was inspired by this display of power and skill. All this effort only retained the *status quo,* a dangerous stalemate in Berlin. It prompts one to wonder what we might be able to do in the way of driving communism backward if, instead of merely responding defensively to their moves, we applied that power and ingenuity to offensive gestures.

George Kennan, *whose name had long been associated with the doctrine of containment against communism, came to view the American effort in Vietnam as a misapplication of his original anticommunist program. As this selection shows, as early as 1966 Kennan was reporting to the Senate Foreign Relations Committee the adverse consequences of our involvement in Vietnam and was expressing doubts about the possibility of victory. A mild and cautious statement, Kennan's presentation nonetheless had a powerful impact as the considered dissent of one of the nation's leading authorities on communism.*

What basic assumptions which underlay American involvement in Vietnam did Kennan challenge? What military and diplomatic consequences did he believe a prolonged war might have? In your opinion, which parts of Kennan's analysis have proven accurate; which parts inaccurate?

George Kennan

Statement Before Senate Foreign Relations Committee

The first point I would like to make is that if we were not already involved as we are today in Vietnam, I would know of no reason why we should wish to become so involved, and I could think of several reasons why we should wish not to.

Vietnam is not a region of major military and industrial importance. It is difficult to believe that any decisive developments of the world situation would be determined in normal circumstances by what happens on that territory. If it were not for the considerations of prestige that arise precisely out of our present involvement, even a situation in which South Vietnam was controlled exclusively by the Vietcong, while regrettable, and no doubt morally unwarranted, would not, in my opinion, present dangers great enough to justify our direct military intervention.

Given the situation that exists today in the relations among the leading Communist powers, and by that I have, of course, in mind primarily the Soviet-Chinese conflict, there is every likelihood that a Communist regime in South Vietnam would follow a fairly independent course.

There is no reason to suspect that such a regime would find it either necessary or desirable in present circumstances to function simply as a passive puppet and instrument of Chinese power. And as for the danger that its establishment there would unleash similar tendencies in neighboring countries, this, I think, would depend largely on the manner in which it came into power. In the light of what has recently happened in Indonesia, and on the Indian subcontinent, the danger of the so-called domino effect, that is the effect that would be produced by a limited Communist success in South Vietnam, seems to me to be considerably less than it was when the main decisions were taken that have led to our present involvement.

Let me stress, I do not say that that danger does not exist, I say that it is less than it was a year or two ago when we got into this involvement.

From the long-term standpoint, therefore, and on principle, I think our military involvement in Vietnam has to be recognized as unfortunate, as something we would not choose deliberately, if the choice were ours to make all over again today, and by the same token, I think it should be our Government's aim to liquidate this involvement just as soon as this can be done without inordinate damage to our own prestige or to the stability of conditions in that area.

It is obvious on the other hand that this involvement is today a fact. It creates a new situation. It raises new questions, ulterior to the long-term problem, which have to be taken into account. A precipitate and

George Kennan, Statement to Hearings before the Committee on Foreign Relations, United States Senate, 89th Congress, 2nd Session, February, 1966.

disorderly withdrawal could represent in present circumstances a disservice to our own interests, and even to world peace, greater than any that might have been involved by our failure to engage ourselves there in the first place.

This is a reality which, if there is to be any peaceful resolution of this conflict, is going to have to be recognized both by the more critical of our friends and by our adversaries.

EXPANSION OF HOSTILITIES IS DANGEROUS

But at the same time, I have great misgivings about any deliberate expansion of hostilities on our part directed to the achievement of something called victory—if by the use of that term we envisage the complete disappearance of the recalcitrance with which we are now faced, the formal submission by the adversary to our will, and the complete realization of our present stated political aims.

I doubt that these things can be achieved even by the most formidable military successes.

There seems to be an impression about that if we bring sufficient military pressure to bear there will occur at some point something in the nature of a political capitulation on the other side. I think this is a most dangerous assumption. I don't say that it is absolutely impossible, but it is a dangerous assumption in the light of the experience we have had with Communist elements in the past.

The North Vietnamese and the Vietcong have between them a great deal of space and manpower to give up if they have to, and the Chinese can give them more if they need it. Fidelity to the Communist tradition would dictate that if really pressed to extremity on the military level these people should disappear entirely from the open scene and fall back exclusively on an underground political and military existence rather than to accept terms that would be openly humiliating and would represent in their eyes the betrayal of the future political prospects of the cause to which they are dedicated.

Any total rooting out of the Vietcong from the territory of South Vietnam could be achieved, if it could be achieved at all, only at the cost of a degree of damage to civilian life and of civilian suffering generally for which I would not like to see this country responsible.

And to attempt to crush North Vietnamese strength to a point where Hanoi could no longer give any support for Vietcong political activity in the South, would almost certainly, it seems to me, have the effect of bringing in Chinese forces at some point, whether formally or in the guise of volunteers, thus involving us in a military conflict with Communist China on one of the most unfavorable theaters of hostility that we could possibly choose.

EFFECT OF CONFLICT ON OTHER INTERESTS AND POLICIES

This is not the only reason why I think we should do everything possible to avoid the escalation of this conflict. There is another one which is no less weighty, and this is the effect the conflict is already having on our policies and interests further afield. This involvement seems to me to represent a grievous misplacement of emphasis in our foreign policies as a whole.

EFFECT ON CONFIDENCE OF OTHER COUNTRIES

Not only are great and potentially more important questions of world affairs not receiving, as a consequence of our involvement in Vietnam, the attention they should be receiving, but in some instances assets we already enjoy and hopefully possibilities we should be developing are being sacrificed to this unpromising involvement in a remote and secondary theater. Our relations with the Soviet Union have suffered grievously as was to be expected, and this at a time when far more important things were involved in those relations than what is ultimately involved in Vietnam and when we had special reason, I think, to cultivate those relations. And more unfortunate still, in my opinion, is the damage being done to the feelings entertained for us by the Japanese people. The confidence and good disposition of the Japanese is the greatest asset we have had and the greatest asset we could have in east Asia. As the only major industrial complex in the entire Far East, and the only place where the sinews of modern war can be produced on a formidable scale, Japan is of vital importance to us and indeed to the prospects generally of peace and stability in east Asia. There is no success we could have in Vietnam that would conceivably warrant, in my opinion, the sacrifice by us of the confidence and good will of the Japanese people. Yet, I fear that we abuse that confidence and good will in the most serious way when we press the military struggle in Vietnam, and particularly when we press it by means of strategic bombing, a process to which the Japanese for historical reasons are peculiarly sensitive and averse.

I mention Japan particularly because it is an outstanding example, both in importance and in the intensity of the feelings aroused, of the psychological damage that is being done in many parts of the world by the prosecution of this conflict, and that will be done in even greater measure if the hostilities become still more bloody and tragic as a result of our deliberate effort.

It is clear that however justified our action may be in our own eyes, it has failed to win either enthusiasm or confidence even among peoples normally friendly to us.

U.S. MOTIVES ARE MISINTERPRETED

Our motives are widely misinterpreted, and the spectacle emphasized and reproduced in thousands of press photographs and stories that appear in the press of the world, the spectacle of Americans inflicting grievous injury on the lives of a poor and helpless people, and particularly a people of different race and color, no matter how warranted by military necessity or by the excesses of the adversary, produces reactions among millions of people throughout the world profoundly detrimental to the image we would like them to hold of this country. I am not saying that this is just or right. I am saying that this is so, and that it is bound in the circumstances to be so. A victory purchased at the price of further such damage would be a hollow one in terms of our world interests, no matter what advantages it might hold from the standpoint of developments on the local scene.

Now, these are the reasons, gentlemen, why I hope that our Government will restrict our military operations in Vietnam to the minimum necessary to assure the security of our forces and to maintain our military presence there until we can achieve a satisfactory peaceful resolution of the conflict. And these are the reasons why I hope that we will continue to pursue vigorously, and I may say consistently, the quest for such a peaceful resolution of the conflict, even if this involves some moderation of our stated objectives, and even if the resulting settlement appears to us as something less than ideal. . . .

U.S. RETREAT WOULD NOT CAUSE LOSS OF CONFIDENCE
OF FREE WORLD

I also find it difficult, for reasons that I won't take time to go into here, to believe that our allies, and particularly our Western European allies, most of whom themselves have given up great territories within recent years, and sometimes in a very statesmanlike way, I find it hard to believe that we would be subject to great reproach or loss of confidence at their hands simply because we followed a defensive rather than an offensive strategy in Vietnam at this time.

In matters such as this, it is not in my experience what you do that is mainly decisive. It is how you do it; and I would submit that there is more respect to be won in the opinion of this world by a resolute and courageous liquidation of unsound positions than by the most stubborn pursuit of extravagant or unpromising objectives.

U.S. COMMITMENT TO SOUTH VIETNAM BEWILDERING

And finally, when I hear it said that to adopt a defensive strategy in South Vietnam would be to rat on our commitment to the Government of that territory I am a little bewildered. I would like to know what that commitment really consists of, and how and when it was incurred. What seems to be involved here is an obligation on our part not only to defend the frontiers of a certain political entity against outside attack, but to assure the internal security of its government in circumstances where that government is unable to assure that security by its own means. Now, any such obligation is one that goes obviously considerably further in its implications than the normal obligations of a military alliance.

If we did not incur such an obligation in any formal way, then I think we should not be inventing it for ourselves and assuring ourselves that we are bound by it today.

But if we did incur it, then I do fail to understand how it was possible to enter into any such commitment otherwise than through the constitutional processes which were meant to come into play when even commitments of lesser import than this were undertaken.

HIGHEST RESPECT FOR U.S. FIGHTING QUALITIES

Now, just two concluding observations: I would like it understood that what I have said here implies nothing but the highest respect and admiration for the fighting qualities of our forces in the field. I have the greatest confidence in them, men and commanders alike. I have no doubt, in fact, that they can and will, if duty requires, produce before this thing is over military results that will surprise both our skeptical friends and our arrogant adversaries. It is not their fighting qualities. It is the purpose to which they are being employed that evokes my skepticism.

UNITED STATES SHOULD NOT SHOULDER POLITICAL BURDEN
OF OTHER COUNTRIES

Secondly, I would like to say I am trying to look at this whole problem not from the moral standpoint but from the practical one. I see in the Vietcong a band of ruthless fanatics, many of them misled, no doubt, by the propaganda that has been drummed into them, but cruel in their methods, dictatorial, and oppressive in their aims, I am not conscious of having any sympathy for them. I think their claim to represent the people of South Vietnam is unfounded. A country which fell under this exclusive power would have my deepest sympathy; and I would hope that this eventuality at any rate would be avoided by a restrained and moderate policy on our part in South Vietnam.

But our country should not be asked, and should not ask of itself, to shoulder the main burden of determining the political realities in any other country, and particularly not in one remote from our shores, from our culture, and from the experience of our people. This is not only not our business, but I don't think we can do it successfully.

*In August 1964 the Johnson administration claimed that North Viet-
namese gunboats attacked an American destroyer in the Gulf of Tonkin.
Without seeking evidence which might have cast serious doubts on the
real nature of the "attack," Congress granted the President authority to
use American forces to prevent further aggression. American bombers
attacked the North, and the war escalated significantly. The following
selection is one of a number of speeches in which President Lyndon Johnson sought to justify the increased commitment of American ground
troops to South Vietnam. It was delivered on a "quiet campus" at Johns
Hopkins in 1965; a few years later the unpopularity of the war would
make presidential appearances on most campuses virtually impossible.*

*According to Johnson, who started the war in Vietnam, and why was
the United States fighting there? What was the nature of the enemy? Why
did Johnson believe that fighting North Vietnam was in the national
interest of the United States? Have these arguments proved sound?*

Lyndon B. Johnson

Speech at Johns Hopkins

Tonight Americans and Asians are dying for a world where each people may choose its own path to change.

This is the principle for which our ancestors fought in the valleys of Pennsylvania. It is the principle for which our sons fight tonight in the jungles of Viet-Nam.

Viet-Nam is far away from this quiet campus. We have no territory there, nor do we seek any. The war is dirty and brutal and difficult. And some 400 young men, born into an America that is bursting with opportunity and promise, have ended their lives on Viet-Nam's steaming soil.

Why must we take this painful road?

Why must this Nation hazard its ease, and its interest, and its power for the sake of a people so far away?

We fight because we must fight if we are to live in a world where every country can shape its own destiny. And only in such a world will our own freedom be finally secure.

This kind of world will never be built by bombs or bullets. Yet the infirmities of man are such that force must often precede reason, and the waste of war, the works of peace.

We wish that this were not so. But we must deal with the world as it is, if it is ever to be as we wish.

THE NATURE OF THE CONFLICT

The world as it is in Asia is not a serene or peaceful place.

The first reality is that North Viet-Nam has attacked the independent nation of South Viet-Nam. Its object is total conquest.

Of course, some of the people of South Viet-Nam are participating in attack on their own government. But trained men and supplies, orders and arms, flow in a constant stream from north to south.

This support is the heartbeat of the war.

And it is a war of unparalleled brutality. Simple farmers are the targets of assassination and kidnapping. Women and children are strangled in the night because their men are loyal to their government. And helpless villages are ravaged by sneak attacks. Large-scale raids are conducted on towns, and terror strikes in the heart of cities.

The confused nature of this conflict cannot mask the fact that it is the new face of an old enemy.

Over this war—and all Asia—is another reality: the deepening shadow of Communist China. The rulers in Hanoi are urged on by Peking. This is a regime which has destroyed freedom in Tibet, which has attacked India, and has been condemned by the United Nations for aggression in Korea. It is a nation which is helping the forces of violence in almost

Public Papers of the Presidents of the United States: Lyndon B. Johnson, Government Printing Office (Washington, D.C., 1966), I (1965), 394-399.

every continent. The contest in Viet-Nam is part of a wider pattern of aggressive purposes.

WHY ARE WE IN VIET-NAM?

Why are these realities our concern? Why are we in South Viet-Nam?

We are there because we have a promise to keep. Since 1954 every American President has offered support to the people of South Viet-Nam. We have helped to build, and we have helped to defend. Thus, over many years, we have made a national pledge to help South Viet-Nam defend its independence.

And I intend to keep that promise.

To dishonor that pledge, to abandon this small and brave nation to its enemies, and to the terror that must follow, would be an unforgivable wrong.

We are also there to strengthen world order. Around the globe, from Berlin to Thailand, are people whose well-being rests, in part, on the belief that they can count on us if they are attacked. To leave Viet-Nam to its fate would shake the confidence of all these people in the value of an American commitment and in the value of America's word. The result would be increased unrest and instability, and even wider war.

We are also there because there are great stakes in the balance. Let no one think for a moment that retreat from Viet-Nam would bring an end to conflict. The battle would be renewed in one country and then another. The central lesson of our time is that the appetite of aggression is never satisfied. To withdraw from one battlefield means only to prepare for the next. We must say in southeast Asia—as we did in Europe—in the words of the Bible: "Hitherto shalt thou come, but no further."

There are those who say that all our effort there will be futile—that China's power is such that it is bound to dominate all southeast Asia. But there is no end to that argument until all of the nations of Asia are swallowed up.

There are those who wonder why we have a responsibility there. Well, we have it there for the same reason that we have a responsibility for the defense of Europe. World War II was fought in both Europe and Asia, and when it ended we found ourselves with continued responsibility for the defense of freedom.

OUR OBJECTIVE IN VIET-NAM

Our objective is the independence of South Viet-Nam, and its freedom from attack. We want nothing for ourselves—only that the people of South Viet-Nam be allowed to guide their own country in their own way.

We will do everything necessary to reach that objective. And we will do only what is absolutely necessary.

In recent months attacks on South Viet-Nam were stepped up. Thus, it became necessary for us to increase our response and to make attacks by air. This is not a change of purpose. It is a change in what we believe that purpose requires.

We do this in order to slow down aggression.

We do this to increase the confidence of the brave people of South Viet-Nam who have bravely borne this brutal battle for so many years with so many casualties.

And we do this to convince the leaders of North Viet-Nam—and all who seek to share their conquest—of a very simple fact:

We will not be defeated.

We will not grow tired.

We will not withdraw, either openly or under the cloak of a meaningless agreement.

We know that air attacks alone will not accomplish all of these purposes. But it is our best and prayerful judgment that they are a necessary part of the surest road to peace.

We hope that peace will come swiftly. But that is in the hands of others besides ourselves. And we must be prepared for a long continued conflict. It will require patience as well as bravery, the will to endure as well as the will to resist.

I wish it were possible to convince others with words of what we now find it necessary to say with guns and planes: Armed hostility is futile. Our resources are equal to any challenge. Because we fight for values and we fight for principles, rather than territory or colonies, our patience and our determination are unending.

Once this is clear, then it should also be clear that the only path for reasonable men is the path of peaceful settlement.

Such peace demands an independent South Viet-Nam—securely guaranteed and able to shape its own relationships to all others—free from outside interference—tied to no alliance—a military base for no other country.

These are the essentials of any final settlement.

We will never be second in the search for such a peaceful settlement in Viet-Nam.

There may be many ways to this kind of peace: in discussion or negotiation with the governments concerned; in large groups or in small ones; in the reaffirmation of old agreements or their strengthening with new ones.

We have stated this position over and over again, fifty times and more, to friend and foe alike. And we remain ready, with this purpose, for unconditional discussions.

And until that bright and necessary day of peace we will try to keep conflict from spreading. We have no desire to see thousands die in battle —Asians or Americans. We have no desire to devastate that which the people of North Viet-Nam have built with toil and sacrifice. We will use our power with restraint and with all the wisdom that we can command.

But we will use it.

This war, like most wars, is filled with terrible irony. For what do the people of North Viet-Nam want? They want what their neighbors also desire: food for their hunger; health for their bodies; a chance to learn; progress for their country; and an end to the bondage of material misery. And they would find all these things far more readily in peaceful association with others than in the endless course of battle. . . .

Every night before I turn out the lights to sleep I ask myself this question: Have I done everything that I can do to unite this country? Have I done everything I can to help unite the world, to try to bring peace and hope to all the peoples of the world? Have I done enough?

Ask yourselves that question in your homes—and in this hall tonight. Have we, each of us, all done all we could? Have we done enough?

We may well be living in the time foretold many years ago when it was said: "I call heaven and earth to record this day against you, that I have set before you life and death, blessing and cursing: therefore choose life, that both thou and thy seed may live."

This generation of the world must choose: destroy or build, kill or aid, hate or understand.

We can do all these things on a scale never dreamed of before.

Well, we will choose life. In so doing we will prevail over the enemies within man, and over the natural enemies of all mankind.

Americans were so preoccupied by the divisive effects of the Viet Nam war on the United States that they sometimes neglected the far more disastrous effects it had on the Vietnamese. In journalist Frances Fitz-Gerald's prize-winning book, Fire in the Lake, *however, the true tragedy of the Viet Nam war unfolds from a perspective sympathetic to the Vietnamese. Highly critical of United States policy, FitzGerald shows how American efforts to "save" an "ally" upset ecological balance, destroyed an economy, gave rise to political corruption and dependence, and devastated a society based upon village and family ties. This selection reveals FitzGerald's sophisticated understanding of Vietnamese culture and history as well as her graceful writing style and keen eye for detail.*

What changes did the war bring to Vietnamese social, political and economic life? How far had American goals for Vietnam (as stated in the previous selection by President Johnson) been fulfilled, according to FitzGerald? How can you account for the discrepancy between the objective and the result?

Frances FitzGerald

Fire in the Lake

Before entering Saigon, the military traffic from Tan Son Nhut airfield slows in a choking blanket of its own exhaust. Where it crawls along to the narrow bridge in a frenzy of bicycles, pedicabs, and tri-Lambrettas, two piles of garbage mark the entrance to a new quarter of the city. Every evening a girl on spindle heels picks her way over the barrier of rotting fruit and onto the sidewalk. Triumphant, she smiles at the boys who lounge at the soft-drink stand, and with a toss of her long earrings, climbs into a waiting Buick.

Behind her, the alleyway carpeted with mud winds back past the façade of the new houses into a maze of thatched huts and tin-roofed shacks called Bui Phat. One of the oldest of the refugee quarters, Bui Phat lies just across the river from the generous villas and tree-lined streets of French Saigon. On its tangle of footpaths, white-shirted boys push their Vespas past laborers in black pajamas and women carrying water on coolie poles. After twelve years and recurrent tides of new refugees, Bui Phat is less an urban quarter than a compost of villages where peasants live with their city children. The children run thick underfoot. The police, it is said, rarely enter this quarter for fear of a gang of teen-age boys, whose leader, a young army deserter, reigns over Bui Phat.

Most of Bui Phat lives beyond the law, the electricity lines, and the water system, but it has its secret fortunes. Here and there amid the chaos of shacks and alleyways, new concrete buildings rear up in a splendor of pastel-faced walls, neon lights, and plastic garden furniture. In one of them there is a half-naked American who suns himself on a porch under a clothesline draped with military uniforms. He does not know, and probably never will know, that the house just down the alleyway is owned and inhabited by an agent of the NLF.

Bui Phat and its likenesses are what the American war has brought to Vietnam. In the countryside there is only an absence: the bare brown fields, the weeds growing in the charred earth of the village, the jungle that has swept back over the cleared land. The grandest ruins are those of the American tanks, for the Vietnamese no longer build fine stone tombs as did their ancestors. The U.S. First Infantry Division has carved its divisional insignia with defoliants in a stretch of jungle—a giant, poisonous graffito—but the Vietnamese have left nothing to mark the passage of their armies and an entire generation of young men. In many places death is not even a physical absence. The villages that once again take root in the rich soil of the Delta fill up with children as quickly as the holes made by the five-hundred-pound and thousand-pound bombs fill up with paddy silt. The desire for survival has been greater than the war itself, for there are approximately two million more people in the south today than there were before the war. But the balance of the

Frances FitzGerald, *Fire in the Lake: The Vietnamese and the Americans in Vietnam,* Little, Brown and Company (Boston, Mass., 1972), 425-437.

nation has changed, and Saigon is no longer the village, it is Bui Phat.

From Dong Ha in the north to Rach Gia, the slow port at the base of the Delta, these new slums, these crushed villages, spread through all of the cities and garrisoned towns. They are everywhere; plastered against sandbag forts, piled up under the guns of the provincial capitals, overwhelming what is left of the Delta's yellow stucco towns. Seaward of Da Nang the tin huts of the refugee settlements lie between the ammunition and the garbage dumps, indistinguishable from either. These huts have been rebuilt many times during the war, for every year there is some kind of disaster—an airplane crash or an explosion in the ammunition depot—that wipes out whole hamlets. Around Qui Nhon, Bien Hoa, and Cam Ranh bay, where the Americans have built jetports and military installations to last through the twentieth century, the thatched huts crowd so closely that a single neglected cigarette or a spark from a charcoal brazier suffices to burn the settlements down. On the streets of tin shacks that run straight as a surrealist's line past the runways and into the sand, babies play naked in the dust and rows of green combat fatigues hang over the barbed wire like dead soldiers.

Out of a population of seventeen million there are now five million refugees. Perhaps 40 or 50 percent of the population, as opposed to the 15 percent before the war, live in and around the cities and towns. The distribution is that of a highly industrialized country, but there is almost no industry in South Vietnam. And the word "city" and even "town" is misleading. What was even in 1965 a nation of villages and landed estates is now a nation of *bidonvilles,* refugee camps, and army bases. South Vietnam is a country shattered so that no two pieces fit together.

In Saigon alone more than three million people live on swampy ground between river and canal in a space made to accommodate a quarter of a million. Saigon now has one of the most dense populations in the world, although few houses rise above two stories, for in the monsoon season whole quarters of the city sink into the marsh. Some districts are little more than gigantic sewers, lakes of filth, above which thatched huts rise on stilts, connected only by rotting boards. In other quarters where the refugees have not had time to build stilts, the sewage inundated even the houses. But there is nowhere else for these people to go. The squatters have already filled up all the free space; their shacks elbow across the main thoroughfares. . . .

The physical suffering of South Vietnam is difficult to comprehend, even in statistics. The official numbers—859,641 "enemy," over 165,268 ARVN soldiers and about 380,000 civilians killed—only begin to tell the toll of death this war has taken. Proportionately, it is as though twenty million Americans died in the war instead of the forty-five thousand to date. But there are more to come. In the refugee camps and isolated villages people die of malnutrition and the children are deformed. In the cities, where there is no sanitation and rarely any running water, the adults die of cholera, typhoid, smallpox, leprosy, bubonic plague, and their children die of the common diseases of dirt, such as scabies and sores. South Vietnam knows nothing like the suffering of India or Bangladesh. Comparatively speaking, it has always been a rich country, and the American aid has provided many people with the means of survival. But its one source of wealth is agriculture, and the American war has wreaked havoc upon its forest and paddy lands. It has given great fortunes to the few while endangering the country's future and forcing the many to live in the kind of "poverty, ignorance, and disease" that South Vietnam never knew before.

Still, the physical destruction is not, perhaps, the worst of it. The destruction of an entire society—"That is, above all, what the Vietnamese blame the Americans for," said one Vietnamese scholar. "Willfully or not, they have tended to destroy what is most precious to us: family, friendship, our manner of expressing ourselves." For all these years, the columns in the Saigon newspapers denouncing Americans for destroying "Vietnamese culture" have sounded somehow fatuous and inadequate to those Americans who witnessed the U.S. bombing raids. But the Vietnamese kept their sights on what is permanent and irreparable. Physical death is everywhere, but it is the social death caused by destruction of the family that is of overriding importance.

The French colonial presence and the first Indochina war swept away the Vietnamese state and the order of the village, but it left the family. And the family was the essence, the cell, as it were, that contained the design for the whole society. To the traditional Vietnamese the nation consisted of a landscape, "our mountains and our rivers," and the past of the family, "our ancestors." The land and the family were the two sources of national as well as personal identity. The Americans have destroyed these sources for many Vietnamese, not merely by killing people but by forcibly separating them, by removing the people from the land and depositing them in the vast swamp-cities.

In a camp on the Da Nang sand-flats a women sits nursing her baby and staring apathetically at the gang of small children who run through the crowded rows of shacks, wheeling and screaming like a flock of sea gulls after a ship's refuse. "It is hard to do anything with the children," she says. Her husband is at first ashamed to talk to the visitors because of his torn and dirty clothes. He has tried, he says, to get a job at the docks, but the Vietnamese interpreter for the Americans demanded a price he could not pay for putting his name on the list. Nowadays he rarely goes out of the barbed-wire enclosure. His hands hang stiffly down, as if paralyzed by their idleness.

An American in Vietnam observes only the most superficial results of this sudden shift of population: the disease, the filth, the stealing, the air of disorientation about the people of the camps and the towns. What he cannot see are the connections within the mind and spirit that have been broken to create this human swamp. The connections between the society and its product, between one man and another, between the nation and its own history—these are lost for these refugees. Land had been the basis of the social contract—the transmission belt of life that carried the generations of the family from the past into the future. Ancestor worshipers, the Vietnamese saw themselves as more than separate egos, as a part of this continuum of life. As they took life from the earth and from the ancestors, so they would find immortality in their children, who in their turn would take their place on the earth. To leave the land and the family forever was therefore to lose their place in the universe and to suffer a permanent, collective death. In one Saigon newspaper story, a young ARVN officer described returning to his home village, after many years to find his family gone and the site of his father's house a patch of thorns revealing no trace of human habitation. He felt, he said, "like someone who has lost his soul."

The soul is, of course, not a purely metaphysical concept, for it signifies a personal identity in life as well as death. For the Vietnamese to leave the land was to leave a part of the personality. When in 1962 the Diem regime forced the peasants to move behind the barbed wire of the strategic hamlets, the peasants found that they no longer trusted each other. And for an excellent reason. Once landowners or tenants, they became overnight improvidents and drifters who depended for their survival on what they could beg or take from others. Their behavior became unpredictable even to those who knew them.

The American war only completed the process the Diem regime had begun, moving peasants out of the villages and into the refugee camps and the cities, the real strategic hamlets of the war. For these farmers, as for their distant ancestors, to leave the hamlet was to step off the brink of the known world. Brought up as the sons of Mr. X or Mr. Y, the inhabitants of such a place, they suddenly found themselves nameless people in a nameless mass where no laws held. They survived, and as the war went on outside their control, they brought up their children in this anarchic crowd.

It was not, of course, the cities themselves that were at fault. To leave the village for the towns was for many Vietnamese far from a personal tragedy. In the 1940's and 1950's the enterprising young men left their villages voluntarily to join the armies or to find some employment in the towns. The balance of village life had long ago been destroyed, and, in any case, who was to say that the constant toil and small entertainment of a peasant's life was preferable even to the harshest of existences in a city? To join the army was in fact to see the world; to move to a town was to leave a life of inevitability for one of possibility. Though, or perhaps because, the hold of the family and the land was so strong, it contained also its contradiction—the desire for escape, for the death of the father and the end of all the burdensome family obligations. But it was one thing to escape into the new but ordered life of the NLF and quite another to escape to the anarchy of the American-occupied cities.

They are not like village children, these fierce, bored urchins who inhabit the shacks and alleyways of Saigon. When a Westerner visits these slums, the women look out shyly from behind their doorways, but the children run out, shoving and scratching at each other for a better view. They scream with hysterical laughter when one of their number falls off the planking and into the sewage. In a few moments they are a mob, clawing at the strangers as if they were animals to be teased and tortured. The anger comes up quickly behind the curiosity. A pebble sails out and falls gently on the stranger's back, and it is followed by a hail of stones.

There are street gangs now in every quarter of Saigon. Led by army deserters and recruited from among the mobs of smaller children, they roam like wolf packs, never sleeping in the same place twice, scavenging or stealing what they need to live on. Many of their numbers are orphans; the rest are as good as orphans, for their parents remain helpless peasants in the city. As a result, these boys are different from other Vietnamese. In a society of strong parental authority and family dependence, they have grown up with almost no discipline at all. Like the old street gangs of Harlem and Chicago, they have special manners, special codes. It is as though they were trying to create an entire society for themselves—a project in which they cannot succeed.

"In an absentminded way," wrote Professor Samuel Huntington in 1968,

the United States in Vietnam may well have stumbled upon the answer to "wars of national liberation." The effective response lies neither in the quest for a conventional military victory, nor in esoteric doctrines and gimmicks of counter-insurgency warfare. It is instead forced-draft urbanization and modernization which rapidly brings the country in question out of the phase in which a rural revolutionary movement can [succeed.]

But there was nothing absentminded about the manner in which the U.S. armed forces went about their program of "forced-draft urbanization." Nor was it a simple oversight that they neglected the corollary of "modernization." Since 1954—indeed since 1950 with the American sponsorship of the French war in Indochina—the United States has had only one concern and that was the war to destroy the revolutionary movement. It has not won that war and it has not destroyed the revolution, but it has changed Vietnam to the point where it is unrecognizable to the Vietnamese.

In 1966 the ministry of social welfare in Saigon wrote in preamble to its program: "With respect to this nation, this Ministry intends to stir up by all ways and means people's patriotic and traditional virtues with a view to shoring up our national ethics [which are] on the verge of ruin." Such a statement would have been perfectly appropriate coming from the priest of a rural Catholic village, but issued by the "government" of a country where numbers of prostitutes, beggars, orphans, juvenile delinquents, war wounded, and the otherwise infirm comprised an important percentage of the population, it seemed a kind of insanity. And in some sense it was, for over the years of war the GVN officials and bourgeoisie of the cities lost their grip on external reality. Cloistered within the high garden walls of their city houses, they looked back through the city, as if it were a transparency, to their old life of the family, the village, and the landed estate. They were dependent on the Americans for plans and programs as well as for the machinery to carry them out, and they lived intellectually in a state of suspended animation. They expected that the Americans would protect them in their sheltered existences, as the French had before them. But instead of protecting them, the Americans drove the peasantry into the cities with them. They created a mass where none had existed, and then they threatened to abandon their protégés.

In April 1968, just after Johnson's announcement of the bombing halt and his withdrawal from the presidential race, a young GVN official sat talking with an American reporter in a café in Tu Do Street. Asked his opinion of the speech, he blurted out suddenly, "You Americans can leave, you can leave whenever you wish. We cannot leave Vietnam. We have little choice." He leaned forward across the table. "Everything here is a theater. Everything is part of the play, even this table is a prop. We are just pawns. We have no say. But we are to be blamed. We have always been pawns."

In a moment of crisis, or seeming crisis, the young official had without thinking confirmed the NLF analysis of the relationship between the Americans and those Vietnamese who cooperated with them. Instead of helping the Saigon government to stand on its own, the Americans made it more and more dependent upon them, economically, politically, militarily. And now the Americans were threatening to withdraw their support, leaving their "allies" as helpless as puppets to control their own destiny.

The American war did not so paralyze the revolutionary movement, but it removed much of its original base and changed the terms under which it operated. The NLF had, after all, pursued a peasant revolution designed to take power from the hands of the foreigners and the few Vietnamese—landlords and officials—who profited from their rule. The Russian, the Chinese, and the North Vietnamese revolutions were also in varying degrees peasant-based, but on a continuum of the four the NLF lay at the extreme end, for there was no industry in the south, and the bourgeoisie, preempted from the trade market by the Chinese, did not constitute a true class. The peasantry was all that existed as a productive force in South Vietnam, and the Front leaders based their program of development upon them. The Stalinist program of bleeding agriculture for the sake of industry was in fact useless to them, for the south had no mineral resources, and the country as a whole no potential to compete in the world market with heavy industry. Out of economic as well as military necessity, the NLF program consisted of agricultural development and the building of small, almost cottage, industries throughout the countryside. Now, after years of exile from the cities, they had to confront a social and economic situation completely new to them.

The economic problem of South Vietnam is not, however, primarily intellectual. It is easy enough to construct theoreis of development, but not so easy to deal with the chaos that the American war has left. In 1954 South Vietnam held great promise as an economic enterprise. Unlike so many countries, it could feed its population and, with some agricultural development, produce enough raw materials to create foreign exchange. Its rich farmland perfectly complemented the mineral resources and the industry of the north. Given a modicum of outside aid, the Vietnamese with their relatively skilled population might have succeeded in breaking through that cycle of poverty and underdevelopment that affects so many countries of the world. But the American war has undermined those possibilities—by the side effects of its own military presence as much as by the bombing. The phenomenon is a curious one. The United States has had no direct economic interest in Vietnam. Over the years of the war it has not taken money out of Vietnam, but has put large amounts in. And yet it has produced much the same effects as the most exploitative of colonial regimes. The reason is that the overwhelming proportion of American funds has gone not into agricultural or industrial development but into the creation of services for the Americans—the greatest service being the Saigon government's army. As a whole, American wealth has gone into creating and supporting a group of people—refugees, soldiers, prostitutes, secretaries, translators, maids, and shoeshine boys—who do not engage in any form of production. Consequently, instead of having no capital, as it had at the moment of the French conquest, South Vietnam has an immense capital debt, for a great percentage of its population depends on the continued influx of American aid. The same was true to a lesser degree in 1954, and Saigon experienced an acute depression in the months between the French withdrawal and the first direct American commitment of aid. But now the balance of the population has changed so that the agriculture of the country scarcely suffices to feed its population, much less to create foreign exchange.

To be sure, as the American troops depart and the supply of dollars declines along with the shooting, many of the refugees will return to their villages and to agriculture. But for many the return will not be so easy. It is not merely that the population has grown and some of the arable land has been permanently destroyed. It is a social problem. Some millions of Vietnamese have now lived in the cities for five, ten years, or more; a half a generation of their children has grown up without ever watching a rice plant harvested. A certain number are used to the luxuries of the West and the freedoms of a Western-dominated city. The life of the peasantry is almost as foreign to them as it is to Americans, and yet they lack the very foundation upon which American society rests. These new city people have no capital—most of the money the United States invested in Vietnamese officials and businessmen has flown to safer investments abroad—and they have no industrial skills. They are not producers, but go-betweens who have engaged in nothing but marketing and services. The American war has altered them and rendered them helpless.

In considering the future of Vietnam, American officials have naturally tended to see these social and economic problems as amenable to American solutions. In 1969 David Lilienthal and a team of economists under commission from AID prepared a plan for the postwar development of the south. The plan, indeed the very fact of its commission, was perhaps the ultimate expression of American hubris. The officials of AID obviously believed even then that the United States could win the war and "modernize" the country to the point where it would pass the "phase" for a "rural insurgency movement." They had, it appeared, learned nothing and forgotten nothing from all those thousands of plans and programs, all those studies produced by MSU professors, the RAND Corporation, and other consultancy firms. They had not learned that economic development does not exist in a void. A political matter in all countries, it is most essentially political in a society that is not organized to make that development possible. AID itself demonstrated this truism in Vietnam. The politics of development were visible even in the landscape.

On the roads outside of Tay Ninh, Dalat, and Bien Hoa, an American visitor could for years see the same constellation of three hamlets. In each case the central hamlet, nominally Buddhist, consisted of no more than a group of palm-leaf hovels where one or two chickens scratched in the dust. The two surrounding Catholic hamlets might have belonged to another country, for they had ample concrete houses, herds of pigs and water buffaloes, and a church—nearly a cathedral—made of USAID cement and embellished with stucco and plaster statuary. For years the local AID advisers tried to bring the Buddhist hamlets up to the status of their Catholic neighbors, but they found it impossible to reverse the order of favoritism. The Catholic communities alone had the organization to demand GVN aid and to put that aid to use.

In many respects the GVN was a larger replica of that nominally Buddhist hamlet. When it received aid, it could not channel it into constructive purposes, nor could it even follow American plans to put it to work. This inability to organize was not "natural" to the GVN leaders, but rather the result of years of dependence on the French and the Americans. With the influx of people into the cities and into the American economy, the disorganization now extended down from the small elite to the very base of the population.

There are no counterparts to the Catholic hamlets in the cities. Though initially Catholic in population, Bui Phat never responded to Catholic leadership as did the villages. The political cadres of the Buddhists and the NLF tried for years to organize in the slums of Saigon, but they never succeeded in forming long-lived, disciplined movements. Their failure owed in part to the difficulty of reaching people who did not belong to any other form of organization—a village or a factory—and who had few interests in common. More profoundly, however, it owed to the fact that the city people did have one thing in common: they depended on the foreigners for their livelihood. When a nationalist political party aimed to assert Vietnamese power, Vietnamese independence, it aimed also to destroy the subsistence of the city people. Beyond the threat of American military power, it was this economic dependency that prevented the city people from rising up to support the NLF during the Tet offensive. And it will be for this reason of dependency that the cities will remain corrupt, anarchic, and miserable so long as the United States continues to dominate the economic life of the country.

If the Lilienthal plan proposed to reconstruct Vietnam through the Saigon government, then it was a contradiction in terms. Like all other aid plans and programs that preceded it, it was designed for a hypothetical country that did not, and furthermore could not, exist while the Americans continued to make plans and programs for it. The United States could, of course, build factories and introduce agricultural extension programs that would benefit a few Vietnamese. It could suppress city politics and maintain the current state of anarchy for many years. But it could not (Professor Huntington to the contrary) build an independent government and move the society beyond its revolutionary "phase." The solution to Vietnamese problems would have to be Vietnamese—and all attempts at such a solution would be suspended for as long as the United States maintained the anti-Communist struggle.

In looking beyond the American withdrawal to a Vietnam governed by Vietnamese, American officials have generally seen nothing but disaster ahead. They have predicted a long period of armed struggle culminating in a severe political repression and the massacre of thousands of their "allies." Many of these predictions have been no more than self-serving propaganda designed to camouflage the destruction the United States itself is perpetrating in Indochina. Others have been sincere expressions of doubt that the Vietnamese can recover from the war without further upheavals and violence. The officials may be right in their predictions. The Vietnamese, after all, have to deal with over a million soldiers and a vast disorganized mass of refugees as well as with the personal and political hostilities that have grown up over the years of war. The difficulty of this task will only increase for as long as the United States continues to fight the war by proxy and to give the Vietnamese no latitude to make a political settlement. In the future the possibility exists that the ARVN will disintegrate into banditry and the NLF and North Vietnamese will repeat their performance in Hue, slaughtering thousands of anti-Communist partisans in an attempt to take control. The American war has devastated the economy while at the same time it has broken down the political power—sectarian as well as Communist—that is necessary to restore it. If no group, or coalition of groups, has the authority to govern by rule of law, the chances are that there will be a severe political repression followed by a draconian attempt to force the urban masses back into some form of production. Such organized violence may in its turn lead to a disorganized reign of terror such as succeeded the North Vietnamese land reform of 1956. But these disasters may well not occur—or at least not on a scale that would make them significant beside the past horrors of war. It is a notable fact that with all the new Vietnamese troops the level of violence has decreased wherever the American troops have pulled out. It is also notable that the Vietnamese who depended economically upon the Americans have survived their withdrawal without any form of community organization or government help. South Vietnam is still a rich country. The withdrawal of all foreign aid would bring a serious economic crisis, but not starvation for thousands of people. Then, too, the American officials, who have witnessed only the division and paralysis their presence has created among their own "allies," tend to underestimate the capacities of the Vietnamese. The American war has created a social and economic chaos, but it has not stripped the Vietnamese of their vitality and powers of resistance. The Vietnamese survived the invasions of the Mongol hordes, and they may similarly survive the American war.

As the inevitability of American defeat and withdrawal from Vietnam became increasingly apparent, Americans tried to look back and assess what had gone wrong. In hearings before the Senate Foreign Relations Committee in 1972 Leslie H. Gelb, an antiwar journalist, summarized the range of explanations which had been advanced to explain American involvement. Does he omit any possible interpretations? How does his view of our failure in Vietnam compare to earlier Americans' views regarding our failure to maintain a friendly government in China?

Leslie H. Gelb

Causes of the War and Lessons Learned

Wars are supposed to tell us about ourselves. Are we a wise and just nation? Or are we foolish and aggressive? Merciless or humane? Well led or misled? Vital or decadent? Hopeful or hopeless? Nations in war and after war, win or lose, try to scratch away at the paste or glue or traditions or values that held their societies together and see of what they are made. It is arguable whether a society should indulge in such self-scrutiny. Societies are, as Edmund Burke wrote, "delicate, intricate wholes" that are more easily damaged than improved when subjected to the glare of Grand Inquisitors.

But in the case of our society and the war in Vietnam, too many people are seeking answers and are entitled to them, and many are only too eager to fill in the blanks. The families and friends of those who were killed and wounded will want to know whether it was worth it after all? Intellectuals will want to know "why Vietnam"? Men seeking and holding political office will demand to know who was responsible? The answers to these questions will themselves become political facts and forces, shaping the United States' role in the world and our lives at home for years to come.

I. CAUSES OF THE WAR: THE RANGE OF EXPLANATIONS

Central to this inquiry is the issue of causes of U.S. involvement in Vietnam. I have found eight discernible explanations advanced in the Vietnam literature. Different authors combine these explanations in various ways, but I will keep them separate for the purpose of analysis. I will, then, sketch my own position.

1. The Arrogance of Power

This view holds that a driving force in American envelopment in Vietnam was the fact that we were a nation of enormous power and like comparable nations in history, we would seek to use this power at every opportunity. To have power is to want to employ it, is to be corrupted by it. The arrogance derives from the belief that to have power is to be able to do anything. Power invokes right and justifies itself. Vietnam was there, a challenge to this power and an opportunity for its exercise, and no task was beyond accomplishment.

There can be no doubt about this strain in the behavior of other great powers and in the American character. But this is not a universal law. Great powers, and especially the United States have demonstrated self-restraint. The arrogance of power, I think, had more to do with

Leslie H. Gelb statement to Hearings before the Committee on Foreign Relations, United States Senate, 92 Congress, 2nd Session, May, 1972.

our persisting in the war than with our initial involvement. It always was difficult for our leaders back in Washington and for operatives in the field to believe that American resources and ingenuity could not devise some way to overcome the adversary.

2. Bureaucratic Politics

There are two, not mutually exclusive, approaches within this view. One has it that national security bureaucrats (the professionals who make up the military services, civilian Defense, AID, State, and the CIA) are afflicted with the curse of machismo, the need to assert and prove manhood and toughness. Career advancement and acceptability within the bureaucracy depended on showing that you were not afraid to propose the use of force. The other approach has it that bureaucrats purposefully misled their superiors about the situation in Vietnam and carefully constructed policy alternatives so as to circumscribe their superiors, thus forcing further involvement in Vietnam.

The machismo phenomenon is not unknown in the bureaucracy. It was difficult, if not damaging, to careers to appear conciliatory or "soft." Similarly, the constriction of options is a well-known bureaucratic device. But, I think, these approaches unduly emphasize the degree to which the President and his immediate advisers were trapped by the bureaucrats. The President was always in a position to ask for new options or to exclude certain others. The role of the bureaucracy was much more central to shaping the programs or the means used to fight the war than the key decisions to make the commitments in the first place.

3. Domestic Politics

This view is quite complicated, and authors argue their case on several different levels. The variants are if you were responsible for losing Vietnam to communism, you would: (a) lose the next election and lose the White House in particular; (b) jeopardize your domestic legislative program, your influence in general, by having to defend yourself constantly against political attack; (c) invite the return of a McCarthyite right-wing reaction; and (d) risk undermining domestic support for a continuing U.S. role abroad, in turn, risking dangerous probes by Russia and China.

There can be no doubt, despite the lack of supporting evidence in the Pentagon Papers, about the importance of domestic political considerations in both the initial commitment to and the subsequent increase in our Vietnam involvement. Officials are reluctant, for obvious reasons, to put these considerations down in writing, and scholars therefore learn too little about them. It should also be noted that domestic political factors played a key part in shaping the manner in which the war was fought—no reserve call-ups, certain limitations on bombing targetting, paying for the war, and the like.

4. Imperialism

This explanation is a variant of the domestic politics explanation. Proponents of this view argue that special interest groups maneuvered the United States into the war. Their goal was to capture export markets and natural resources at public expense for private economic gain.

The evidence put forward to support this "devil theory" has not been persuasive. Certain groups do gain economically from wars, but their power to drive our political system into war tends to be exaggerated and over-dramatized.

5. Men Making Hard Choices Pragmatically

This is the view that our leaders over the years were not men who were inspired by any particular ideology, but were pragmatists weighing the evidence and looking at each problem on its merits. According to this perspective, our leaders knew they were facing tough choices, and their decisions always were close ones. But having decided 51 to 49 to go ahead, they tried to sell and implement their policies one hundred percent.

This view cannot be dismissed out-of-hand. Most of our leaders, and especially our Presidents, occupied centrist political positions. But Vietnam is a case, I believe, where practical politicians allowed an anticommunist world view to get the best of them.

6. Balance of Power Politics

Intimately related to the pragmatic explanations is the conception which often accompanies pragmatism—the desire to maintain some perceived balance-of-power among nations. The principal considerations in pursuing this goal were: seeing that "the illegal use of force" is not allowed to succeed, honoring commitments, and keeping credibility with allies and potential adversaries. The underlying judgment was that failure to stop aggression in one place would tempt others to aggress in ever more dangerous places.

These represent the words and arguments most commonly and persuasively used in the executive branch, the Congress, and elsewhere. They seemed commonsensical and prudential. Most Americans were prepared to stretch their meaning to Vietnam. No doubt many believed these arguments on their own merits, but in most cases, I think, the broader tenet of anti-communism made them convincing.

7. The Slippery Slope

Tied to the pragmatic approach, the conception of balance of power and the arrogance of power, is the explanation which holds that United States involvement in Vietnam is the story of the slippery slope. According to this view, Vietnam was not always critical to U.S. national security; it became so over the years as each succeeding administration piled commitment on commitment. Each administration sort of slid further into the Vietnam quagmire, not really understanding the depth of the problems in Vietnam and convinced that it could win. The catchwords of this view are optimism and inadvertence.

While this explanation undoubtedly fits certain individuals and certain periods of time, it is, by itself, a fundamental distortion of the Vietnam experience. From the Korean War, stated American objectives for Vietnam were continuously high and absolute. U.S. involvement, not U.S. objectives, increased over time. Moreover, to scrutinize the range of official public statements and the private memos as revealed in the Pentagon Papers makes it difficult to argue that our leaders were deceived by the enormity of the Vietnam task before them. It was not necessary for our leaders to believe they were going to win. It was sufficient for them to believe that they could not afford to lose Vietnam to communism.

8. Anti-Communism

The analysts who offer this explanation hold that anti-communism was the central and all-pervasive fact of U.S. foreign policy from at least 1947 until the end of the sixties. After World War II, an ideology whose very existence seemed to threaten basic American values had combined with the national force of first Russia and then China. This combination of ideology and power brought our leaders to see the world in "we-they" terms and to insist that peace was indivisible. Going well beyond balance of power considerations, every piece of territory became critical, and every besieged nation, a potential domino. Communism came to be seen as an infection to be quarantined rather than a force to be judiciously and appropriately balanced. Vietnam, in particular became the cockpit of confrontation between the "Free World" and Totalitarianism; it was where the action was for 20 years.

In my opinion, simple anti-communism was the principal reason for

United States involvement in Vietnam. It is not the whole story, but it is the biggest part.

As of this point in my own research, I advance three propositions to explain why, how, and with what expectations the United States became involved in the Vietnam war.

First, U.S. involvement in Vietnam is not mainly or mostly a story of step by step, inadvertent descent into unforeseen quicksand. It is primarily a story of why U.S. leaders considered that it was vital not to lose Vietnam by force to Communism. Our leaders believed Vietnam to be vital not for itself, but for what they thought its "loss" would mean internationally and domestically. Previous involvement made further involvement more unavoidable, and, to this extent, commitments were inherited. But judgments of Vietnam's "vitalness"—beginning with the Korean War—were sufficient in themselves to set the course for escalation.

Second, our Presidents were never actually seeking a military victory in Vietnam. They were doing only what they thought was minimally necessary at each stage to keep Indochina, and later South Vietnam, out of Communist hands. This forced our Presidents to be brakemen, to do less than those who were urging military victory and to reject proposals for disengagement. It also meant that our Presidents wanted a negotiated settlement without fully realizing (though realizing more than their critics) that a civil war cannot be ended by political compromise.

Third, our Presidents and most of their lieutenants were not deluded by optimistic reports of progress and did not proceed on the basis of wishful thinking about winning a military victory in South Vietnam. They recognized that the steps they were taking were not adequate to win the war and that unless Hanoi relented, they would have to do more and more. Their strategy was to persevere in hope that their will to continue—if not the practical effects of their actions—would cause the Communists to relent.

4

promise
and aspiration

The "Kennedy mystique" began to develop while John Kennedy still occupied the White House, but it took on ever larger proportions after his assassination. Arthur Schlesinger, Jr., an adviser and admirer of the President, made the Kennedy family seem larger than life in his laudatory history A Thousand Days. *This selection from the book told much about the Kennedys—their values, their pleasures, their outlook on life—and it revealed even more about the Kennedy myth, for the people in these pages always seem a little too charming and a little too clever. In many places the picture is cliché-ridden: the frolicking, carefree children, the wife who is a "sanctuary of comfort and affection," and the vibrant, immaculately groomed President who is equally at home on a boat, at a dinner dance, or at his desk. Schlesinger attributed Kennedy's successes to his "presidential government" of advisers; his administration's failure came from what Schlesinger called the "permanent government" of bureaucrats.*

What qualities does this selection reveal in John Kennedy? What qualities should a president have? Why was Kennedy remembered with such devotion? What was the difference, in Schlesinger's terms, between the "presidential government" and the "permanent government"? Was there validity in this distinction, and do you agree with Schlesinger that the office of the President was much weaker than most people believed?

Arthur M. Schlesinger, Jr.

Kennedy:
In the White House

The day began at quarter to eight. George Thomas, his devoted and humorous Negro valet, would knock at the door of the Kennedy bedroom. As he sat down before his breakfast tray, surrounded by the morning papers and urgent cables and reports which may have come in during the night, Caroline and John would rush in, greet their father and turn on the television to watch animated cartoons. Then more presidential reading, with the television going full blast. At nine o'clock a calisthenics program came on, and Kennedy liked to watch the children tumble on the bedroom floor in rhythm with the man on the screen. Then, taking one of the children by the hand, he would walk over to the presidential office in the West Wing.

After a morning of work and a swim, often with David Powers, in the White House pool, he returned to the Mansion for luncheon. He preferred to lunch alone or with Jacqueline; very occasionally he brought guests. After luncheon came the nap. Impressed by Churchill's eloquence in praise of afternoon rest, he had begun this practice in the Senate. It was a genuine sleep, in pajamas and under covers. He went off at once; and in forty-five minutes would awaken and chat as he dressed. This was Jacqueline's hour of the day, as the morning was the children's.

This historian, it must be said, had not realized how constricted the living quarters of an American President were. The first floor of the Mansion was given over to public rooms and reserved for state occasions. The third floor was rarely mentioned. The private life of the Kennedys took place on the second floor under conditions which an average Park Avenue tycoon would regard as claustrophobic. A long dark corridor, brightened by a set of Catlin's Indian paintings, transected the floor. Bedrooms debouched from each side. A yellow oval room, marvelously light and lovely, was used for tea or drinks before dinner; it had served earlier Presidents as an office. Another room at the west end of the corridor was Jacqueline's room by day and the sitting room in the evening. Dinner guests resorted to the President's own bathroom. It was not a house for spacious living. Yet, until Theodore Roosevelt persuaded the Congress to build the West Wing, Presidents not only raised their families in these crowded quarters but ran the country from them.

It never seemed unduly crowded in these days. The atmosphere was always one of informality. When his family was away, the President used to have his afternoon appointments on the second floor. But generally he returned to the West Wing after his nap, where he worked until seven-thirty or eight at night. Jacqueline liked to guard the evenings for relaxation, and the President welcomed the relief from the incessant business of the day. These were the times when he confided

Arthur M. Schlesinger, Jr., *A Thousand Days: John F. Kennedy in the White House,* Houghton Mifflin Co. (Boston, 1965), 665-689. Copyright © 1965 by Arthur Schlesinger, Jr. Reprinted by permission of Houghton Mifflin Company.

public affairs to his subconscious mind, exposed himself to new people and ideas and recharged his intellectual energies. One of Jacqueline's charms, Robert Kennedy once said, was that "Jack knows she'll never greet him with 'What's new in Laos?' " From time to time, of course, she did, as one crisis or another dominated the headlines, and he would tell Bundy to show her the cables. But her central effort was to assure him a sanctuary of comfort and affection.

After the first year, they left the White House very seldom for private dinners elsewhere, though Kennedy always enjoyed the food and conversation at Joseph Alsop's. Instead, Jacqueline would arrange small dinners of six, eight or ten in the Mansion. They were informal and gay, the most agreeable occasions in the world. One memorable evening celebrated Stravinsky's seventy-fifth birthday. The composer, who had been rehearsing all day, was both excited and tired. A Chicago newspaper publisher, also present, insisted on talking across him at dinner to the President about such issues as Katanga and Medicare. Stravinsky said to me later, "They were speaking about matters which I did not understand and about which I did not care. I became an alien in their midst." But then the President toasted him and Stravinsky, obviously moved, responded with immense charm. On less formal evenings Jacqueline would sometimes put on phonograph records and there might be a moment of dancing. The President often vanished silently into his bedroom to work or make phone calls, reappearing in time to bid his guests goodnight. Occasionally there were films in the projection room in the East Wing. Kennedy was not a great movie fan and tended, unless the film was unusually gripping, to walk out after the first twenty or thirty minutes.

Private relationships are always a puzzle for Presidents. "The Presidency," Kennedy once remarked, "is not a very good place to make new friends"—or sometimes to keep old ones either. They watched with fascination how White Housitis affected their acquaintances, leading some to grievance and others to sycophancy and discussed a book which might be written called "The Poison of the Presidency." By 1963 the dinners became somewhat less frequent. More and more the President fell back on the easy and reliable company of tried friends—William Walton, the Benjamin Bradlees, the Charles Bartletts, the David Ormsby Gores, the Franklin Roosevelts.

The state dinners were inevitable, but Jacqueline made them bearable by ending the old regimented formality of solemn receiving lines and stilted conversation and changing them into elegant and cheerful parties, beautifully mingling informality and dignity. When asked about White House dinners, people would now say with surprise that they really had a very good time. But the gala occasions were the small dinner dances. Jacqueline conceived them as a means of restoring a larger social gaiety to her husband's life. When several months of unrelenting pressure had gone by, she would feel that the time had come for another dancing party and begin to look for a pretext to give one, whether to say hello or farewell to the Radziwills, welcome Kenneth Galbraith or honor Eugene Black. There were not many such parties—only five in the whole time in the White House—and they were all blithe and enchanting evenings. The President seemed renewed by them and walked with a springier step the next day.

The Kennedys liked to preserve the weekends as much as possible for themselves and the children. In 1961 they took a house at Glen Ora in Virginia; but the President found it confining and in later years preferred to go to Roosevelt's old refuge of Shangri-La at Catoctin Mountain in Maryland, renamed by Eisenhower Camp David after his grandson. In the winter there was Palm Beach, where they went for longer periods at Christmas and Easter, and in the summer Hyannis Port and Newport. Sailing relaxed him most of all—the sun, the breeze, the water; above all, no telephone. He could get along quite happily even without the sun and used to insist on taking his friends out on dark and chilly days. The guests would huddle together against the cold while the President sat in the stern in a black sweater, the wind blowing his hair, blissfully happy with a steaming bowl of fish chowder. . . .

Seated at his desk or in the rocking chair in front of the fireplace, immaculately dressed in one of his two-buttoned, single-breasted suits, he radiated a contained energy, electric in its intensity. Occasionally it would break out, especially during long and wandering meetings. His fingers gave the clue to his impatience. They would suddenly be in constant action, drumming the table, tapping his teeth, slashing impatient pencil lines on a pad, jabbing the air to underscore a point. Sometimes the constraint of the four walls seemed too much, and he would stride across the room, pausing wryly to look at the mass of indentations left on the floor by his predecessor's golf cleats, throw open the doors to the lawn and walk up and down the colonnade. One day, while talking, he rose from his desk, picked up his cane, inverted it and started making golf swings; then, looking up with a smile, he said, "I'm getting to be more like Ike every day!"

He had to an exceptional degree the talent for concentration. When he put on his always surprising horn-rimmed glasses and read a document, it was with total intentness; in a moment he would have seized its essence and returned to the world he had left. He was for the same reason a superb listener. "Whoever he's with," someone said, "he's with them completely." He would lean forward, his eyes protruding slightly, concerned with using the occasion not to expound his own thoughts but to drag out of the talker whatever could be of use to him. Isaiah Berlin was reminded of a remark made about Lenin: that he could exhaust people by listening to them. In this way he ventilated problems in great detail without revealing his own position and without making his visitors conscious that he was holding back.

His manners were distinguished, and the more timid or lowly the people, the greater his consideration. "Mr. Kennedy's almost awesome egalitarianism," Secret Service Chief Baughman later wrote, was "in some ways even greater than Mr. Truman's." His moments of irritation were occasional but short. They came generally because he felt that he had been tricked, or because a crisis caught him without warning, or because someone in the government had leaked something to the press. The air would rock for a moment; his years in the Navy and in Massachusetts politics had not been in vain and, when pressed, his vocabulary was vivid. But, though he got mad quickly, he stayed mad briefly. He was a man devoid of hatred. He detested qualities but not people. Calm would soon descend, and in time the irritation would become a matter for jokes.

"Humour," said Hazlitt, "is the describing the ludicrous as it is in itself; wit is the exposing it, by comparing or contrasting it with something else. Humour is, as it were, the growth of nature and accident; wit is the product of art and fancy." Franklin Roosevelt was a man of humor, Kennedy a man of wit. Irony was his most distinctive mode ("Washington is a city of southern efficiency and northern charm"). Explaining the origins of *Six Crises,* Nixon wrote about his visit to Kennedy after the Bay of Pigs: "When I told him that I was considering the possibility of joining the 'literary' ranks, of which he is himself so distinguished a member, he expressed the thought that every public man should write a book at some time in his life, both for the mental discipline and because it tends to elevate him in popular esteem to the respected status of an 'intellectual.' " Only the solemnity with which Kennedy's remark was received could possibly have exceeded the ambiguity with which it was uttered.

His irony could be gentle or sharp, according to mood, and it was directed at himself as often as at others. It helped him to lighten crises and to hold people and problems in balance; it was an unending source of refreshment and perspective, and an essential part of his own apparatus of self-criticism. Detachment was one of his deepest reflexes. When the first volume of Eisenhower's presidential reminiscences came out, he said drily to me, "Apparently Ike never did anything wrong. . . . When we come to writing the memoirs of this administration, we'll do it differently." And self-criticism was a vital strength in his luminous and rational intelligence, so consecutive and objective, so lucidly in possession of his impulses and emotions. . . .

He always shrank from portentous discussions of himself and the Presidency (or anything else). Pressed, he turned questioners aside: "I have a nice home, the office is close by and the pay is good." In the autumn of 1961 Kennedy was sitting on the lawn of his mother-in-law's house in Newport, smoking a fragrant pre-Castro cigar, while in the background the sun was setting and a great battle cruiser was entering the bay. It was the time of Berlin and the Soviet resumption of testing; in California Nixon was having his troubles with former Governor Goodwin Knight in internal Republican politics. As the warship steamed along, the American flag flying high, a friend felt a patriotic glow and was moved to ask Kennedy: "What do you *feel* at a moment like this? What is it *like* to be President?" The President smiled, flicked the ash from his cigar and said, "Well, it's a lot better than mucking around with Goody Knight in California." Once James Reston asked him what he hoped to achieve by the time he rode down Pennsylvania Avenue with his successor. "He looked at me," Reston later wrote, "as if I were a dreaming child. I tried again: Did he not feel the need of some goal to help guide his day-to-day decisions and priorities? Again a ghastly pause. It was only when I turned the question to immediate, tangible problems that he seized the point and rolled off a torrent of statistics." Reston concluded that Kennedy had no large designs; but I suspect that the President was simply stupefied by what he regarded as the impracticality of the question. He was possessed not by a blueprint but by a process.

In order to get the country moving again, he had to get the government moving. He came to the White House at a time when the ability of the President to do this had suffered steady constriction. The clichés about the 'most powerful office on earth' had concealed the extent to which the mid-century Presidents had much less freedom of action than, say, Jackson or Lincoln or even Franklin Roosevelt. No doubt the mid-century Presidents could blow up the world, but at the same time they were increasingly hemmed in by the growing power of the executive bureaucracy and of Congress—and at a time when crisis at home and abroad made clear decision and swift action more imperative than ever before. The President understood this. "Before my term has ended," he said in his first State of the Union address, "we shall have to test anew whether a nation organized and governed such as ours can endure. The outcome is by no means certain."

Kennedy was fully sensitive—perhaps oversensitive—to the limitations imposed by Congress on the presidential freedom of maneuver. But, though he was well aware of the problem within the executive domain, I do not think he had entirely appreciated its magnitude. The textbooks had talked of three coordinate branches of government: the executive, the legislative, the judiciary. But with an activist President it became apparent that there was a fourth branch: the Presidency itself. And, in pursuing his purposes, the President was likely to encounter almost as much resistance from the executive branch as from the others. By 1961 the tension between the permanent government and the presidential government was deep in our system. . . .

The Bay of Pigs was a crucial episode in the struggle. This disaster was a clear consequence of the surrender of the presidential government to the permanent government. The inherited executive bureaucracy rallied in support of an undertaking which the new administration would never conceivably have designed for itself. The CIA had a heavy investment in this project; other barons, having heavy investments in their own pre-Kennedy projects doubtless wished to show that the newcomers could not lightly reject whatever was bubbling up in the pipeline, however repugnant it might be to the preconceptions of the New Frontier. But the result, except for leading the President to an invaluable overhaul of his own operating methods, was ironically not to discredit the permanent government; instead, it became in certain ways more powerful than ever. The reason for this was that, one risk having failed, all risks were regarded with suspicion; and, since the permanent government almost never wished to take risks (except for the CIA, where risks were the entrenched routine), this strengthened those who wanted to keep things as they were as against those who wanted to change things. The fiasco was also a shock to the President's hitherto supreme confidence in his own luck; and it had a sobering effect throughout the presidential government. No doubt this was in many ways to the good; but it also meant that we never quite recaptured again the youthful, adventurous spirit of the first days. "Because this bold initiative flopped," I noted in June 1961, "there is now a general predisposition against boldness in all fields." With one stroke the permanent government had dealt a savage blow to the élan of the newcomers—and it had the satisfaction of having done so by persuading the newcomers to depart from their own principles and accept the permanent government's plan. . . .

Kennedy tried in a number of ways to encourage innovation in the permanent government. His call for "dissent and daring" in the first State of the Union message concluded: "Let the public service be a proud and lively career." He took particular pleasure in the rehabilitation of government servants who had been punished for independence of thought in the past. Early on, for example, Reed Harris, whom

Senator McCarthy had driven from USIA a decade before, came back to work under Edward R. Murrow, who himself had been one of McCarthy's bravest critics. The President looked for an appropriate occasion to invite Robert Oppenheimer to the White House and soon found one. He was vigilant in his opposition to any revival of McCarthyism. One of his few moments of anger in press conferences came when a woman reporter asked him why "two well-known security risks" had been given assignments in the State Department. Kennedy remarked icily that she "should be prepared to substantiate" her charges and unconditionally defended the character and record of the officials involved.

But Kennedy's habit of reaching into the permanent government was disruptive as well as exciting for the bureaucracy. For the permanent government had its own set of requirements and expectations—continuity of policy, stability of procedure, everything within channels and according to the book. These were essential; without them government would collapse. Yet an active President, with his own requirements and expectations, was likely to chafe under the bureaucratic minuet. . . .

He considered results more important than routine. "My experience in government," he once said, "is that when things are noncontroversial, beautifully coordinated, and all the rest, it must be that not much is going on." He was not, like Roosevelt, a deliberate inciter of bureaucratic disorder; he found no pleasure in playing off one subordinate against another. But his total self-reliance, his confidence in his own priorities and his own memory, freed him from dependence on orderly administrative arrangements. In any case, the Constitution made it clear where the buck stopped. "The President," he once said, "bears the burden of the responsibility. . . . The advisers may move on to new advice." The White House, of course, could not do everything, but it could do something. "The President can't administer a department," he said drily on one occasion, "but at least he can be a stimulant." This Kennedy certainly was, but on occasion he almost administered departments too.

His determination was to pull issues out of the bureaucratic ruck in time to defend his own right to decision and his own freedom of innovation. One devoted student of his methods, Prime Minister Harold Wilson, later spoke of the importance of getting in on emerging questions "by holding meetings of all relevant ministers at an early stage before the problem gets out of hand. That's one of the techniques the world owes to Kennedy." In this and other respects he carried his intervention in the depths of government even further than Roosevelt. . . .

His first instrument was the White House staff. This was a diverse group, and Kennedy wanted it that way. Bundy liked to compare the staff to prisms through which the President could look at public problems; and he knew precisely the angle of each refraction. One of his talents was the capacity to attract natural oppositionists—Galbraith, Kaysen, Murrow and others—and put them to work for government. He had some of these on his staff, along with some who were natural public servants; together they provided the mix which met his needs.

He was infinitely accessible to the Special Assistants. One could nearly always get him by phone; and, while Ken O'Donnell guarded one entrance to the presidential office with a wise concern for the President's time and energy, Evelyn Lincoln presided over the other with welcoming patience and warmth. For the half hour or so before luncheon and then again in the last hour of the afternoon, the door between Mrs. Lincoln's office and the President's room was generally ajar—a signal to the staff that he was open for business. One put one's head in the door, was beckoned in; then the report was made or document cleared briskly across his desk. Everything was transacted in a kind of shorthand. Kennedy's mind raced ahead of his words; and, by the time he was midway in a thought, he was likely to assume that the drift was evident and, without bothering to complete one sentence, he would begin the next. In the early evening, however, after the Huntley-Brinkley news program, the pressure would be off. Then he would frequently be in a mood to lean back in his chair and expand on the events of the day.

He liked to regard his staff as generalists rather than specialists and had a distressing tendency to take up whatever happened to be on his desk and hand it to whoever happened to be in the room. But a measure of specialization was inevitable, and the staff on the whole contrived its own clandestine structure, taking care to pass on a presidential directive to the person in whose area it lay. He never forgot anything, however, and he was perfectly capable weeks or months later of demanding to know what one had done about such-and-such.

He expected his staff to cover every significant sector of federal activity —to know everything that was going on, to provide speedy and exact answers to his questions and, most of all, to alert him to potential troubles. When a crisis was sprung without notice, there would be ejaculations of incredulity or despair; "For God's sake, do I have to do everything around here myself?" These passed swiftly; he wasted little time in recrimination and always buckled down promptly to the problem of what to do next. For those who failed him, remorse was a far sharper spur than reprimands would have been.

He wanted the staff to get into substance. He constantly called for new ideas and programs. If a staff member told him about a situation, he would say, "Yes, but what can I do about it?" and was disappointed if no answer was forthcoming. The Special Assistants were not to get between the President and the operating chiefs of the departments and agencies; but they were to make sure that the departmental and agency recommendations took full account of the presidential and national interests. When the operating chiefs had business which was important enough for the White House to be informed but not important enough to justify a direct call to the President, they had a place to register their recommendation or make their point. Above all, the responsibility of the staff, Kennedy said, was to make certain that "important matters are brought here in a way which permits a clear decision after alternatives have been presented." He added, "Occasionally, in the past, I think the staff has been used to get a pre-arranged agreement which is only confirmed at the President's desk, and that I don't agree with."

When a decision was in the offing, the next step was to call a meeting. Kennedy disliked meetings, especially large ones, and insisted that they be honed to the edge of action. He convened the cabinet far less even than Roosevelt. "Cabinet meetings," he once told John Sharon, "are simply useless. Why should the Postmaster General sit there and listen to a discussion of the problems of Laos? . . . I don't know how Presidents functioned with them or relied on them in the past." (Very few good ones had.) Instead, he asked for weekly reports from cabinet members outlining their activities and proposals. In consequence, he did not use the cabinet as effectively as he might have either to mobilize the government or to advance public understanding of administration policies. Perhaps the best cabinet meeting was in the midst of the Bay of Pigs when there were genuine exchange and assurances of reciprocal support.

If he had to have a meeting, he preferred a small one with candid discussion among the technicians and professionals who could give him the facts on which decision was to be based. Policy people were less essential because he could supply policy himself. Kennedy would listen quietly to the presentation, then ask pertinent questions and expect precise replies. He had a disconcerting capacity, derived in part from his larger perspective and in part from his more original intelligence, to raise points which the experts, however diligently they had prepared themselves, were hard put to answer. Rambling made him impatient, but his courtesy was unshakable; there were only those drumming fingers. At the end, he would succinctly sum up the conclusions.

Just a few months before the Gulf of Tonkin incident provoked a dramatic widening of the war in Viet Nam, Lyndon Johnson announced the blueprint for a Great Society Program which would not only end poverty and racial injustice but would dramatically elevate the quality of American life through beautification projects, urban renewal, and educational reform. Assisted by the inspiration of John Kennedy's legacy and by the practical political know-how of President Johnson, dozens of Great Society programs passed Congress. They represented Johnson's most fervent hopes for America and for his own historical reputation.

Though well-intentioned, the Great Society never survived its centralized bureaucratic management or the foreign war which demanded even greater amounts of America's treasure. Ironically, Johnson's important place in history is secure, but he will be remembered less for these ill-fated domestic reforms than for the bitter war which seared American honor and tranquility.

How did Johnson view government's relationship to the people? Does a centralized government represent a greater or lesser threat to personal liberty than local government? What were Johnson's Great Society priorities? If one proposed a Great Society today, how might concerns have changed?

Lyndon B. Johnson

The Great Society:
Speech at Ann Arbor

I have come today from the turmoil of your capital to the tranquility of your campus to speak about the future of your country.

The purpose of protecting the life of our nation and preserving the liberty of our citizens is to pursue the happiness of our people. Our success in that pursuit is the test of our success as a nation.

For a century we labored to settle and to subdue a continent. For half a century we called upon unbounded invention and untiring industry to create an order of plenty for all of our people.

The challenge of the next half century is whether we have the wisdom to use that wealth to enrich and elevate our national life, and to advance the quality of our American civilization.

Your imagination, your initiative, and your indignation will determine whether we build a society where progress is the servant of our needs, or a society where old values and new visions are buried under unbridled growth. For in your time we have the opportunity to move not only toward the rich society and the powerful society, but upward to the Great Society.

The Great Society rests on abundance and liberty for all. It demands an end to poverty and racial injustice, to which we are totally committed in our time. But that is just the beginning.

The Great Society is a place where every child can find knowledge to enrich his mind and to enlarge his talents. It is a place where leisure is a welcome chance to build and reflect, not a feared cause of boredom and restlessness. It is a place where the city of man serves not only the needs of the body and the demands of commerce but the desire for beauty and the hunger for community.

It is a place where man can renew contact with nature. It is a place which honors creation for its own sake and for what it adds to the understanding of the race. It is a place where men are more concerned with the quality of their goals than the quantity of their goods.

But most of all, the Great Society is not a safe harbor, a resting place, a final objective, a finished work. It is a challenge constantly renewed, beckoning us toward a destiny where the meaning of our lives matches the marvelous products of our labor.

So I want to talk to you today about three places where we begin to build the Great Society—in our cities, in our countryside, and in our classrooms.

Many of you will live to see the day perhaps fifty years from now, when there will be 400 million Americans—four-fifths of them in urban areas. In the remainder of this century urban population will double, city land will double, and we will have to build homes, highways, and

Public Papers of the Presidents of the United States: Lyndon B. Johnson, Government Printing Office (Washington, D.C., 1965), I (1963-1964), 704-707.

facilities equal to all those built since this country was first settled. So in the next forty years we must rebuild the entire urban United States.

Aristotle said: "Men come together in cities in order to live, but they remain together in order to live the good life." It is harder and harder to live the good life in American cities today.

The catalogue of ills is long: there is the decay of the centers and the despoiling of the suburbs. There is not enough housing for our people or transportation for our traffic. Open land is vanishing and old landmarks are violated.

Worst of all expansion is eroding the precious and time-honored values of community with neighbors and communion with nature. The loss of these values breeds loneliness and boredom and indifference.

Our society will never be great until our cities are great. Today the frontier of imagination and innovation is inside those cities and not beyond their borders. . . .

A second place where we begin to build the Great Society is in our countryside. We have always prided ourselves on being not only America the strong and America the free, but America the beautiful. Today that beauty is in danger. The water we drink, the food we eat, the very air that we breathe, are threatened with pollution. Our parks are overcrowded, our seashores overburdened. Green fields and dense forests are disappearing.

A few years ago we were greatly concerned about the "Ugly American." Today we must act to prevent an ugly America.

For once the battle is lost, once our natural splendor is destroyed, it can never be recaptured. And once man can no longer walk with beauty or wonder at nature his spirit will wither and his sustenance be wasted.

A third place to build the Great Society is in the classrooms of America. There your children's lives will be shaped. Our society will not be great until every young mind is set free to scan the farthest reaches of thought and imagination. We are still far from that goal. . . .

Each year more than 100,000 high school graduates, with proved ability, do not enter college because they cannot afford it. And if we cannot educate today's youth, what will we do in 1970 when elementary school enrollment will be 5 million greater than 1960? And high school enrollment will rise by 5 million. College enrollment will increase by more than 3 million.

In many places, classrooms are overcrowded and curricula are outdated. Most of our qualified teachers are underpaid, and many of our paid teachers are unqualified. So we must give every child a place to sit and a teacher to learn from. Poverty must not be a bar to learning, and learning must offer an escape from poverty.

But more classrooms and more teachers are not enough. We must seek an educational system which grows in excellence as it grows in size. This means better training for our teachers. It means preparing youth to enjoy their hours of leisure as well as their hours of labor. It means exploring new techniques of teaching, to find new ways to stimulate the love of learning and the capacity for creation.

These are three of the central issues of the Great Society. While our government has many programs directed at those issues, I do not pretend that we have the full answer to those problems. . . .

But I do promise this: We are going to assemble the best thought and the broadest knowledge from all over the world to find those answers for America. I intend to establish working groups to prepare a series of White House conferences and meetings—on the cities, on natural beauty, on the quality of education, and on other emerging challenges. And from these meetings and from this inspiration and from these studies we will begin to set our course toward the Great Society.

The solution to these problems does not rest on a massive program in Washington, nor can it rely solely on the strained resources of local authority. They require us to create new concepts of cooperation, a creative federalism, between the national capital and the leaders of local communities.

Within your lifetime powerful forces, already loosed, will take us toward a way of life beyond the realm of our experience, almost beyond the bounds of our imagination.

For better or for worse, your generation has been appointed by history to deal with those problems and to lead America toward a new age. You have the chance never before afforded to any people in any age. You can help build a society where the demands of morality, and the needs of the spirit, can be realized in the life of the nation.

So, will you join in the battle to give every citizen the full equality which God enjoins and the law requires, whatever his belief, or race, or the color of his skin?

Will you join in the battle to give every citizen an escape from the crushing weight of poverty?

Will you join in the battle to make it possible for all nations to live in enduring peace—as neighbors and not as mortal enemies?

Will you join in the battle to build the Great Society, to prove that our material progress is only the foundation on which we will build a richer life of mind and spirit?

There are those timid souls who say this battle cannot be won; that we are condemned to a soulless wealth. I do not agree. We have the power to shape the civilization that we want. But we need your will, your labor, your hearts, if we are to build that kind of society.

Those who came to this land sought to build more than just a new country. They sought a new world. So I have come here today to your campus to say that you can make their vision our reality. So let us from this moment begin our work so that in the future men will look back and say: It was then, after a long and weary way, that man turned the exploits of his genius to the full enrichment of his life.

The early Civil Rights movement was inextricably connected with the name and philosophy of Martin Luther King. In this selection a prominent black writer, John A. Williams, examined King's background and philosophy, stressing his Southern middle class origins and implicitly questioning his movement's relevance to the bulk of black people who were urban and oppressed. Williams even questioned the heretofore unquestionable: how much success King could even claim in the southern desegregation battles? Clearly Williams, himself a middle class black, believed that lower-class militancy, not bourgeois nonviolence, was the inevitable trend for black people. He concluded that the black middle class would turn toward the ghetto, not toward the trappings of white respectability as King's organization tended to do. This selection reveals much about Martin Luther King and also about his more militant followers. It also suggests John Williams' agonizing reappraisal of his own relationship to the black revolution.

What was Williams' view of the early desegregation struggles in the South? What kinds of things did King's movement fight for; what didn't they fight for? After his death, King became a hero to many Americans—both white and black. Does this selection suggest any reasons for his popularity? Has Williams' view of the proper role for the black middle class prevailed?

John A. Williams

The King
God Didn't Save

The late sociologist, E. Franklin Frazier, pointed out in his *Black Bourgeoisie* (The Macmillan Company, 1962) that after World War I the middle-class values began to change; lightness of color, for example, became less important than solid achievements in the professions. But there are still a goodly number of fair-skinned Negroes, older people to be sure, who consider themselves superior to Negroes with darker skins. Black societies in cities like Washington, D.C., and Atlanta, are still touched with the color-bug.

King himself, apparently, had some color hang-up. Over a period of about two years I had a series of running conversations with Person B. Of King's personal attitude toward women with dark skin, Person B told me: "Martin often said he was willing to fight and die for black people, but he was damned if he could see anything pretty in a *black* woman." Person B was lighter in complexion than King. But coming out of a home where his mother appeared to be pure Negro, and coming out of an organization in which his most trusted aid, Ralph Abernathy, could not be mistaken for anything but a Negro, King's color consciousness seems to have been a direct throwback to the social values of black Atlanta.

Another person I spoke to in pursuing answers to King's life, was Mrs. Hugh Butts, née Dobbs, who grew up with M. L. She said that when the Kings moved onto Boulevard Street in Atlanta, where her own parents lived, it was a "step up for them," meaning the Kings. Ella Baker told me there had been a long-time rivalry between the Kings and the Dobbs.

Musing about King in her West Side Manhattan brownstone, Mrs. Butts saw his accumulation of degrees and roster of schools attended as "symbols" of his middle-class position. "He wanted all the right things behind his name." Says Richard Hammer in *Commentary* (May, 1968) King was "well educated, something the Negro in the South prizes to an inordinate degree."

Black people of my generation and the generation before were taught that education is something no one can take away from you. The emphasis in black families was on education, and Louis Lomax states that in Georgia, "Everybody preached against such things as adultery and stealing, but the one venial sin was ignorance." He goes on to say that, "The education proffered us was of a poor quality, but this was more than overshadowed by the all but unbearable pressure that forced us to do our studies or be literally thrashed into insensibility."

And if a young man could take graduate studies in the white universities of the North, his status was increased manyfold. Morehouse College has sent countless numbers of its graduates north where an

Reprinted by permission of Coward, McCann & Geoghegan, Inc. from *The King God Didn't Save* by John A. Williams. Copyright © 1970 by John A. Williams, 151-162.

overwhelming majority of them have made good in professional and academic circles. The A.B. soon enough became almost nothing in terms of status; the M.A. became the target, and, finally, the Ph.D. How grand to roll around on the tongue the word "doctor"! How marvelous to be addressed as "doctor"!

A man clawing out his status doesn't stop with getting an education; there are attendant titles to earn. In the *Negro Handbook Biographical Dictionary* (Johnson, 1966) King is listed as an Elk and a member of Alpha Phi Alpha Fraternity. Of the former, E. Franklin Frazier wrote: ". . . . the Order of Elks is a means of power and income for middle class Negroes. . . . Because of the predominantly working class membership of the Order of Elks, a middle class Negro, if he is a doctor or college professor, will generally 'explain' his membership in the Elks on the grounds that it is necessary for his profession, or that he can render 'service.' "

Of the fraternities Frazier said, "It is through the Greek letter fraternities that the so-called intellectual members of the black bourgeoisie often gain recognition and power." Alpha Phi Alpha is the oldest black fraternity and by that accident, the most prestigious, and a handy organization for a young man on the way up to join. I too was once a member of that fraternity, and perhaps for the very same reasons.

Status, education and otherwise, would of course have been extremely empty things without other resources. Lerone Bennett comments: "Because of their church connections and financial interests, King's grandfather and, later, his father, were members of the ruling elite of Atlanta's Negro community which was considered by some the distilled essence of what E. Franklin Frazier called the Black Puritan class." In addition, young King was heir to the fabled Ebenezer Baptist Church, which was family-owned, passing from the fiery Adam Daniel Williams to his daughter Alberta's husband, Martin King, Sr. Next in line was Martin, Jr., and last, Adam Daniel, his brother, called A. D. (A. D. drowned during a bizarre midnight swim in his pool in the summer of 1969.)

The Kings were very much a part of the Atlanta scene, had contributed its generations to its development, its standards of culture, approved generally or not, and had a vested interest in maintaining their positions in it. Lomax: ". . . the black South had a stout and healthy middle class society in operation. We did not think of, nor did we wish for a day when we would melt into white society."

During an interview with Bayard Rustin I said, "I'm struck by the appearance that Martin was almost always involved with the black middle class, and perhaps didn't get to the guts of the black people until Chicago. Would you agree?"

We were lunching over his desk. Downstairs, on Park Avenue South, the traffic honked and snorted its way past. Rustin chewed and thought and finally said, "Well, I think I have to agree with that, but I think that was inevitable."

That inevitability sprang naturally from his middle-class background, as determinedly achieved and as tenaciously clung to as that had been for his parents in their beginning. That he was so involved in this "society without substance," as Frazier called it, is the direct result of national white attitudes toward black people. Because those attitudes were so pronouncedly racist, it was natural that within the oppressed community there would be reflected caste systems that were also to some degree racist. Now, it is time to return again to Montgomery, where it all took hold, the *Zeitgeist*—spirit of the times, as King liked to call it—the confluence of an eager, hero-seeking press, cracker intransigence, the Supreme Court's decision of 1954 and the restlessness of American blacks. It is somehow both fitting and paradoxical that Montgomery forged the cradle of the Confederacy as well as the cradle of the contemporary civil rights movement.

All these many, many years I've wondered what would have happened there in 1954 if it had not been for the presence of Mrs. Rosa Parks, who is credited for the action that sparked the movement. She was a seamstress. This is a bland image, calling to mind the fairy tale cliché of poor but honest. I've known black seamstresses who were rich, but I don't think this was the case with Mrs. Parks. What *was* the case was her middle-class standing in the black community.

What if Mrs. Parks had not been as King wrote, "a charming" woman; what if she had not had a "radiant personality," or an "impeccable" character, or possessed a "deep-rooted" dedication? What if she had just stepped out of a bar, had not been soft-spoken but raucous; suppose her slip had been hanging and her hair a little awry, her stocking seams twisted? What if she had let the bus driver have a shot in the face with her handbag?

I think then that her attempt to gain redress against the bus company and the Southern system would have first been thwarted by the Negroes in her own community, for not being exactly the right kind of person it was willing to go to bat for. Obviously, Claudette Colvin, a student, and others before her did not completely fill the requirements for the sort of people the community leaders would support. Mrs. Parks did enjoy status in the community and, as in any community, the black leaders in Montgomery were more willing to move on behalf of a substantial citizen than an unsubstantial one.

"Fortunately," King wrote, "Mrs. Parks was ideal for the role assigned to her by history."

King's presence in Montgomery had been as carefully plotted as the presence of, say, the Kennedys in the U.S. Senate. The Dexter Avenue Baptist Church was the place where the coming big men of the black Baptist organization served; it was a step on the escalator. King himself, with barely muted pride, described that first pastorate. The church was comparatively small, with a membership of around three hundred people, but it occupied a central place in the community. Many influential and respected citizens—professional people with substantial incomes—were among its members . . . [Dexter] was sort of a silk-stocking church catering only to a certain class. Often it was referred to as the 'big folks' church.' "

Lomax comments on Dexter: "As King well knew before he assumed the pastorate, the Dexter Avenue church did not enjoy a good reputation among Montgomery's black masses. . . . The plain implication was that nonprofessional and uneducated Negroes were not welcome at the Dexter Avenue altar. . . . It was this class discrimination in his own church, then, that first demanded Martin's attention." Lomax recalls that King's predecessor once became involved in an argument with a bus driver and then called for other black passengers to walk off the bus. "Not only did the Negroes remain in their seats, but one member of Dexter Avenue Church rebuked [the Reverend] Johns for his actions, saying, 'you should know better!' "

William Robert Miller writes more of the Dexter congregation in his biography, *Martin Luther King, Jr.:* ". . . the Dexter congregation included teachers from Alabama State College, as well as upper-income professionals, giving it a tone more intellectual and less emotional than the average."

Given King's upbringing, education, and his father's plans for him, King would very probably have refused to pastor a lesser church. No minister, as Lomax implies, accepts the leadership of a church without knowledge of its solvency or lack thereof, or of the composition of its congregation. King was later quoted as saying that he didn't understand the shouting and stamping, the "emotionalism" of Negro religion. It "embarrassed" him. Certainly an "intellectual" congregation appealed to him, also its financial ranking. Today's spiritual leaders do not live on faith alone. Religion is, after all, a business. The spires of the churches may stretch for the clouds, but the foundations are settled in dollars, or their pastors would like them to be.

It is not for me to say what the intellectual quality of King's congregation was at that time since I knew none of the parishioners. Intellectuals (often erroneously) tend to be associated with colleges or universities, and Alabama State College is the one King most often makes references to in *Stride*. I've never known anyone from Alabama State College, and have spoken to only one man on the faculty, and that, long after the boycott, long after King had gone on to greater fame. That professor refused to allow me to interview him because, he said, "Governor Wallace pays my salary; I have nothing to say to you."

In the cracker states the black colleges, many of which are physically similar to high schools, were established by state governments to prevent the educational development of black people. White people, of course, know this, and a growing number of black people, especially the young, are becoming aware of it. State governments sought and secured black people who were willing to abide by the rules of the system. The agreement was unwritten and unspoken; both parties simply *knew* what was being agreed to. (There were cases, however, and fortunately, when the rules were broken by the black teachers.) There could be no security for black teachers, if they did not go along with the system. Such thoroughly compromised people, in the main, have been the "intellectuals" on the faculties of the black colleges, and their major task was to provide their students with educations that could not be utilized. This is one of the reasons why, for close to a decade now, Negro students in the black colleges of crackerland have been demonstrating. They are starting to understand the system and how it operates, and they are angrily demanding a change.

James Forman's book, *Sammy Younge, Jr.* (Grove Press, 1968) details the problems black students had with their college teachers at Tuskegee, some miles north of Montgomery. The frightening part of the book is that the numbers of black teachers who collaborate with the system are not declining as rapidly as I once believed. Administrators of black colleges are on the firing line as often and as much as white college administrators—and they know it. I went to a meeting late in 1968 at which each person present had to introduce himself and present his credentials. One man did so with this phrase.

"My name is——and I was president of——College when I left it last night."

There was laughter, of course, but we all understood the ramifications of his statement, given the times.

There is no more telling example of King's long-time devotion to the black middle class than what happened to Montgomery after he left it. Lomax says in his *Negro Revolt:*

"Martin King left Montgomery, his work undone; the buses are integrated, but the schools are not; neither are the parks, playgrounds or other public facilities . . . one of the questions now plaguing the social scientists is why such a deep-rooted movement as the Montgomery boycott resulted in nothing more than the integration of the buses."

The answer, I think, is that the middle class in Montgomery felt it had pushed far enough; that *it* did not need open schools, parks, or playgrounds; that was a part of the unwritten contract with the system. The man in the underclass is determined to try to hold onto his dignity in the face of all the racist efforts to the contrary. The black man wishes his cup of coffee, his cheeseburger, his bus ride, his stroll through a public park, good schools for his children—to be free from the slightest hint that he possesses, or has been forced to possess, second-class citizenship. These needs are far more pressing for the black man in the street than for the middle class.

The middle-class man will eat his cheeseburger and drink his coffee in his split-level home in a middle-class neighborhood. His children and the children of his neighbors go to nearby schools, and since the neighborhood is middle class, so is the school. It goes without saying, almost, that the teachers are members in good standing of the same class. The middle-class black man will use his car for transportation, rather than suffer the daily indignity of using public transportation, and he will buy his clothes out of town so that he will not be demeaned in stores where he may not try on garments at all.

Montgomery, Alabama, had a black population of well over 45,000, or more than 35 percent of the total when King first went there. If his congregation at Dexter numbered only around 300 people, he was very possibly dealing with not the middle, but the black *upper* class of Montgomery. (Black people shy away from being considered upper class; this smacks suspiciously of behaving like Whitey.) Three hundred people do not a successful bus boycott make; nor do 5,000, which figure probably exhausted the number of middle-class blacks. Montgomery was a failure because of limited goals, uncertainty of approach, limited numbers of troops, and a failure to utilize consistently the city's entire black population.

On the other side of the coin, the white press so thoroughly indoctrinated King and his people with the idea that the capitulation of the bus company was a victory for the blacks, that they believed it; believed too that other things would inevitably fall like tin soldiers, all in a neat line.

The fact that the racist barriers did not fall down into a neat line, however, in Montgomery or anywhere else in this land, is the very reason why there is more black unity today among all classes than has ever existed before in the United States. Untold numbers of middle-class blacks have turned back to the ghetto, operating on the theory that they cannot "get loose," *i.e.*, gain a functioning place in American society, unless *all* black people gain it as well.

There is irony in the fact that Martin King was greatly, although indirectly responsible for what the white pollsters and newsmen call "the new militancy" in the black middle class. Many Negroes King's age, but generally older, believed that he was changing the racial climate for the better. The older people had children barely in their teens when the bus boycott was under way, and these youngsters moved, if not physically, at first, spiritually, with King. His nonviolent "militancy" was the *only* attack possible on the existing system; they had to go for it. Certainly there was the NAACP and the National Urban League, but these were Northern-based operations, and they chose to bang away in the courts, a time-consuming process, and one that was not guaranteed to pay off.

By 1960 the middle-class youngsters in the all-black colleges in crackerland were itching for speedier returns for practicing nonviolence than they had so far received. Perhaps having reached college age and going to institutions of higher learning sharpened their awareness. That is what college is supposed to do, and even state-supported crackerland colleges cannot escape forever what is common knowledge to everyone. Since college, at least in the United States, is the great stepping stone to middle-class life, the youngsters in the colleges automatically sought to transform things as they were into things as they wished them to be.

Although fading from memory, the Montgomery boycott nevertheless still evoked thoughts of the possibility of transferring the techniques that had made it appear to be a success to other areas of public accommodation protest. Time was fast slipping by. People who would be heard from in the early and middle sixties were emerging from their teens, people like John Lewis, Stokely Carmichael, and Rap Brown.

SNCC leaders have all come from the college-oriented middle class: Charles McDew, James Forman, John Lewis, Stokely Carmichael, and Rap Brown. Committed in the beginning to nonviolence, they were met and violently beaten. In the beginning, like their elders, they held the faith that they were dealing with a basically moral enemy. They had that faith shoved down their throats.

The "Honkie" and "Whitey" cries were born in despair, rejection, frustration, and white violence, and they did not spring first or only from the throats of Stokely or Rap. The treatment accorded SNCC was directly responsible for their formation of the Black Panthers. The leader of the most well-known group, the Oakland Panthers, is Huey P. Newton, another college-trained man, now in jail.

Older black middle-class people came to their own truths during the New York rebellion of 1964 and Watts I in 1965. There came talk that the cops where whipping black heads left and right, whether the owners of those heads were involved in the rebellions or not, or middle class or not. The talk was backed up by extensive documentation. Bread-winning middle-class blacks were being treated just like any Negro down at the pool hall. Newark and Detroit sent millions (and there are millions) of middle-class black people bounding down off the fence.

By 1967 the black middle class was apprehensively sniffing a strange, spine-tingling odor in the air. While King was still propounding non-violence, blacks raised the question of the possibility of black genocide at the hands of whites. Some whites, too, remarked that attitudes seemed to be swinging in that direction. Quietly, and purposefully, the middle class set out on a double-pronged venture. Return to the ghetto; unite with the man in the street. Supply him with help, education, encouragement—anything he needed to be a completely functioning man. And: Obtain arms. Although the white middle class is far, far ahead of the blacks in this respect, if Armageddon comes, there are going to be a number of very, very surprised white people. I hope black pepole have been trained well enough not to be surprised by whites, for there are many surprises lying in wait there, too.

*The black civil rights movement stimulated the growth of ethnic con-
sciousness among other minority groups. Hundreds of books and articles
published since the late 1960's have dealt with minority problems—from
cultural oppression to political non-representation to economic disadvantage. The following selection provides one example of the kind of intro-
spection which must be the first step in a minority group's self-assertion.
In this piece, Rubén Salazar uses concrete cases to discuss one of the
major problems of Mexican-Americans: the psychological implications
caused by the dominant culture's disdain for the Spanish language and
heritage. Studies such as Salazar's have helped end prohibitions on the
use of Spanish in many areas with Mexican, Puerto Rican, or Cuban-
American populations, and schools are now experimenting with bilingual
programs in the lower grades. Still, old attitudes of cultural chauvinism
are never far beneath the surface, and Spanish-speaking people must continue the work of restoring their past and making bilingualism a badge
of honor rather than disgrace.*

*In what ways, according to Salazar, are Spanish-speaking people con-
ditioned to feel ashamed of their language and heritage? What other
ethnic groups experience similar treatment? What are some remedies
which have been, or might be, adopted?*

Rubén Salazar

Stranger in One's Land

You know it almost from the beginning: speaking Spanish makes you different. Your mother, father, brothers, sisters, and friends all speak Spanish. But the bus driver, the teacher, the policeman, the store clerk, the man who comes to collect the rent—all the people who are doing important things—do not. Then the day comes when your teacher—who has taught you the importance of many things—tells you that speaking Spanish is wrong. You go home, kiss your mother, and say a few words to her in Spanish. You go to the window and look out and your mother asks you what's the matter?

Nada, mamá, you answer, because you don't know what is wrong. . . .

Howard A. Glickstein, then Acting Staff Director of the Commission asked witness Edgar Lozano, a San Antonio high school student, whether he has ever been punished for speaking Spanish at school. Yes, in grammar, in junior high, and in senior high schools, he answers.

". . . they took a stick to me," says Edgar. "It really stayed in your mind. Some things, they don't go away as easy as others."

Edgar relates with some bitterness and anger the times he was beaten by teachers for speaking Spanish at school after "getting a lecture about, if you want to be an American, you have got to speak English."

Glickstein tries to ask Edgar another question and the boy, this time more sad than angry, interrupts and says:

"I mean, how would you like for somebody to come up to you and tell you what you speak is a dirty language? You know, what your mother speaks is a dirty language? You know, that is the only thing I ever heard at home.

"A teacher comes up to you and tells you, 'No, no. You know that is a filthy language, nothing but bad words and bad thoughts in that language.'

"I mean, they are telling you that your language is bad. . . . Your mother and father speak a bad language, you speak a bad language. I mean you communicate with dirty words, and nasty ideas.

". . . that really stuck to my mind."

Edgar, like many Mexican Americans before him, had been scarred with the insults of an Anglo world which rejects everything except carbon copies of what it has decreed to be "American." You start being different and you end up being labeled as un-American.

What can a school, in which teacher and student speak not only different languages but are also on different emotional wave lengths, do to a Mexican American child?

This kind of school, Dr. Jack Forbes of Berkeley's Far West Laboratory for Educational Research and Development, told the Commission:

"Tends to lead to a great deal of alienation, a great deal of hostility,

Rubén Salazar, *Stranger in One's Land,* U.S. Government Printing Office, U.S. Commission on Civil Rights Clearing House Publication, No. 19 (May, 1970).

it tends to lead also to a great deal of confusion, where the child comes out of that school really not knowing who he is, not knowing what he should be proud of, not knowing what language he should speak other than English, being in doubt as to whether he should completely accept what Anglo people have been telling him and forget his Mexican identity, or whether he should listen to what his parents and perhaps other people have said and be proud of his Mexican identity."

The word "Mexican" has been and still is in many places in the Southwest a word of contempt. Mexican Americans refer to themselves as Mexicanos or Chicanos with the ease of those who know and understand each other. But when some Anglos talk about "Mexicans" the word takes on a new meaning, almost the counterpart of "nigger."

The Mexican Americans' insistence on keeping the Spanish language is but one aspect of cultural differences between Anglos and Mexican Americans.

Values differ between these two groups for a variety of historical reasons. Mexicans have deep rural roots which have produced a sense of isolation. Spanish Catholicism has given Mexicans an attitude of fatalism and resignation. Family ties are extremely important and time, or clock-watching, is not.

Luis F. Hernández, assistant professor of education at San Fernando Valley State College in Los Angeles, has described the differences this way:

"Mexican American values can be said to be directed toward tradition, fatalism, resignation, strong family ties, a high regard for authority, paternalism, personal relations, reluctance to change, a greater orientation to the present than to the future and a greater concern for being than doing.

"The contrasting Anglo-American values can be said to be directed toward change, achievement, impersonal relations, efficiency, progress, equality, scientific rationalization, democracy, individual action and reaction, and a greater concern for doing than being."

Distortion of or deletion of Mexicans' contribution to the Southwest in history books can inhibit a Mexican American child from the beginning of his schooling.

State Senator Joe Bernal of Texas told the Commission that "schools have not given us any reason to be proud" of being Mexican Americans. People running the schools "have tried to take away our language," the senator continued, and so Mexican American children very early are made to feel ashamed of the Spanish language and of being Mexican.

The children start building up defenses such as insisting on being called "Latin" or "Hispano" or "Spanish American" because, said Bernal, "they want no reference made to being Mexican." One of the reasons for this, Bernal told the Commission, is that "it has been inculcated" in the minds of grammar school children that the Mexican "is no good" by means of, for instance, overly and distortedly emphasizing the Battle of the Alamo and ignoring all contributions made by Mexicans in the Southwest.

To be Spanish, of course, is something else. Spanish has a European connotation and Europe is the motherland.

Carey McWilliams in his *North From Mexico* explains that "the Hispanic heritage of the Southwest has two parts: the Spanish and the Mexican-Indian. Originally one heritage, unified in time, they have long since been polarized. Carefully distinguished from the Mexican, the Spanish heritage is now enshrined throughout the Southwest. It has become the sacred or templar tradition of which the Mexican-Indian inheritance is the secular or profane counterpart. . . ."

Dr. Forbes noticed on his arrival in San Antonio for the hearing that things have not changed.

". . . the San Antonio greeter magazine which I picked up in a hotel lobby and which had the statement about the history of San Antonio said nothing about the Mexican heritage of this region, talking only about the glorious Spanish colonial era and things of this nature. . . ."

To be Spanish is fine because white is important and Spain is white.

Dr. Forbes reminded the Commission that "first of all, the Mexican American population is in great part a native population in the Southwest. It is not an immigrant population. Now this nativity in the Southwest stems not only from the pre-1848 period during the so-called Spanish colonial and Mexican periods, but it also stems from the fact that many people who today identify as Mexican Americans or in some areas as Hispanos, are actually of local Indian descent. . . ."

Aurelio Manuel Montemayor, who taught in San Felipe High School at Del Rio, Texas, explained to the Commission how in his view all this is ignored in the school curriculum.

Quoting from a State-approved textbook, Montemayor said the book related how "the first comers to America were mainly Anglo-Saxons but soon came Dutchmen, Swedes, Germans, Frenchmen, Africans, then the great 19th century period of immigration added to our already melting pot. Then later on, it [the textbook] said, the Spaniards came."

"So my students," continued Montemayor, "had no idea where they came from" and wondered whether "they were part of American society."

Betty Friedan's book, The Feminine Mystique, *helped stimulate a new awareness among women and contributed to the birth of the "women's liberation" movement. One of the organizers of the National Organization for Women (NOW), Friedan challenged the ideas that women were happiest in the home and that they found fulfillment solely from their roles as wives and mothers. Applying psychologist Erik Erikson's theories about "identity crises" to women (Erikson dealt primarily with men) and adapting the "self-actualization" research of Abraham Maslow, Friedan concludes that only by breaking out of the prison of the "feminine mystique" can women fulfill their "unique possibilities as separate human beings" and lead satisfying lives.*

Why did Friedan believe that most young women have difficulty picturing themselves in later life? Why do you think the early research on "identity crises" tended to focus on men? How much impact on society do you think Friedan's book has had? Does Friedan's book have any relevance for men?

Betty Friedan

The Feminine Mystique

I discovered a strange thing, interviewing women of my own generation over the past ten years. When we were growing up, many of us could not see ourselves beyond the age of twenty-one. We had no image of our own future, of ourselves as women.

I remember the stillness of a spring afternoon on the Smith campus in 1942, when I came to a frightening dead end in my own vision of the future. A few days earlier, I had received a notice that I had won a graduate fellowship. During the congratulations, underneath my excitement, I felt a strange uneasiness, there was a question that I did not want to think about.

"Is this really what I want to be?" The question shut me off, cold and alone, from the girls talking and studying on the sunny hillside behind the college house. I thought I was going to be a psychologist. But if I wasn't sure, what did I want to be? I felt the future closing in—and I could not see myself in it at all. I had no image of myself, stretching beyond college. I had come at seventeen from a Midwestern town, an unsure girl; the wide horizons of the world and the life of the mind had been opened to me. I had begun to know who I was and what I wanted to do. I could not go back now. I could not go home again, to the life of my mother and the women of our town, bound to home, bridge, shopping, children, husband, charity, clothes. But now that the time had come to make my own future, to take the deciding step, I suddenly did not know what I wanted to be.

I took the fellowship, but the next spring, under the alien California sun of another campus, the question came again, and I could not put it out of my mind. I had won another fellowship that would have committed me to research for my doctorate, to a career as professional psychologist. "Is this really what I want to be?" The decision now truly terrified me. I lived in a terror of indecision for days, unable to think of anything else.

The question was not important, I told myself. No question was important to me that year but love. We walked in the Berkeley hills and a boy said: "Nothing can come of this, between us. I'll never win a fellowship like yours." Did I think I would be choosing, irrevocably, the cold loneliness of that afternoon if I went on? I gave up the fellowship, in relief. But for years afterward, I could not read a word of the science that once I had thought of as my future life's work; the reminder of its loss was too painful.

I never could explain, hardly knew myself, why I gave up this career. I lived in the present, working on newspapers with no particular plan. I married, had children, lived according to the feminine mystique as a suburban housewife. But still the question haunted me. I could sense no purpose in my life, I could find no peace, until I finally faced it and worked out my own answer.

I discovered, talking to Smith seniors in 1959, that the question is no less terrifying to girls today. Only they answer it now in a way that my generation found, after half a lifetime, not to be an answer at all. These girls, mostly seniors, were sitting in the living room of the college house, having coffee. It was not too different from such an evening when I was a senior, except that many more of the girls wore rings on their left hands. I asked the ones around me what they planned to be. The engaged ones spoke of weddings, apartments, getting a job as a secretary while husband finished school. The others, after a hostile silence, gave vague answers about this job or that, graduate study, but no one had any real plans. A blonde with a ponytail asked me the next day if I had believed the things they had said. "None of it was true," she told me. "We don't like to be asked what we want to do. None of us know. None of us even like to think about it. The ones who are going to be married right away are the lucky ones. They don't have to think about it."

But I noticed that night that many of the engaged girls, sitting silently around the fire while I asked the others about jobs, had also seemed angry about something. "They don't want to think about not going on," my ponytailed informant said. "They know they're not going to use their education. They'll be wives and mothers. You can say you're going to keep on reading and be interested in the community. But that's not the same. You won't really go on. It's a disappointment to know you're going to stop now, and not go on and use it."

In counterpoint, I heard the words of a woman, fifteen years after she left college, a doctor's wife, mother of three, who said over coffee in her New England kitchen:

The tragedy was, nobody ever looked us in the eye and said you have to decide what you want to do with your life, besides being your husband's wife and children's mother. I never thought it through until I was thirty-six, and my husband was so busy with his practice that he couldn't entertain me every night. The three boys were in school all day. I kept on trying to have babies despite an Rh discrepancy. After two miscarriages, they said I must stop. I thought that my own growth and evolution were over. I always knew as a child that I was going to grow up and go to college, and then get married, and that's as far as a girl has to think. After that, your husband determines and fills your life. It wasn't until I got so lonely as the doctor's wife and kept screaming at the kids because they didn't fill my life that I realized I had to make my own life. I still had to decide what I wanted to be. I hadn't finished evolving at all. But it took me ten years to think it through.

The feminine mystique permits, even encourages, women to ignore the question of their identity. The mystique says they can answer the question "Who am I?" by saying "Tom's wife . . . Mary's mother." But I don't think the mystique would have such power over American women if they did not fear to face this terrifying blank which makes them unable to see themselves after twenty-one. The truth is—and how long it has been true, I'm not sure, but it was true in my generation and it is true of girls growing up today—an American woman no longer has a private image to tell her who she is, or can be, or wants to be. . . .

Another girl, a college junior from South Carolina told me:

I don't want to be interested in a career I'll have to give up.

My mother wanted to be a newspaper reporter from the time she was twelve, and I've seen her frustration for twenty years. I don't want to be interested in world affairs. I don't want to be interested in anything beside my home and being a wonderful wife and mother. Maybe education is a liability. Even the brightest boys at home want just a sweet, pretty girl. Only sometimes I wonder how it would feel to be able to stretch and stretch and stretch, and learn all you want, and not have to hold yourself back.

Her mother, almost all our mothers, were housewives, though many had started or yearned for or regretted giving up careers. Whatever they told us, we, having eyes and ears and mind and heart, knew that their lives were somehow empty. We did not want to be like them, and yet what other model did we have?

The only other kind of women I knew, growing up, were the old-maid high-school teachers; the librarian; the one woman doctor in our town, who cut her hair like a man; and a few of my college professors. None of these women lived in the warm center of life as I had known it at home. Many had not married or had children. I dreaded being like them, even the ones who taught me truly to respect my own mind and use it, to feel that I had a part in the world. I never knew a woman, when I was growing up, who used her mind, played her own part in the world, and also loved, and had children.

I think that this has been the unknown heart of woman's problem in America for a long time, this lack of a private image. Public images that defy reason and have very little to do with women themselves have had the power to shape too much of their lives. These images would not have such power, if women were not suffering a crisis of identity.

The strange, terrifying jumping-off point that American women reach —at eighteen, twenty-one, twenty-five, forty-one—has been noticed for many years by sociologists, psychologists, analysts, educators. But I think it has not been understood for what it is. It has been called a "discontinuity" in cultural conditioning; it has been called woman's "role crisis." It has been blamed on the education which made American girls grow up feeling free and equal to boys—playing baseball, riding bicycles, conquering geometry and college boards, going away to college, going out in the world to get a job, living alone in an apartment in New York or Chicago or San Francisco, testing and discovering their own powers in the world. All this gave girls the feeling they could be and do whatever they wanted to, with the same freedom as boys, the critics said. It did not prepare them for their role as women. The crisis comes when they are forced to adjust to this role. Today's high rate of emotional distress and breakdown among women in their twenties and thirties is usually attributed to this "role crisis." If girls were educated for their role as women, they would not suffer this crisis, the adjusters say.

But I think they have seen only half the truth. . . .

It is my thesis that the core of the problem for women today is not sexual but a problem of identity—a stunting or evasion of growth that is perpetuated by the feminine mystique. It is my thesis that as the Victorian culture did not permit women to accept or gratify their basic sexual needs, our culture does not permit women to accept or gratify their basic need to grow and fulfill their potentialities as human beings, a need which is not solely defined by their sexual role. . . .

There have been identity crises for man at all the crucial turning points in human history, though those who lived through them did not give them that name. It is only in recent years that the theorists of psychology, sociology and theology have isolated this problem, and given it a name. But it is considered a man's problem. It is defined, for man, as the crisis of growing up, of choosing his identity, "the decision as to what one is and is going to be," in the words of the brilliant psychoanalyst Erik H. Erikson:

I have called the major crisis of adolescence the identity crisis; it occurs in that period of the life cycle when each youth must forge for himself some central perspective and direction, some working unity, out of the effective remnants of his childhood and the hopes of his anticipated adulthood; he must detect some meaningful resemblance between what he has come to see in himself and what his sharpened awareness tells him others judge and expect him to be. . . . In some people, in some classes, at some periods in history, the crisis will be minimal; in other people, classes and periods, the crisis will be clearly marked off as a critical period, a kind of "second birth," apt to be aggravated either by widespread neuroticisms or by pervasive ideological unrest.

In this sense, the identity crisis of one man's life may reflect, or set off, a rebirth, or new stage, in the growing up of mankind. "In some periods of his history, and in some phases of his life cycle, man needs a new ideological orientation as surely and sorely as he must have air and food," said Erikson, focusing new light on the crisis of the young Martin Luther, who left a Catholic monastery at the end of the Middle Ages to forge a new identity for himself and Western man.

The search for identity is not new, however, in American thought—though in every generation, each man who writes about it discovers it anew. In America, from the beginning, it has somehow been understood that men must thrust into the future; the pace has always been too rapid for man's identity to stand still. In every generation, many men have suffered misery, unhappiness, and uncertainty because they could not take the image of the man they wanted to be from their fathers. The search for identity of the young man who can't go home again has always been a major theme of American writers. And it has always been considered right in America, good, for men to suffer these agonies of growth, to search for and find their own identities. The farm boy went to the city, the garment-maker's son became a doctor, Abraham Lincoln taught himself to read—these were more than rags-to-riches stories. They were an integral part of the American dream. The problem for many was money, race, color, class, which barred them from choice—not what they would be if they were free to choose.

Even today a young man learns soon enough that he must decide who he wants to be. If he does not decide in junior high, in high school, in college, he must somehow come to terms with it by twenty-five or thirty, or he is lost. But this search for identity is seen as a greater problem now because more and more boys cannot find images in our culture—from their fathers or other men—to help them in their search. The old frontiers have been conquered, and the boundaries of the new are not so clearly marked. More and more young men in America today suffer an identity crisis for want of any image of man worth pursuing, for want of a purpose that truly realizes their human abilities.

But why have theorists not recognized this same identity crisis in women? In terms of the old conventions and the new feminine mystique women are not expected to grow up to find out who they are, to choose their human identity. Anatomy is woman's destiny, say the theorists of femininity; the identity of women is determined by her biology.

But is it? More and more women are asking themselves this question. As if they were waking from a coma, they ask, "Where am I . . . what am I doing here?" For the first time in their history, women are becoming aware of an identity crisis in their own lives, a crisis which began many generations ago, has grown worse with each succeeding generation, and will not end until they, or their daughters, turn an unknown corner and make of themselves and their lives the new image that so many women now so desperately need.

In a sense that goes beyond any one woman's life, I think this is the crisis of women growing up—a turning point from an immaturity that has been called femininity to full human identity. I think women had to suffer this crisis of identity, which began a hundred years ago, and have to suffer it still today, simply to become fully human. . . .

In the late thirties, Professor Maslow began to study the relationship between sexuality and what he called "dominance feeling" or "self-esteem" or "ego level" in women—130 women, of college education or of comparable intelligence, between twenty and twenty-eight, most of whom were married, of Protestant middle-class city background. He found, contrary to what one might expect from the psychoanalytical theories and the conventional images of femininity, that the more "dominant" the woman, the greater her enjoyment of sexuality—and the greater her ability to "submit" in a psychological sense, to give herself freely in love, to have orgasm. It was not that these women higher in "dominance" were more "highly sexed," but they were, above all, more completely themselves, more free to be themselves—and this seemed inextricably linked with a greater freedom to give themselves in love. These women were not, in the usual sense, "feminine," but they enjoyed sexual fulfillment to a much higher degree than the conventionally feminine women in the same study.

I have never seen the implications of this research discussed in popular psychological literature about femininity or women's sexuality. It was, perhaps, not noticed at the time, even by the theorists, as a major landmark. But its findings are thought-provoking for American women today, who lead their lives according to the dictates of the feminine mystique. Remember that this study was done in the late 1930's, before the mystique became all-powerful. For these strong, spirited, educated women, evidently there was no conflict between the driving force to be themselves and to love. . . .

Professor Maslow found that the higher the dominance, or strength of self in a woman, the less she was self-centered and the more her concern was directed outward to other people and to problems of the world. On the other hand, the main preoccupation of the more conventionally feminine low-dominance women was themselves and their own inferiorities. From a psychological point of view, a high-dominance woman was more like a high-dominance man than she was like a low-dominance woman. Thus Professor Maslow suggested that either you have to describe as "masculine" both high-dominance men and women or drop the terms "masculine" and "feminine" altogether because they are so "misleading." . . .

There are many things that emerged from this study which bear directly on the problem of women in America today. For one thing, among the public figures included in this study, Professor Maslow was able to find only two women who had actually fulfilled themselves—Eleanor Roosevelt and Jane Addams. (The men included Lincoln, Jefferson, Einstein, Freud, G. W. Carver, Debs, Schweitzer, Kreisler, Goethe, Thoreau, William James, Spinoza, Whitman, Franklin Roosevelt, Beethoven.) Apart from public and historical figures, he studied at close range a small number of unnamed subjects who met his criteria—all in their 50's and 60's—and he screened 3,000 college students, finding only twenty who seemed to be developing in the direction of self-actualization; here also, there were very few women. As a matter of fact, his findings implied that self-actualization, or the full realization of human potential, was hardly possible at all for women in our society. . . .

"We measure ourselves by many standards," said the great American psychologist William James, nearly a century ago. "Our strength and our intelligence, our wealth and even our good luck, are things which warm our heart and make us feel ourselves a match for life. But deeper than all such things, and able to suffice unto itself without them, is the sense of the amount of effort which we can put forth."

If women do not put forth, finally, that effort to become all that they have it in them to become, they will forfeit their own humanity. A woman today who has no goal, no purpose, no ambition patterning her days into the future, making her stretch and grow beyond that small score of years in which her body can fill its biological function, is committing a kind of suicide. For that future half a century after the child-bearing years are over is a fact that an American woman cannot deny. Nor can she deny that as a housewife, the world is indeed rushing past her door while she just sits and watches. The terror she feels is real, if she has no place in that world.

The feminine mystique has succeeded in burying millions of American women alive. There is no way for these women to break out of their comfortable concentration camps except by finally putting forth an effort—that human effort which reaches beyond biology, beyond the narrow walls of home, to help shape the future. Only by such a personal commitment to the future can American women break out of the housewife trap and truly find fulfillment as wives and mothers—by fulfilling their own unique possibilities as separate human beings.

5

technology's children

In this selection the prominent environmental scientist, Barry Com-
moner, examines the inordinate intensification of pollution rates since
World War II. Noting changes in agricultural fertilizers, detergents, elec-
tric power facilities, and packaging industries, Commoner concludes that
the adverse impact on the environment from new developments has
probably greatly outweighed the social gains they brought. This excerpt
from his widely-read book, The Closing Circle, *shows Commoner's ability*
to make complex scientific processes comprehensible to non-scientists and
to stimulate concern about the environment.

According to Commoner, what has been the major cause of rising pol-
lution levels since World War II? What does he believe Americans must
do if they are to stop the growth of pollution? Must Americans halt their
overall economic growth? What are some other examples of replacing
natural materials with synthetic ones? What have been the social gains and
the environmental costs?

Barry Commoner

The Technological Flaw

We have now arrived at the following position in the search for the causes of the environmental crisis in the United States. We know that *something* went wrong in the country after World War II, for most of our serious pollution problems either began in the postwar years or have greatly worsened since then. While two factors frequently blamed for the environmental crisis, population and affluence, have intensified in that time, these increases are much too small to account for the 200 to 2,000 per cent rise in pollution levels since 1946. The product of these two factors, which represents the total output of goods (total production equals population times production per capita), is also insufficient to account for the intensification of pollution. Total production—as measured by GNP—has increased by 126 per cent since 1944 while most pollution levels have risen by at least several times that rate. Something else besides growth in population and affluence must be deeply involved in the environmental crisis. . . .

The growth of the United States economy is recorded in elaborate detail in a variety of government statistics—huge volumes tabulating the amounts of various goods produced annually; the expenditures involved, the value of the goods sold, and so forth. Although these endless columns of figures are rather intimidating, there are some useful ways to extract meaningful facts from them. In particular, it is helpful to compute the rate of growth of each productive activity, a procedure that nowadays can be accomplished by committing the tables of numbers to an appropriate programmed computer. In order to compare one kind of economic activity with another, it is useful to arrange the computer to yield a figure for the percentage increase, or decrease, in production or consumption.

Not long ago, two of my colleagues and I went through the statistical tables and selected from them the data for several hundred items, which together represent a major and representative part of over-all United States agricultural and industrial production. For each item, the average annual percentage change in production or consumption was computed for the years since 1946, or since the earliest date for which the statistics were available. Then we computed the over-all change for the entire twenty-five-year period—a twenty-five-year growth rate. When this list is rearranged in decreasing order of growth rate, a picture of *how* the United States economy has grown since World War II begins to emerge.

The winner of this economic sweepstakes, with the highest postwar growth rate, is the production of nonreturnable soda bottles, which has increased about 53,000 per cent in that time. The loser, ironically, is the horse; work animal horsepower has declined by 87 per cent of its original postwar value. The runners-up are an interesting but seemingly mixed bag. In second place is production of synthetic fibers, up 5,980 per cent;

Barry Commoner, *The Closing Circle: Nature, Man, and Technology,* Alfred A. Knopf (New York, 1971), 142-175.

third is mercury used for chlorine production, up 3,920 per cent; succeeding places are held as follows: mercury used in mildew-resistant paint, up 3,120 per cent; air conditioner compressor units, up 2,850 per cent; plastics, up 1,960 per cent; fertilizer nitrogen, up 1,050 per cent; electric housewares (such as can-openers and corn-poppers), up 1,040 per cent; synthetic organic chemicals, up 950 per cent; aluminum, up 680 per cent; chlorine gas, up 600 per cent; electric power, up 530 per cent; pesticides, up 390 per cent; wood pulp, up 313 per cent; truck freight, up 222 per cent; consumer electronics (TV sets, tape recorders), up 217 per cent; motor fuel consumption, up 190 per cent; cement, up 150 per cent.

Then there is a group of productive activities that, as indicated earlier, have grown at about the pace of the population (i.e., up about 42 per cent): food production and consumption, total production of textiles and clothes, household utilities, and steel, copper, and other basic metals.

Finally there are the losers, which increase more slowly than the population or actually shrink in total production: railroad freight, up 17 per cent; lumber, down 1 per cent; cotton fiber, down 7 per cent; returnable beer bottles, down 36 per cent; wool, down 42 per cent; soap, down 76 per cent; and, at the end of the line, work animal horsepower, down 87 per cent.

What emerges from all these data is striking evidence that while production for most basic needs—food, clothing, housing—has just about kept up with the 40 to 50 per cent or so increase in population (that is, production *per capita* has been essentially constant), the *kinds* of goods produced to meet these needs have changed drastically. New production technologies have displaced old ones. Soap powder has been displaced by synthetic detergents; natural fibers (cotton and wool) have been displaced by synthetic ones; steel and lumber have been displaced by aluminum, plastics, and concrete; railroad freight has been displaced by truck freight; returnable bottles have been displaced by nonreturnable ones. On the road, the low-powered automobile engines of the 1920's and 1930's have been displaced by high-powered ones. On the farm, while per capita production has remained about constant, the amount of harvested acreage has decreased; in effect, fertilizer has displaced land. Older methods of insect control have been displaced by synthetic insecticides, such as DDT, and for controlling weeds the cultivator has been displaced by the herbicide spray. Range-feeding of livestock has been displaced by feedlots.

In each of these cases, what has changed drastically is the technology of production rather than over-all output of the economic good. Of course, part of the economic growth in the United States since 1946 has been based on some newly introduced goods: air conditioners, television sets, tape recorders, and snowmobiles, all of which have increased absolutely without displacing an older product.

Distilled in this way, the mass of production statistics begins to form a meaningful pattern. In general, the growth of the United States economy since 1946 has had a surprisingly small effect on the degree to which individual needs for basic economic goods have been met. That statistical fiction, the "average American," now consumes, each year, about as many calories, protein, and other foods (although somewhat less of vitamins); uses about the same amount of clothes and cleaners; occupies about the same amount of newly constructed housing; requires about as much freight; and drinks about the same amount of beer (twenty-six gallons per capita!) as he did in 1946. However, his food is now grown on less land with much more fertilizer and pesticides than before; his clothes are more likely to be made of synthetic fibers than of cotton or wool; he launders with synthetic detergents rather than soap; he lives and works in buildings that depend more heavily on aluminum, concrete, and plastic than on steel and lumber; the goods he uses are increasingly shipped by truck rather than rail; he drinks beer out of nonreturnable bottles or cans rather than out of returnable bottles or at the tavern bar. He is more likely to live and work in air-conditioned surroundings than before. He also drives about twice as far as he did in 1946, in a heavier car, on synthetic rather than natural rubber tires, using more gasoline per mile, containing more tetraethyl lead, fed into an engine of increased horsepower and compression ratio.

These primary changes have led to others. To provide the raw materials needed for the new synthetic fibers, pesticides, detergents, plastics, and rubber, the production of synthetic organic chemicals has also grown very rapidly. The synthesis of organic chemicals uses a good deal of chlorine. Result: chlorine production has increased sharply. To make chlorine, an electric current is passed through a salt solution by way of a mercury electrode. Consequently, mercury consumption for this purpose has increased—by 3,930 per cent in the twenty-five-year postwar period. Chemical products, along with cement for concrete and aluminum (also winners in the growth race), use rather large amounts of electric power. Not surprisingly, then, that item, too, has increased considerably since 1946.

All this reminds us of what we have already been told by advertising —which incidentally has *also* grown; for example, the use of newsprint for advertising has grown faster than its use for news—that we are blessed with an economy based on very modern technologies. What the advertisements do not tell us—as we are urged to buy synthetic shirts and detergents, aluminum furniture, beer in no-return bottles, and Detroit's latest creation—is that *all this "progress" has greatly increased the impact on the environment.*

This pattern of economic growth is the major reason for the environmental crisis. A good deal of the mystery and confusion about the sudden emergence of the environmental crisis can be removed by pinpointing, pollutant by pollutant, how the postwar technological transformation of the United States economy has produced not only the much-heralded 126 per cent rise in GNP, but also, at a rate about ten times faster than the growth of GNP, the rising levels of environmental pollution.

Agriculture is a good place to start. . . . Between 1949 and 1968 total United States agricultural production increased by about 45 per cent. Since the United States population grew by 34 per cent in that time, the over-all increase in production was just about enough to keep up with population; crop production *per capita* increased 6 per cent. In that period, the annual use of fertilizer nitrogen increased by 648 per cent, surprisingly larger than the increase in crop production. One reason for this disparity also turns up in the agricultural statistics: between 1949 and 1968 harvested acreage *declined* by 16 per cent. Clearly, more crop was being produced on less land (the yield per acre increased by 77 per cent). Intensive use of fertilizer nitrogen is the most important means of achieving this improvement in yield per acre. Thus, the intensive use of fertilizer nitrogen allowed "agribusiness" to just about meet the population's need for food—and at the same time to reduce the acreage used for that purpose.

These same statistics also explain the resulting water pollution problem. In 1949, an average of about 11,000 tons of fertilizer nitrogen were used *per USDA unit of crop production,* while in 1968 about 57,000 tons of nitrogen were used for the *same* crop yield. This means that the efficiency with which nitrogen contributes to the growth of the crop declined fivefold. Obviously, a good deal of the fertilizer nitrogen did not enter the crop and must have ended up elsewhere in the ecosystem. . . .

What the new fertilizer technology has accomplished for the farmer is clear: more crop can be produced on less acreage than before. Since the cost of fertilizer, relative to the resultant gain in crop sales, is lower than that of any other economic input, and since the Land Bank pays the farmer for acreage not in crops, the new technology pays him well. The cost—in environmental degradation—is borne by his neighbors in town who find their water polluted. The new technology is an economic success—but only because it is an ecological failure. . . .

In marketing terms, detergents are probably one of the most successful of modern technological innovations. In a scant twenty-five years this new invention has captured more than two thirds of the laundry market from one of man's oldest, best-established, and most useful inventions— soap. This technological displacement is typical of many that have occurred since World War II: the replacement of a natural organic product by an unnatural synthetic one. In each case the new technology has worsened the environmental impact of the economic good.

Soap is produced by reacting a natural product, fat, with alkali. A typical fat used in soap-making is palm oil. This is produced by the palm tree, using water and carbon dioxide as raw materials, and sunlight to provide the necessary energy. These are all freely available, renewable resources. No environmental impact results from the synthesis of the palm oil molecule. Of course, with inadequate husbandry a palm plantation can deplete the soil, and when the oil is extracted from the coconut, fuel is used and the resultant burning contributes to air pollution. The manufacture of soap from oil and alkali also consumes fuel and produces wastes.

Once used and sent down the drain, soap is broken down by the bacteria of decay—for the natural fat is readily attacked by the bacterial enzymes. In most places, this bacterial action takes place within the confines of a sewage treatment plant. What is then emitted to surface waters is only carbon dioxide and water, since fat contains only carbon, hydrogen, and oxygen atoms. Hence there is little or no impact on the aquatic ecosystem due to biological oxygen demand (which accompanies bacterial degradation of organic wastes) arising from soap wastes. Nor is the product of soap degradation, carbon dioxide, usually an important ecological intrusion since it is already in plentiful supply from other environmental sources. In its production and use, soap has a relatively light impact on the environment.

In comparison with soap, the production of detergents is likely to exert a more intense environmental impact. Detergents are synthesized from organic raw materials originally present in petroleum along with a number of other substances. To obtain the raw materials, the petroleum is subjected to distillation and other energy-consuming processes—and the burned fuel pollutes the air. Then the purified raw materials are used in a series of chemical reactions, involving chlorine and high temperatures, finally yielding the active cleaning agent. This is then mixed with a variety of additives, designed to soften hard water, bleach stains, "brighten" wash (this additive strongly reflects light and dazzles the eye to achieve a simulated whiteness), and otherwise gladden the heart of the advertising copy writer. Suitably boxed, this is the detergent. The total energy used to produce the active agent alone—and therefore the resultant air pollution—is probably three times that needed to produce oil for soap manufacture. And to produce the needed chlorine, mercury is used—and released to the environment as a pollutant. In substituting man-made chemical processes for natural ones, detergent manufacture inevitably produces a greater environmental stress than does the manufacture of soap. . . .

Another pollution problem arises from the phosphate content of detergents, whether degradable or not, for phosphate can stimulate algal overgrowths, which on their death overburden the aquatic ecosystem with organic matter. Phosphate is added to detergents for two purposes: to combat hard water (because it helps to tie up materials, such as calcium, which cause water hardness) and to help suspend dirt particles so that they can be readily rinsed away. Soap itself accomplishes the second of these functions, but not the first. In hard water, soap is rather ineffective, but can be improved by adding a water-softening agent such as phosphate. Thus, phosphate is needed only to solve the hard-water problem. But where water is hard, it can be treated by a household water-softener, a device which could also be built into washing machines. In other words, successful washing can be accomplished without resorting to phosphate, which when added to detergents, worsens their already serious environmental effects. Thus the actual need to replace soap is slight. As a recent chemical engineering textbook states: "There is absolutely no reason why old-fashioned soap cannot be used for most household and commercial cleaning." . . .

Electric power is one of the fast-growing features of the postwar United States economy. This industry is also the source of major pollution problems: sulfur dioxide, nitrogen oxides, and dust emitted by fossil-fuel burning plants; radioactive emissions and the small but enormously catastrophic potential of an accident from the operation of nuclear power plants; and the emission of waste heat to the air and nearby surface waters by both types of plants. This growth in the use of electric power is, justifiably, associated with the modernity of our economy and—with much less cause—to our supposed "affluence." The statistics appear to be straightforward enough. In the United States, annual power consumption is about 20,540 kilowatt hours per capita (the United States consumes 34 per cent of the world's electric power output), as opposed to about 2,900 kw-h per capita for Chile, 260 kw-h per capita for India, and 230 kw-h per capita for Thailand. However, electric power, unconverted, is not in itself capable of satisfying any known human need, and its contribution to human welfare needs to be measured in terms of the economic goods that power can produce. Here we discover another serious failing—when measured in terms of human welfare—of postwar technology: the new productive technologies are more costly than the technologies they have displaced, in consumption of electric power and other forms of fuel-generated energy *per unit economic good*. For example, aluminum, which has increasingly displaced steel and lumber as a construction material, requires for its production about 15 times more fuel energy than steel and about 150 times more fuel energy than lumber. Even taking into account that less aluminum, by weight, is needed for a given purpose than steel, the power discrepancy remains. For example, the energy required to produce metal for an aluminum beer can is 6.3 times that needed for a steel beer can.

The displacement of natural products by synthetic organic chemicals and of lumber and steel by concrete has a similar effect, for both chemical manufacturing and the production of cement for concrete are intense consumers of electric power. Aluminum and chemical production alone account for about 28 per cent of total industrial use of electric power in the United States. Thus the expansion of power production in the United States is not an accurate measure of increased economic good, being badly inflated by the growing tendency to displace power-thrifty goods with power-consumptive ones. The cost of this inefficiency is heavily borne by the environment.

Another technological displacement is readily visible to the modern householder in the daily acquisition of rubbish, most of it from packaging. It is a useful exercise to examine the statistics relevant to some economic good—beer, let us say—and determine from them the origin of the resultant impact on the environment. We can begin the exercise by recalling that the relevant economic good is chiefly the beer, not the bottle or can in which it is delivered. The relevant pollutant is the non-returnable bottle or can, for these, when "disposed of" in rubbish, cannot be assimilated in any natural ecological cycle. Therefore, they either accumulate or must be reprocessed at some expenditure of energy and cost in power-produced pollutants. The exercise consists in determining the relative effects of the three factors that might lead to an increased output of pollution, in this case, in the period from 1950 to 1967. In that time, the total consumption of nonreturnable beer bottles increased by 595 per cent and the consumption of beer increased by 37 per cent. Since the population increased by 30 per cent, the "affluence" factor, or the amount of beer consumed per capita, remained essentially constant (actually a 5 per cent increase). The remainder of the increased output of pollutant—beer bottles—is due to the technological factor—that is, the number of nonreturnable bottles produced per gallon of beer, which increased by 408 per cent. The relative importance of the three factors is evident.

It will be argued, of course, that the use of a nonreturnable beer bottle is more desirable than a returnable one to the individual beer drinker. After all, some human effort must be expended to return the bottle to the point of purchase. We can modify the earlier evaluation, then, by asserting that for the sake of whatever improvement in well-being is involved in avoiding the effort of returning the bottle, the production of beer in nonreturnable bottles incurs a 408 per cent intensification of environmental impact. No such subtlety is involved in comparing the environmental impacts of two alternative nonreturnable beer containers: steel beer cans and aluminum ones. The energy involved in producing the aluminum can—and therefore the amount of combustion and the resultant output of pollutants—is 6.3 times that required for a steel can.

Similar computations can be made for the added environmental impact incurred when extra layers of packaging are added to foods and other goods or when plastic wrappers (nondegradable) are substituted for degradable cellulosic ones. In general, modern industrial technology has encased economic goods of no significantly increased human value in increasingly larger amounts of environmentally harmful wrappings. Result: the mounting heaps of rubbish that symbolize the advent of the technological age.

It should be recognized that such computations of environmental impact are still in a primitive, only partially developed stage. What is needed, and what—it is to be hoped—will be worked out before long, is an ecological analysis of every major aspect of the production, use, and disposition of goods. What is needed is a kind of "ecological impact inventory" for each productive activity, which will enable us to attach a sort of pollution price tag to each product. We would then know, for example, for each pound of detergent: how much air pollution is generated by the electric power and fuel burned to manufacture its chemical ingredients; how much water pollution is due to the mercury "loss" by the factory in the course of manufacturing the chlorine needed to produce it; the water pollution due to the detergent and phosphate entering sewage systems; the ecological effect of fluoride and arsenic (which may contaminate the phosphate), and of mercury, which might contaminate any alkali used to compound the detergent. Such pollution price tags are needed for all major products if we are to judge their relative *social* value. The foregoing account shows how far we are from this goal, and once again reminds us how blind we are about the environmental effects of modern technology.

The Port Huron Statement, written largely by Tom Hayden, was the founding document of the Students for a Democratic Society (SDS), established in Michigan in 1962. The statement is both a critique of American society and social relationships and a limited program of action. It calls for a revitalization of American politics through "participatory democracy." Why, do you think, these comfortable, well-educated youth found the American Dream empty? What are the strengths and limitations of their programs and analyses? In the late 1960's SDS became the major fountainhead of campus radicalism and militancy. In what ways is the Port Huron Statement radical; in what ways is it an example of conventional liberalism?

Tom Hayden et al.

Port Huron Statement

We are people of this generation, bred in at least modest comfort, housed now in universities, looking uncomfortably to the world we inherit.

When we were kids the United States was the wealthiest and strongest country in the world; the only one with the atom bomb, the least scarred by modern war, an initiator of the United Nations that we thought would distribute Western influence throughout the world. Freedom and equality for each individual, government of, by, and for the people—these American values we found good, principles by which we could live as men. Many of us began maturing in complacency.

As we grew, however, our comfort was penetrated by events too troubling to dismiss. First, the permeating and victimizing fact of human degradation, symbolized by the Southern struggle against racial bigotry, compelled most of us from silence to activism. Second, the enclosing fact of the Cold War, symbolized by the presence of the Bomb, brought awareness that we ourselves, and our friends, and millions of abstract "others" we knew more directly because of our common peril, might die at any time. We might deliberately ignore, or avoid, or fail to feel all other human problems, but not these two, for these were too immediate and crushing in their impact, too challenging in the demand that we as individuals take the responsibility for encounter and resolution.

While these and other problems either directly oppressed us or rankled our consciences and became our own subjective concerns, we began to see complicated and disturbing paradoxes in our surrounding America. The declaration "all men are created equal . . ." rang hollow before the facts of Negro life in the South and the big cities of the North. The proclaimed peaceful intentions of the United States contradicted its economic and military investments in the Cold War status quo.

We witnessed, and continue to witness, other paradoxes. With nuclear energy whole cities can easily be powered, yet the dominant nation-states seem more likely to unleash destruction greater than that incurred in all wars of human history. Although our own technology is destroying old and creating new forms of social organization, men still tolerate meaningless work and idleness. While two-thirds of mankind suffers undernourishment, our own upper classes revel amidst superfluous abundance. Although world population is expected to double in forty years, the nations still tolerate anarchy as a major principle of international conduct and uncontrolled exploitation governs the sapping of the earth's physical resources. Although mankind desperately needs

Tom Hayden et al., Port Huron Statement, mimeographed (n.p., Students for a Democratic Society, 1962).

revolutionary leadership, America rests in national stalemate, its goals ambiguous and tradition-bound instead of informed and clear, its democratic system apathetic and manipulated rather than "of, by, and for the people."

Not only did tarnish appear on our image of American virtue, not only did disillusion occur when the hypocrisy of American ideals was discovered, but we began to sense that what we had originally seen as the American Golden Age was actually the decline of an era. The world-wide outbreak of revolution against colonialism and imperialism, the entrenchment of totalitarian states, the menace of war, overpopulation, international disorder, supertechnology—these trends were testing the tenacity of our own commitment to democracy and freedom and our abilities to visualize their application to a world in upheaval.

Our work is guided by the sense that we may be the last generation in the experiment with living. But we are a minority—the vast majority of our people regard the temporary equilibriums of our society and world as eternally-functional parts. In this is perhaps the outstanding paradox: we ourselves are imbued with urgency, yet the message of our society is that there is no viable alternative to the present. Beneath the reassuring tones of the politicians, beneath the common opinion that America will "muddle through," beneath the stagnation of those who have closed their minds to the future, is the pervading feeling that there simply are no alternatives, that our times have witnessed the exhaustion not only of Utopias, but of any new departures as well. Feeling the press of complexity upon the emptiness of life, people are fearful of the thought that at any moment things might be thrust out of control. They fear change itself, since change might smash whatever invisible framework seems to hold back chaos for them now. For most Americans, all crusades are suspect, threatening. The fact that each individual sees apathy in his fellows perpetuates the common reluctance to organize for change. The dominant institutions are complex enough to blunt the minds of their potential critics, and entrenched enough to swiftly dissipate or entirely repel the energies of protest and reform, thus limiting human expectancies. Then, too, we are a materially improved society, and by our own improvements we seem to have weakened the case for further change.

Some would have us believe that Americans feel contentment amidst prosperity—but might it not be better called a glaze above deeply-felt anxieties about their role in the new world? And if these anxieties produce a developed indifference to human affairs, do they not as well produce a yearning to believe there *is* an alternative to the present, that something *can* be done to change circumstances in the school, the workplaces, the bureaucracies, the government? It is to this latter yearning, at once the spark and engine of change, that we direct our present appeal. The search for truly democratic alternatives to the present, and a commitment to social experimentation with them, is a worthy and fulfilling human enterprise, one which moves us and, we hope, others today. On such a basis do we offer this document of our convictions and analysis: as an effort in understanding and changing the conditions of humanity in the late twentieth century, an effort rooted in the ancient, still unfulfilled conception of man attaining determining influence over his circumstances of life.

VALUES

Making values explicit—an initial task in establishing alternatives—is an activity that has been devalued and corrupted. The conventional moral terms of the age, the politician moralities—"free world," "people's democracies"—reflect realities poorly, if at all, and seem to function more as ruling myths than as descriptive principles. But neither has our experience in the universities brought us moral enlightenment. Our professors and administrators sacrifice controversy to public relations; their curriculums change more slowly than the living events of the world; their skills and silence are purchased by investors in the arms race; passion is called unscholastic. The questions we might want raised—what is really important? can we live in a different and better way? if we wanted to change society, how would we do it?—are not thought to be questions of a "fruitful, empirical nature," and thus are brushed aside.

Unlike youth in other countries we are used to moral leadership being exercised and moral dimensions being clarified by our elders. But today, for us, not even the liberal and socialist preachments of the past seem adequate to the forms of the present. Consider the old slogans: Capitalism Cannot Reform Itself, United Front Against Fascism, General Strike, All Out on May Day. Or, more recently, No Cooperation with Commies and Fellow Travellers, Ideologies are Exhausted, Bipartisanship, No Utopias. These are incomplete, and there are few new prophets. It has been said that our liberal and socialist predecessors were plagued by vision without program, while our own generation is plagued by program without vision. All around us there is astute grasp of method, technique—the committee, the ad hoc group, the lobbyist, the hard and soft sell, the make, the projected image—but if pressed critically, such expertise is incompetent to explain its implicit ideals. It is highly fashionable to identify oneself by old categories, or by naming a respected political figure, or by explaining "how we would vote" on various issues.

Theoretic chaos has replaced the idealistic thinking of old—and, unable to reconstitute theoretic order, men have condemned idealism itself. Doubt has replaced hopefulness—and men act out a defeatism that is labelled realistic. The decline of utopia and hope is in fact one of the defining features of social life today. The reasons are various: the dreams of the older left were perverted by Stalinism and never re-created; the congressional stalemate makes men narrow their view of the possible; the specialization of human activity leaves little room for sweeping thought; the horrors of the twentieth century, symbolized in the gas-ovens and concentration camps and atom bombs, have blasted hopefulness. To be idealistic is to be considered apocalyptic, deluded. To have no serious aspirations, on the contrary, is to be "toughminded."

In suggesting social goals and values, therefore, we are aware of entering a sphere of some disrepute. Perhaps matured by the past, we have no sure formulas, no closed theories—but that does not mean values are beyond discussion and tentative determination. A first task of any social movement is to convince people that the search for orienting theories and the creation of human values are complex but worthwhile. We are aware that to avoid platitudes we must analyze the concrete conditions of social order. But to direct such analysis we must use the guideposts of basic principles. Our own social values involve conceptions of human beings, human relationships, and social systems.

We regard *men* as infinitely precious and possessed of unfulfilled capacities for reason, freedom, and love. In affirming these principles we are aware of countering perhaps the dominant conceptions of man in the twentieth century: that he is a thing to be manipulated, and that he is inherently incapable of directing his own affairs. We oppose the depersonalization that reduces human beings to the status of things—if anything, the brutalities of the twentieth century teach that means and ends are intimately related, that vague appeals to "posterity" cannot justify the mutilations of the present. We oppose, too, the doctrine of human incompetence because it rests essentially on the modern fact that men have been "competently" manipulated into incompetence—we see little reason why men cannot meet with increasing skill the complexities and responsibilities of their situation, if society is organized not for minority, but for majority, participation in decision-making.

Men have unrealized potential for self-cultivation, self-direction, self-understanding, and creativity. It is this potential that we regard as crucial and to which we appeal, not to the human potentiality for violence, unreason, and submission to authority. The goal of man and society should be human independence: a concern not with image of popularity but with finding a meaning in life that is personally authentic; a quality of mind not compulsively driven by a sense of powerlessness, nor one which unthinkingly adopts status values, nor one which represses all threats to its habits, but one which has full, spontaneous access to present and past experiences, one which easily unites the fragmented parts of personal history, one which openly faces problems which are troubling and un-resolved; one with an intuitive awareness of possibilities, an active sense of curiosity, an ability and willingnesss to learn.

This kind of independence does not mean egotistic individualism—the object is not to have one's way so much as it is to have a way that is one's own. Nor do we deify man—we merely have faith in his potential.

Human relationships should involve fraternity and honesty. Human interdependence is contemporary fact; human brotherhood must be willed, however, as a condition of future survival and as the most ap-propriate form of social relations. Personal links between man and man are needed, especially to go beyond the partial and fragmentary bonds of function that bind men only as worker to worker, employer to employee, teacher to student, American to Russian.

Loneliness, estrangement, isolation describe the vast distance between man and man today. These dominant tendencies cannot be overcome by better personnel management, nor by improved gadgets, but only when a love of man overcomes the idolatrous worship of things by man. As the individualism we affirm is not egoism, the selflessness we affirm is not self-elimination. On the contrary we believe in generosity of a kind that im-prints one's unique individual qualities in the relation to other men, and to all human activity. Further, to dislike isolation is not to favor the abolition of privacy; the latter differs from isolation in that [it] occurs or is abolished according to individual will.

We would replace power rooted in possession, privileged, or circum-stance by power and uniqueness rooted in love, reflectiveness, reason, and creativity. As a *social system* we seek the establishment of a democracy of individual participation, governed by two central aims: that the individ-ual share in those social decisions determining the quality and direction of his life; that society be organized to encourage independence in men and provide the media for their common participation.

In a participatory democracy, the political life would be based on sev-eral root principles:

that decision-making of basic social consequence be carried on by pub-lic groupings;

that politics be seen positively, as the art of collectively creating an acceptable pattern of social relations;

that politics has the function of bringing people out of isolation and into community, thus being a necessary, though not sufficient, means of finding meaning in personal life;

that the political order should serve to clarify problems in a way instrumental to their solution; it should provide outlets for the expression of personal grievance and aspiration; opposing views should be organized so as to illuminate choices and facilitate the attainment of goals; channels should be commonly available to relate men to knowledge and to power so that private problems—from bad recreation facilities to personal alienation—are formulated as general issues.

The economic sphere would have as its basis the principles:

that work should involve incentives worthier than money or survival. It should be educative, not stultifying; creative, not mechanical; self-directed, not manipulated, encouraging independence, a respect for others, a sense of dignity and a willingness to accept social responsibility, since it is this experience that has crucial influence on habits, perceptions and individual ethics;

that the economic experience is so personally decisive that the individual must share in its full determination;

that the economy itself is of such social importance that its major resources and means of production should be open to democratic participation and subject to democratic social regulation.

Like the political and economic ones, major social institutions—cultural, educational, rehabilitative, and others—should be generally organized with the well-being and dignity of man as the essential measure of success.

In social change or interchange, we find violence to be abhorrent because it requires generally the transformation of the target, be it a human being or a community of people, into a depersonalized object of hate. It is imperative that the means of violence be abolished and the institutions —local, national, international—that encourage nonviolence as a condition of conflict be developed.

These are our central values, in skeletal form. It remains vital to understand their denial or attainment in the context of the modern world. . . .

TOWARDS AMERICAN DEMOCRACY

Every effort to end the Cold War and expand the process of world industrialization is an effort hostile to people and institutions whose interests lie in perpetuation of the East-West military threat and the postponement of change in the "have not" nations of the world. Every such effort, too, is bound to establish greater democracy in America. The major goals of a domestic effort would be:

1 *America must abolish its political party stalemate.*

Two genuine parties, centered around issues and essential values, demanding allegiance to party principles shall supplant the current system of organized stalemate which is seriously inadequate to a world in flux. . . . What is desirable is sufficient party disagreement to dramatize major issues, yet sufficient party overlap to guarantee stable transitions from administration to administration.

Every time the President criticizes a recalcitrant Congress, we must ask that he no longer tolerate the Southern conservatives in the Democratic Party. Every time a liberal representative complains that "we can't expect everything at once" we must ask if we received much of anything from Congress in the last generation. Every time he refers to "circumstances beyond control" we must ask why he fraternizes with racist scoundrels. Every time he speaks of the "unpleasantness of personal and party fighting" we should insist that pleasantry with Dixiecrats is inexcusable when the dark peoples of the world call for American support.

2 *Mechanisms of voluntary association must be created through which political information can be imparted and political participation encouraged.*

Political parties, even if realigned, would not provide adequate outlets for popular involvement. Institutions should be created that engage people with issues and express political preference, not as now with huge business lobbies which exercise undemocratic *power* but which carry political *influence* (appropriate to private, rather than public, groupings) in national decision-making enterprise. Private in nature, these should be organized around single issues (medical care, transportation systems reform, etc.), concrete interest (labor and minority group organizations); multiple issues or general issues. These do not exist in America in quantity today. If they did exist, they would be a significant politicizing and educative force bringing people into touch with public life and affording them means of expression and action. Today, giant lobby representatives of business interests are dominant, but not educative. The Federal government itself should counter the latter forces whose intent is often public deceit for private gain, by subsidizing the preparation and decentralized distribution of objective materials on all public issues facing government.

3 *Institutions and practices which stifle dissent should be abolished, and the promotion of peaceful dissent should be actively promoted.*

The First Amendment freedoms of speech, assembly, thought, religion and press should be seen as guarantees, not threats, to national security. While society has the right to prevent active subversion of its laws and institutions, it has the duty as well to promote open discussion of all issues—otherwise it will be in fact promoting real subversion as the only means of implementing ideas. To eliminate the fears and apathy from national life it is necessary that the institutions bred by fear and apathy be rooted out: the House Un-American Activities Committee, the Senate Internal Security Committee, the loyalty oaths on Federal loans, the Attorney General's list of subversive organizations, the Smith and McCarran Acts. The process of eliminating the blighting institutions is the process of restoring democratic participation. Their existence is a sign of the decomposition and atrophy of participation.

4 *Corporations must be made publicly responsible.*

It is not possible to believe that true democracy can exist where a minority utterly controls enormous wealth and power. The influence of corporate elites on foreign policy is neither reliable nor democratic; a way must be found to subordinate private American foreign investment to a democratically-constructed foreign policy. . . .

Labor and government as presently constituted are not sufficient to "regulate" corporations. A new re-ordering, a new calling of responsibility is necessary: more than changing "work rules" we must consider changes in the rules of society by challenging the unchallenged politics of American corporations. Before the government can really begin to control business in a "public interest," the public must gain more substantial control of government: this demands a movement for political as well as economic realignments. We are aware that simple government "regulation," if achieved, would be inadequate without increased worker participation in management decision-making, strengthened and independent regulatory power, balances of partial and/or complete public ownership, various means of humanizing the conditions and types of work itself, sweeping welfare programs and regional *public* development authorities. These are examples of measures to re-balance the economy toward public—and individual—control.

5 *The allocation of resources must be based on social needs. A truly "public sector" must be established, and its nature debated and planned.*

At present the majority of America's "public sector," the largest part of our public spending, is for the military. When great social needs are so pressing, our concept of "government spending" is wrapped up in the "permanent war economy." . . .

The main *private* forces of economic expansion cannot guarantee a steady rate of growth, nor acceptable recovery from recession—especially in a demilitarizing world. Government participation will inevitably expand enormously, because the stable growth of the economy demands increasing "public" investments yearly. Our present outpour of more than $500 billion might double in a generation, irreversibly involving government solutions. And in future recessions, the compensatory fiscal action by the government will be the only means of avoiding the twin disasters of greater unemployment and a slackening rate of growth. Furthermore, a close relationship with the European Common Market will involve competition with numerous planned economies and may aggravate American unemployment unless the economy here is expanding swiftly enough to create new jobs.

All these tendencies suggest that not only solutions to our present social needs but our future expansion rests upon our willingness to enlarge the "public sector" greatly. Unless we choose war as an economic solvent, future public spending will be of non-military nature—a major intervention into civilian production by the government. . . .

6 *America should concentrate on its genuine social priorities: abolish squalor, terminate neglect, and establish an environment for people to live in with dignity and creativeness.*

A. A program against *poverty* must be just as sweeping as the nature of poverty itself. It must not be just palliative, but directed to the abolition of the structural circumstances of poverty. At a bare minimum it should include a *housing* act far larger than the one supported by the Kennedy Administration, but one that is geared more to low- and middle-income needs than to the windfall aspirations of small and large private entrepreneurs, one that is more sympathetic to the quality of communal life than to the efficiency of city-split highways. Second, *medical care* must become recognized as a lifetime human right just as vital as food, shelter and clothing—the Federal government should guarantee health insurance as a basic social service turning medical treatment into a social habit, not just an occasion of crisis, fighting sickness among the aged, not just by making medical care financially feasible but by reducing sickness among children and younger people. Third, existing institutions should be expanded so the Welfare State cares for *everyone's* welfare according to need. *Social Security* payments should be extended to everyone and should be proportionately greater for the poorest. A *minimum wage* of at least $1.50 should be extended to all workers (including the 16 million currently not covered at all). Programs for equal *educational opportunity* are as important a part of the battle against poverty.

B. A full-scale public initiative for civil rights should be undertaken despite the clamor among conservatives (and liberals) about gradualism, property rights, and law and order. The executive and legislative branches of the Federal government should work by enforcement *and* enactment against any form of exploitation of minority groups. No Federal cooperation with racism is tolerable—from financing of schools, to the development of Federally-supported industry, to the social gatherings of the President. Laws hastening school desegregation, voting rights, and economic protection for Negroes are needed right now. The moral force of the Executive Office should be exerted against the Dixiecrats specifically, and the national complacency about the race question generally. Especially in the North, where one-half of the country's Negro people now live, civil rights is not a problem to be solved in isolation from other problems. The fight against poverty, against slums, against the stalemated Congress, against McCarthyism, are all fights against the discrimination that is nearly endemic to all areas of American life.

C. The promise and problems of long-range *Federal economic development* should be studied more constructively. It is an embarrassing paradox that the Tennessee Valley Authority is a wonder to most foreign visitors but a "radical" and barely influential project to most Americans. The Kennedy decision to permit private facilities to transmit power from the $1 billion Colorado River Storage Project is a disastrous one, interposing privately-owned transmitters between publicly-owned generators and their publicly (and cooperatively) owned distributors. The contrary trend, to public ownership of power, should be generated in an experimental way.

The Area Redevelopment Act of 1961 is a first step in recognizing the underdeveloped areas of the United States. It is only a drop in the bucket financially and is not keyed to public planning and public works on a broad scale. It consists only of a few loan programs to lure industries and some grants to improve public facilities to lure these industries. The current public works bill in Congress is needed—and a more sweeping, higher-priced program of regional development with a proliferation of "TVAs" in such areas as the Appalachian region are needed desperately. However, it has been rejected already by Mississippi because the improvement it bodes for the unskilled Negro worker. This program should be enlarged, given teeth, and pursued rigorously by Federal authorities.

D. We must meet the growing complex of "city" problems; over 90 percent of Americans will live in urban areas within two decades. Juvenile delinquency, untended mental illness, crime increase, slums, urban tenantry and non-rent controlled housing, the isolation of the individual in the city—all are problems of the city and are major symptoms of the present system of economic priorities and lack of public planning. Private property control (the real estate lobby and a few selfish landowners and businesses) is as devastating in the cities as corporations are on the national level. But there is no comprehensive way to deal with these problems now amidst competing units of government, dwindling tax resources, suburban escapism (saprophitic to the sick central cities), high infrastructure costs and no one to pay them.

The only solutions are national and regional. "Federalism" has thus far failed here because states are rural-dominated; the Federal government has had to operate by bootlegging and trickle-down measures dominated by private interests, with their appendages through annexation or federation. A new external challenge is needed, not just a Department of Urban Affairs but a thorough national *program* to help the cities. The *model* city must be projected—more community decision-making and participation, true integration of classes, races, vocations—provision for beauty, access to nature and the benefits of the central city as well, privacy without privatism, decentralized "units" spread horizontally with central, regional democratic control—provision for the basic facility-needs, for everyone, with units of planned *regions* and thus public, democratic control over the growth of the civic community and the allocation of resources.

E. *Mental health institutions* are in dire need; there were fewer mental hospital beds in relation to the numbers of mentally-ill in 1959 than there were in 1948. Public hospitals, too, are seriously wanting; existing structures alone need an estimated $1 billion for rehabilitation. Tremendous staff and faculty needs exist as well, and there are not enough medical students enrolled today to meet the anticipated needs of the future.

F. Our *prisons* are too often the enforcers of misery. They must be either re-oriented to rehabilitative work through public supervision or be abolished for their dehumanizing social effects. Funds are needed, too, to make possible a decent prison environment.

G. *Education* is too vital a public problem to be completely entrusted to the province of the various states and local units. In fact, there is no good reason why America should not progress now toward internationalizing rather than localizing, its education system—children and young adults studying everywhere in the world, through a United Nations program, would go far to create mutual understanding. In the meantime, the need for teachers and classrooms in America is fantastic. This is an area where "minimal" requirements should hardly be considered as a goal—there always are improvements to be made in the education system, e.g., smaller classes and many more teachers for them, programs to subsidize the education for the poor but bright, etc.

H. America should eliminate *agricultural policies* based on scarcity and pent-up surplus. In America and foreign countries there exist tremendous needs for more food and balanced diets. The Federal government should finance small farmers' cooperatives, strengthen programs of rural electrification, and expanded policies for the distribution of agricultural surpluses throughout the world (by Food-for-Peace and related UN programming). Marginal farmers must be helped to either become productive enough to survive "industrialized agriculture" or given help in making the transition out of agriculture—the current Rural Area Development program must be better coordinated with a massive national "area re-development" program.

I. *Science* should be employed to constructively transform the conditions of life throughout the United States and the world. Yet at the present time the Department of Health, Education, and Welfare and the National Science Foundation together spend only $300 million annually for scientific purposes in contrast to the $6 billion spent by the Defense Department and the Atomic Energy Commission. One-half of all research and development in America is directly devoted to military purposes. Two imbalances must be corrected—that of military over non-military investigation, and that of biological-natural-physical science over the sciences of human behavior. Our political system must then include planning for the human use of science: by anticipating the political consequences of scientific innovation, by directing the discovery and exploration of space, by adapting science to improved production of food, to international communications systems, to technical problems of disarmament, and so on. For the newly-developing nations, American science should focus on the study of cheap sources of power, housing and building materials, mass educational techniques, etc. Further, science and scholarship should be seen less as an apparatus of conflicting power blocs, but as a bridge toward supra-national community: the International Geophysical Year is a model for continuous further cooperation between the science communities of all nations.

The youthful discontent of the late 1960's surprised many adults: pro-
testors had benefited from economic boom and unprecedented educa-
tional opportunity. Why were they complaining? Peter Drucker, an
economic analyst, studies population dynamics and concludes that people
should have foreseen this time of turbulence because the baby boom had
lowered the age of the country's center of population gravity and given
the population as a whole a cast of immaturity. And what about the
future? Contrary to people who predict the rapid growth of a "counter-
culture" which rejects dominant values, Drucker suggests that demo-
graphic and economic data indicate that the nation will experience a
return to traditional or "old-fashioned" values. His emphasis on demog-
raphy provides another perspective on the years of protest in the late
1960's.

What does Drucker think are the consequences of a rapid shift in the
age of the population's center of gravity? If he is right, what might hap-
pen in the 1980's, 1990's, and 2000's as the baby boom generation gets
older? What economic factors does he believe will help make the 1970's a
rather conservative decade? Do his predictions appear to be proving true
or false?

Peter Drucker

The Surprising Seventies

A great many people, especially the better educated, take it for granted that today's "youth culture" is the wave of the future. They assume that as the present generation of college students become the young adults of tomorrow, their new life-styles will come to dominate American society and our economy. Practically all of the popular forecasters have been telling us that this will mean a dwindling concern with affluence and the production of material goods.

Maybe so. But the only facts that we know for sure about the future make these predictions look quite unreliable. To me it seems far more probable that during the Seventies this country will return to a preoccupation with the traditional economic worries. Indeed, during the next decade economic performance—with jobs, savings, and profits at the center —may well become more important than it was in the Sixties. Productivity rather than creativity is likely to be the key word. Charles Reich's Consciousness III, in my view, is a description of what happened in the recent past, rather than a forecast of what will happen in the future. No doubt the next ten years will be turbulent; but their central issues and concerns may be familiar ones.

For the only thing we can know with certainty about America's near future—the next ten or twenty years—are a few facts about its population. We can foresee its size, its structure, and its dynamics, because everyone who will enter college or the work force between now and the late Eighties already is alive. We know, for example, that this year marks a true watershed. It is the last year, for as long as we can see ahead, in which teen-agers—that is, 17- and 18-year-olds—will form the center of gravity of our population. Consequently, tomorrow's population dynamics are sure to be radically different from those of the past ten years, the decade of the Youth Revolution.

Everyone knows that the United States had a baby boom after World War II, but few people realize how violent and unprecedented it was. Within a few short years, mainly between 1948 and 1953, the number of babies born in this country rose by almost 50 percent. This is by far the biggest increase in births ever recorded here or, up until then, in any other country. It destroyed the axiom on which population forecasts had always been based: the assumption that birthrates change only at a snail's pace, except in times of major catastrophe, such as war, pestilence, or famine.

We still have no explanation for this extraordinary baby boom. It may never happen again. But it did happen—not only in the United States, but also in the Soviet Union and in all of the other industrially developed states but one. Great Britain was the sole exception.

Peter F. Drucker, "The Surprising Seventies," *Harper's Magazine.* Copyright © 1971 by Harper's Magazine. Reprinted from the July 1971 issue by special permission, 35-39.

AN ERUPTION OF TEEN-AGERS

If the baby boom was unprecedented, so was the baby bust ten years later. The boom crested in 1953. For the next six years the number of births still increased, but at a much slower rate. By 1955 one- and two-year-olds made up a smaller proportion of the total population than they had in the preceding years, and by 1960 the total number of births had started to drop sharply. It kept on dropping for seven years. Like the preceding rise, this was the sharpest fall recorded in population history. Almost 4.3 million babies were born in 1960, but only 3.5 million in 1967—a drop of 20 percent. Today the birthrate is still bumping along at about the same low level and shows little sign of going up.

Because of the violent fluctuations, seventeen-year-olds became in 1964 the largest single age group in the country. For the next seven years—that is, until 1971—the seventeen-year-old group has been larger every year than it was the year before. Throughout that period, then, age 17 has been the center of population gravity in this country.

Now, seventeen is a crucial age. It is the age at which the youngster generally moves out from the family. Until this time, he has taken much of his behavior, and many of his attitudes and opinions—indeed, his way of life—from the family. At seventeen, however, he is likely to make his first career decisions and to take his opinions, attitudes, and concerns increasingly from his peer group, rather than from his family. Seventeen, in other words, has for centuries been the age of the youth rebellion.

In 1960 the center of population gravity in this country was in the thirty-five-to-forty age group—older than it had ever been before. Suddenly, within five years, the center shifted all the way down to age 17—younger than it had been in our history since the early nineteenth century. The psychological impact of this shift proved unusually strong because so many of these seventeen-year-olds—almost half of the young men —did not join the work force but instead stayed on in school, outside of adult society and without adult responsibilities.

The youth revolution was therefore predictable ten or twelve years ago. It was in fact predicted by whoever took the trouble to look at population figures. No one could have predicted then what form it would take; but even without Vietnam or racial confrontation, something pretty big was surely bound to result from such a violent shift in age structure and population dynamics.

We are now about to undergo another population shift, since the seventeen-year-olds will no longer be the largest single group in the population. Perhaps more importantly, this is the last year in which this group will be larger than the seventeen-year-old group of the year before.

From now on, the center of population gravity will shift steadily upward, and by 1975 the dominant age year will be twenty-one or twenty-two. From 1977 to 1985, the total number of seventeen-year-olds in the population will drop sharply.

THE SHOCK OF GROWING UP

In urban and developed economies such as ours, the four years that separate age 17 from age 21 are the true generation gap. No period in a man's life—except perhaps the jump from fulltime work at age 64 and eleven months to complete retirement at sixty-five—involves greater social or psychological changes. Seventeen-year-olds are traditionally (and for good reasons) rebellious, in search of a new identity, addicted to causes, and intoxicated with ideas. But young adults from twenty-one to thirty-five—and especially the young adult women—tend to be the most conventional group in the population, and the one most concerned with concrete and immediate problems. This is the time of life when the first baby arrives, when one has to get the mortgage on one's first house and start paying interest on it. This is the age in which concern with job, advancement, career, income, furniture, and doctors' bills moves into the fore. And this is the age group which, for the next fifteen years, is increasingly going to dominate American society and to constitute its center of gravity.

This group is even more likely than comparable age groups in the past to concern itself with the prosaic details of grubby materialism. For the shift between the economic reality they knew when they dominated our population as seventeen-year olds, and the economic reality they will experience when, still dominant in terms of population, they become young marrieds, is going to be unusually jarring. In the past, most seventeen-year-olds went to work, began to earn a living and to think about money, jobs, prices, and budgets. The affluent seventeen-year-old of the past ten years—especially the very large proportion that went to college (half of the males, and almost two-fifths of the females)—have never known anything but what the economists call "discretionary income." They may not have had a great deal of money in their jeans, but however much it was they could spend it any way they wanted without worrying about the consequences. It made little difference whether they blew it on the whims of the moment or put it into a savings account. The necessities—shoes, the dentist, food, and, in most cases, tuition—were still being provided by their parents. Now, within a few short years, they will suddenly have to take care of these things themselves. Even if a young woman marries a young man with a good income—an accountant, for instance, a college professor, or a meteorologist in the Weather Bureau—she will suddenly feel herself deprived. Suddenly she will have no discretionary income at all. The demands on her purse will inevitably be much greater than her resources because her expectations have risen much faster than her income will. She now expects health care, decent schools, housing, a clean environment, and a hundred other things her grandmother never dreamed of and even her mother did not take for granted when she first started out in married life.

She and her husband, therefore, will probably demonstrate a heightened concern with economics. Ralph Nader, rather than the Weathermen, is likely to foreshadow the popular mood. And no matter how radical Ralph Nader may sound, his is a highly conventional view of the "system." Indeed, his are the values of our oldest tradition: populism. Nader believes in economic performance above all; he makes it the central touchstone of a good society.

Many sociologists and psychologists in the past few years have pointed out that the significant gap in society today may be not that between generations—that is, between middle-class, affluent parents and their college-age children—but that between the kids in college and the young hard-hats who have gone to work after high school. Usually it is the kids in college, the kids of the youth revolution, who are touted as the harbingers of tomorrow, with the hard-hats representing yesterday. But it may well be the other way around. It is just conceivable that the nineteen-year-old hard-hat—precisely because he is already exposed to the realities of economic life which are soon to shock college graduates—prefigures the values, the attitudes, and the concerns to which today's rebellious youth will switch tomorrow.

JOBS WILL BECOME MORE IMPORTANT

The shock the individual college graduate will feel on entering the job market may be severe. The shock to the job market itself may be even stronger. During each year of the next decade, we will have to find jobs for 40 percent more people than in each of the past ten years. The babies of the baby boom are only now entering the work force in large numbers, because so many of them delayed going to work by entering college. There has been a great deal of talk about the "young, educated employee," but he is only beginning to come out of the colleges, and the full impact his group will make is still three or four years away.

The first implication of this is, of course, that jobs are likely to be of increasing concern to the young during the next ten years. The shift from "abundant jobs for college graduates" in 1969 to a "scarcity of jobs for college graduates" in 1971 is not, as most commentators believe, merely a result of the 1970–1971 mini-recession. It is a result of the overabundance of college graduates, which will continue until the end of the decade even if the economy starts expanding again at a fast clip.

At the same time that many more young, college-trained people are out looking for jobs, the largest single source of jobs available to them in the Sixties—that is, teaching jobs—will almost completely dry up.

During the past two decades the number of children in school expanded at an unprecedented rate, and, as every anguished taxpayer well knows, new schools had to be built to accommodate them. The reason, obviously, was that the babies born during the postwar boom were then reaching school age. Yet the teachers in the schools during the Fifties and early Sixties were mostly elderly; the last period of massive hiring had been in the Twenties, an era when high schools grew as fast as colleges have recently. Between 1955 and 1970, therefore, an unusually large number of teachers reached retirement age, became disabled, or died. As a result, some five million college-educated young people found teaching jobs available during this period.

During the next ten years, however, no more than two million teaching jobs will open up; some forecasts put the figure as low as one million. One reason is that the school-age population will be smaller, as a result of the decline in birthrates that began a decade ago. Another reason is that teachers today are the youngest group of workers in the country, so fewer vacancies will occur because of death and retirement.

This decreasing demand for teachers will be partly offset by an increasing demand for computer programmers, medical technologists, and employees of local governments. These jobs, like teaching, traditionally have attracted women with technical training. But an education in the liberal arts, which is what many college women choose, does not quality them for such positions.

Some college-educated girls will probably not even enter the work force but make straight for marriage, home, and a family. If they do, however, this will only increase the economic pressure on them and their husbands, and intensify their concern with incomes, prices, and jobs. A good many young women will decide to work and, as they look for jobs in fields other than teaching, they will begin to compete with young men; it is hardly coincidence that there has been a sharp increase these past two years in the number of women applicants in law and accounting, for instance. (There are fewer women in management or the professions today than there were twenty years ago—a staple of Women's Libbers' complaints—but the explanation may lie as much in the tremendous demand for teachers since the Fifties as in male chauvinism.) The woman who looks for work in business or government because there is no place for her in the public school is, of course, increasing the pressure for jobs. . . .

I do not assert that population dynamics will determine the psychology, politics, or even economics of the years to come. I would consider that absurd. No one factor, I am convinced, is decisive. But it seems equally absurd to omit population as an important factor in determining the characteristics of any era, especially of a time marked by swings as extreme as those we are going through now. The new big issues that emerged these past twenty years—race and civil rights, the urban crisis, the environment—will not go away. For this reason alone, the Seventies will surely not be at all like the Fifties or the Thirties. But a study of population dynamics indicates that they will not be like the Sixties either.

Whether they will be conservative in their mood or liberal, reactionary or revolutionary, no one can yet foresee. But in the issues that matter to them, in their values, and, above all, in their needs, the Seventies may be a very traditional—indeed, a quite old-fashioned——decade.

6

the nixon years

Spiro T. Agnew shot across the political skyline between 1968 and 1973. He went from a self-proclaimed unknown—Spiro Agnew is not a household word, he conceded after receiving the GOP's vice-presidential nomination in 1968—to perhaps the best known vice-president in recent American history. He nearly ended up being the first vice-president to go to jail; only through intensive plea-bargaining was Agnew able to escape indictment—and almost sure conviction—for a variety of crimes.

Agnew's carefully-calculated and extravagantly-phrased attacks upon the press, black militants, and antiwar demonstrators helped set much of the bitter tone of the first Nixon administration. At the same time, Agnew's proclaimed respect for the "common man" made him a political folk hero to Richard Nixon's "silent majority." All the while, the vice-president hobnobbed with wealthy Republican celebrities, like Bob Hope and Frank Sinatra, and continued to solicit bribes from powerful corporations in his home state of Maryland.

Whom does Agnew blame for the nation's problems? Why? What might be the consequences of Agnew's view of dissent?

Spiro T. Agnew

Impudence in the Streets

A little over a week ago, I took a rather unusual step for a Vice President. I said something. Particularly, I said something that was predictably unpopular with the people who would like to run the country without the inconvenience of seeking public office. I said I did not like some of the things I saw happening in this country. I criticized those who encouraged government by street carnival and suggested it was time to stop the carousel.

It appears that by slaughtering a sacred cow I triggered a holy war. I have no regrets. I do not intend to repudiate my beliefs, recant my words, or run and hide.

What I said before, I will say again. It is time for the preponderant majority, the responsible citizens of this country, to assert *their* rights. It is time to stop dignifying the immature actions of arrogant, reckless, inexperienced elements within our society. The reason is compelling. It is simply that their tantrums are insidiously destroying the fabric of American democracy.

By accepting unbridled protest as a way of life, we have tacitly suggested that the great issues of our times are best decided by posturing and shouting matches in the streets. America today is drifting toward Plato's classic definition of a degenerating democracy—a democracy that permits the voice of the mob to dominate the affairs of government.

Last week I was lambasted for my lack of "mental and moral sensitivity." I say that any leader who does not perceive where persistent street struggles are going to lead this nation lacks mental acuity. And any leader who does not caution this nation on the danger of this direction lacks moral strength.

I believe in Constitutional dissent. I believe in the people registering their views with their elected representatives, and I commend those people who care enough about their country to involve themselves in its great issues. I believe in legal protest within the Constitutional limits of free speech, including peaceful assembly and the right of petition. But I do not believe that demonstrations, lawful or unlawful, merit my approval or even my silence where the purpose is fundamentally unsound. In the case of the Vietnam Moratorium, the objective announced by the leaders—immediate unilateral withdrawal of all our forces from Vietnam—was not only unsound but idiotic. The tragedy was that thousands who participated wanted only to show a fervent desire for peace, but were used by the political hustlers who ran the event.

It is worth remembering that our country's founding fathers wisely shaped a Constitutional republic, not a pure democracy. The representative government they contemplated and skillfully constructed never intended that elected officials should decide crucial questions by counting

Spiro T. Agnew, Address at Pennsylvania Republican Dinner, October 30, 1969, as reprinted in *Speaking Freely* (Washington, D.C.: Public Affairs Press, 1970), 16-24.

the number of bodies cavorting in the streets. They recognized that freedom cannot endure dependent upon referendum every time part of the electorate desires it.

So great is the latitude of our liberty that only a subtle line divides use from abuse. I am convinced that our preoccupation with emotional demonstration, frequently crossing the line to civil disruption and even violence could inexorably lead us across that line forever.

Ironically, it is neither the greedy nor the malicious but the self-righteous who are guilty of history's worst atrocities. Society understands greed and malice and erects barriers of law to defend itself from these vices. But evil cloaked in emotional causes is well disguised and often undiscovered until it is too late.

We have just such a group of self-proclaimed saviours of the American soul at work today. Relentless in their criticism of intolerance in America, they themselves are intolerant of those who differ with their views. In the name of academic freedom, they destroy academic freedom. Denouncing violence, they seize and vandalize buildings of great universities. Fiercely expressing their respect for truth, they disavow the logic and discipline necessary to pursue truth.

They would have us believe that they alone know what is good for America—what is true and right and beautiful. They would have us believe that their reflexive action is superior to our reflective action; that their revealed righteousness is more effective than our reason and experience.

Think about it. Small bands of students are allowed to shut down great universities. Small groups of dissidents are allowed to shout down political candidates. Small cadres of professional protestors are allowed to jeopardize the peace efforts of the President of the United States.

It is time to question the credentials of their leaders. And, if in questioning we disturb a few people, I say it is time for them to be disturbed. If, in challenging, we polarize the American people, I say it is time for a positive polarization.

It is time for a healthy in-depth examination of policies and a constructive realignment in this country. It is time to rip away the rhetoric and to divide on authentic lines. It is time to discard the fiction that in a country of 200 million people, everyone is qualified to quarterback the government.

For too long we have accepted superficial categorization—young versus old, white versus black, rich versus poor. Now it is time for an alignment based on principles and values shared by all citizens regardless of age, race, creed, or income. This, after all, is what America is all about.

America's pluralistic society was forged on the premise that what unites us in ideals is greater than what divides us as individuals. Our political and economic institutions were developed to enable men and ideas to compete in the marketplace on the assumption that the best would prevail. Everybody was deemed equal and by the rules of the game they could become superior. The rules were clear and fair: in politics, win an election; in economics, build a better mousetrap. And as time progressed, we added more referees to assure equal opportunities and provided special advantages for those whom we felt had entered life's arena at a disadvantage.

The majority of Americans respect these rules—*and with good reason.* Historically, they have served as a bulwark to prevent totalitarianism, tyranny, and privilege—the old world spectres which drove generations of immigrants to American sanctuary. Pragmatically, the rules of America work. This nation and its citizens—collectively and individually—have made more social, political and economic progress than any civilization in world history.

The principles of the American system did not spring up overnight. They represent centuries of bitter struggle. Our laws and institutions are not even purely American—only our federal system bears our unique imprimatur.

We owe our values to the Judeo-Christian ethic which stresses individualism, human dignity, and a higher purpose than hedonism. We owe our laws to the political evolution of government by consent of the governed. Our nation's philosophical heritage is as diverse as its cultural background. We are a melting pot nation that has for over two centuries distilled something new and, I believe, sacred.

Now, we have among us a glib, activist element who would tell us our values are lies, and I call them impudent. Because anyone who impugns a legacy of liberty and dignity that reaches back to Moses, is impudent.

I call them snobs for most of them disdain to mingle with the masses who work for a living. They mock the common man's pride in his work, his family and his country. It has also been said that I called them intellectuals. I did not. I said that they characterized themselves as intellectuals. No true intellectual, no truly knowledgeable person, would so despise democratic institutions.

America cannot afford to write off a whole generation for the decadent thinking of a few. America cannot afford to divide over their demagoguery, to be deceived by their duplicity, or to let their license destroy liberty. We can, however, afford to separate them from our society— with no more regret than we should feel over discarding rotten apples from a barrel.

The leaders of this country have a moral as well as a political obligation to point out the dangers of unquestioned allegiance to any cause. We must be better than a charlatan leader of the French Revolution, remembered only for his words: "There go the people; I am their leader; I must follow them."

And the American people have an obligation, too—an obligation to exercise their citizenship with a precision that precludes excesses.

I recognize that many of the people who participated in the past Moratorium Day were unaware that its sponsors sought immediate unilateral withdrawal. Perhaps many more had not considered the terrible consequences of immediate unilateral withdrawal.

I hope that all citizens who really want peace will take the time to read and reflect on the problem. I hope that they will take into consideration the impact of abrupt termination; that they will remember the more than 3,000 innocent men, women and children slaughtered after the Viet Cong captured Hue last year and the more than 15,000 doctors, nurses, teachers and village leaders murdered by the Viet Cong during the war's early years. The only sin of these people was their desire to build their budding nation of South Vietnam.

Chanting "Peace Now" is no solution, if "Peace Now" is to permit a wholesale bloodbath. And saying that the President should understand the people's view is no solution. It is time for the people to understand the views of the President they elected to lead them.

First, foreign policy cannot be made in the streets.

Second, turning out a good crowd is not synonymous with turning out a good foreign policy.

Third, the test of a President cannot be reduced to a question of public relations. As the eighteenth century jurist, Edmund Burke, wrote: "Your representative owes you not his industry only but his judgment; and he betrays instead of serving you, if he sacrifices it to your opinion."

Fourth, the impatience—the understandable frustration over this war —should be focused on the government that is stalling peace while continuing to threaten and invade South Vietnam—and that government's capital is not in Washington. It is in Hanoi.

This was not Richard Nixon's war, but it will be Richard Nixon's peace if we only let him make it.

Finally—and most important—regardless of the issue, it is time to stop demonstrating in the streets and start doing something constructive about our institutions. America must recognize the dangers of constant carnival. Americans must reckon with irresponsible leadership and reckless words. The mature and sensitive people of this country must realize that their freedom of protest is being exploited by avowed anarchists and communists who detest everything about this country and want to destroy it.

This is a fact. These are the few; these are not necessarily leaders. But they prey upon the good intentions of gullible men everywhere. They pervert honest concern to something sick and rancid. They are vultures who sit in trees and watch lions battle, knowing that win, lose or draw, they will be fed.

Abetting the merchants of hate are the parasites of passion. These are the men who value a cause purely for its political mileage. These are the politicians who temporize with the truth by playing both sides to their own advantage. They ooze sympathy for "the cause" but balance each sentence with equally reasoned reservations. Their interest is personal, not moral. They are ideological eunuchs whose most comfortable position is straddling the philosophical fence, soliciting votes from both sides.

Aiding the few who seek to destroy and the many who seek to exploit is a terrifying spirit, the new face of self-righteousness. Former H.E.W. Secretary John Gardner described it: "Sad to say, it's fun to hate . . . that is today's fashion. Rage and hate in a good cause! Be vicious for virtue, self-indulgent for higher purposes, dishonest in the service of a higher honesty."

This is what is happening in this nation. We *are* an effete society if we let it happen here.

I do not overstate the case. If I am aware of the danger, the convicted rapist Eldridge Cleaver is aware of the potential. From his Moscow hotel room he predicted, "Many complacent regimes thought that they would be in power eternally—and awoke one morning to find themselves up against the wall. I expect that to happen in the United States in our lifetime."

People cannot live in a state of perpetual electric shock. Tired of a convulsive society, they settle for an authoritarian society. As Thomas Hobbes discerned three centuries ago, men will seek the security of a Leviathan state as a comfortable alternative to a life that is "nasty, brutish and short."

Will Congress settle down to the issues of the nation and reform the institutions of America as our President asks? Can the press ignore the pipers who lead the parades? Will the heads of great universities protect the rights of all their students? Will parents have the courage to say no to their children? Will people have the intelligence to boycott pornography and violence? Will citizens refuse to be led by a series of Judas goats down tortuous paths of delusion and self-destruction?

Will we defend fifty centuries of accumulated wisdom? For that is our heritage. Will we make the effort to preserve America's bold, successful experiment in truly representative government? Or do we care so little that we will cast it all aside?

Because on the eve of our nation's 200th birthday, we have reached the crossroads. Because at this moment totalitarianism's threat does not necessarily have a foreign accent. Because we have a home-grown menace, made and manufactured in the U.S.A. Because if we are lazy or foolish, this nation could forfeit its integrity, never to be free again.

I do not want this to happen to America. And I do not think that you do either. We have something magnificent here, something worth fighting for, and now is the time for all good men to fight for the soul of their country. Let us stop apologizing for our past. Let us conserve and create for the future.

Seymour Martin Lipset and Earl Raab have made one of the earliest attempts to place Richard Nixon and the Watergate happenings in a broad historical perspective. They examine what they believe are the two strains in Nixon's background and in American politics: the provincial and the cosmopolitan. Although Nixon's association with the Eisenhower administration gained him support from the cosmopolitan wing of the Republican party, Lipset and Raab suggest that his earlier Orange County provincial and conspiratorial outlook surfaced when he faced the pressures of the presidency. Lipset and Raab are distinguished observers of the American political process, and their views on the Watergate mentality are bound to influence future historians of the subject.

From what sections of the political spectrum did Richard Nixon draw his support? Do Lipset and Raab provide any clues as to why Nixon could, in one year, win a landslide election and, in the next, see such rapid erosion in his support? How valid or useful are the categories "cosmopolitan" and "provincial"?

Seymour Martin Lipset
Earl Raab

An Appointment with Watergate

As the witnesses testified before the Ervin Committee, one could hear the rustling of a two-hundred-year-old American ghost. The Watergate affair, standing as it does for the whole bag of "White House horrors," was not just the creation of evil men; it was the symptomatic rumbling of a deep strain in American society, of which Richard Nixon has come to seem the almost perfect embodiment. To characterize the behavior which has emerged as "dirty tricks" is to minimize it. To characterize it as "fascist" is to evade its specific American meaning. The United States, and the Nixon administration, had an appointment with Watergate. The form this appointment has taken is significant because of its similarity to certain episodes in America's past; and also significant because of the ways in which it departs from those characteristic episodes.

Watergate begins with the idea, first expressed in the testimony of James McCord and Bernard L. Barker, that the people involved were engaged in a holy mission to combat the secret internal enemies of the United States. Throughout the testimony before the Senate Committee, there runs a self-justifying description of the background of the Watergate horrors: disruptive demonstrations, violence, trashing, bombings, burnings, civil disobedience—much of it conducted by shadowy figures who were never apprehended. And against that background, there was the failure, as the Watergate conspirators saw it, of large segments of the American public to understand the danger fully and the frustrating need this bred to submit to constraints in fighting it.

John Mitchell, who had come to volunteer nothing, said that the Nixon mission was so important that Mitchell would have done anything "short of treason and high crimes" to insure the President's reelection. Jeb Stuart Magruder, who had come, clean-cut, to volunteer everything, was more explicit. He said that "because of that atmosphere that had occurred, to all of us who had worked in the White House, there was that feeling of resentment and frustration at being unable to deal with them on a legal basis." And about the clandestine activities of various members of the Nixon team—the break-in and bugging which gave Watergate its name, the Ellsberg break-in, the proposed raid on the Brookings Institution, the "enemies list," the plans for a new intelligence unit, and so forth—he said: ". . . Although I was aware they were illegal, we had become somewhat inured to using such activities in accomplishing what we thought was a cause, a legitimate cause."

There is a direct line between the rhetoric of the Watergate conspirators and the statement in 1799 of a prominent Bostonian, Jedediah Morse, who said that the new country had internal

Seymour Martin Lipset and Earl Raab, "An Appointment With Watergate," *Commentary* (Sept., 1973), 35-43. Reprinted from *Commentary*, by permission; copyright © 1973 by the American Jewish Committee.

enemies whose professed design is to subvert and overturn our holy religion and our free and excellent government. . . . Among those fruits of their endeavors may be reckoned our unhappy and threatening political divisions; the increasing abuse of our wise and faithful rulers; the virulent opposition to some of the laws of our country; and the measures of the Supreme Executive; . . . the industrious circulation of baneful and corrupting books, and the consequent wonderful spread of infidelity, impiety, and immorality.

But what links Jedediah Morse to Jeb Stuart Magruder is more than a matter of conspiracy theory. It is also a matter of circumstance. In detail, of course, the circumstances of 1799 were different from those of the late 1960's, but their essential nature was remarkably similar, just as both were similar to those of the 1920's. In each case, an important segment of the American population felt that it was being displaced in power and status; in each case this feeling generated a cultural and moralistic "backlash" among the segment in question; and in each case a conspiracy theory was developed to provide ideological justification for the backlash. . . .

NIXON AS PROVINCIAL

The displacing developments of the 1920's were interrupted by the Depression and the war, but galloping megalopolization brought them back in the 1960's and in force. In addition, of course, those who had previously been ruled out of America's "achieving society," the blacks, now declared themselves in. America's closed frontiers were closing in even further with the evident decline of American power and expansion abroad. Huge, highly-taxing welfare programs were concocted in Washington. The still resentful non-metropolitans, the entrenched labor forces in the cities, the postwar *nouveaux riches,* all began to feel insecure about their old or newly-won power and status.

This feeling was reinforced and given body by all those activities of the late 1960's ticked off by the Watergate witnesses: disruptive demonstrations, riots, violence, bombings, flag-burnings, civil disobedience. The attack on the culture was made explicit by the drug revolution, the sexual revolution, the gay revolution, and so forth. The moralists of the 1920's had complained bitterly about knee-length skirts; how were their descendants to feel about another eight inches of elevation? And most humiliating of all was our inability to defeat a small and underdeveloped Communist enemy in Southeast Asia. How was all this possible except as a consequence of demoralization and betrayal in high places?

When George Wallace received the support of a quarter of the American people in the opinion polls, he was clearly expressing the virulence of their backlash sentiments. Nevertheless, while everybody (including Henry Kissinger) waited, breathlessly anticipating a repressive right-wing movement like the KKK of the 20's, no such movement ever developed. Instead of the KKK, we got Watergate. Why? The answer to that question lies to a considerable extent in the political career of Richard Nixon and the complex relation of that career to America's backlash tradition.

It has often been pointed out that Nixon was originally the product of provincial America. He was raised in the backwater environments of Yorba Linda and Whittier in the 1920's, an area in which the Klan was relatively strong. Of course, most people in the area did not support the KKK, but they were affected by the same anxieties of displacement which lay behind the Klan. In a latter-day TV interview, Nixon himself said that the fundamental cause of unrest in this country is not war, poverty, or prejudice but "a sense of insecurity that comes from the old values being torn away." And not only did Nixon grow up in this area; it was also here that he first ran for political office immediately after World War II.

The backlash "package" of the 1920's included anti-radicalism; and after World War II, with the quick outbreak of the cold war, the revelation of widespread Communist espionage, and then the Korean war, militant anti-Communism became a leading backlash staple. Since almost all Americans were anti-Communist in one degree or another, and since there was a real Communist threat in Berlin, Czechoslovakia, Korea, China, and Western Europe, it is perhaps more accurate to say that anti-Communism was often used as the centerpiece of a backlash syndrome. Thus, to many on the political Right, Communism was made to symbolize the immoralities of "modernism" in general. As Senator Joseph McCarthy put it: "The great difference between our Western Christian world and the atheistic Communist world is not political . . . it is moral."

In this environment Nixon ran against Jerry Voorhis for Congress; and a few years later, against Helen Gahagan Douglas for Senator. In the Voorhis campaign he charged that his opponent had the support of radical groups, and that a vote for Nixon was a vote "to preserve the American way of life." To an American Legion post he declared that "the infiltration of Communists into public office is part of a design to impose a Communist form of government on the American people." This kind of public antagonism to Communism was a standard part of the temper of the times; indeed it was Jerry Voorhis himself who had authored the group) to register with the Department of Justice. The fact that Nixon law requiring Communists (and any other left- or right-wing subversive could attack the author of such a bill as soft on Communism helped give him his reputation as "Tricky Dick." And it also began Nixon's identification with the ideological backlash syndrome.

Nationally this identification was established for Nixon by his prominent role in the Congressional investigations and especially in the prosecution of Alger Hiss. In that role, he conducted himself with dogged persistence, but without any marked McCarthy-like excesses. Nevertheless he was pictured as the heavy villain by everyone who refused to accept the fact that Hiss was guilty. Nixon himself, in his *Six Crises,* pointed to the underlying support for Hiss as

the symbol of a considerable number of perfectly loyal citizens whose theaters of operation are the nation's mass media and universities, its scholarly foundations, and its government bureaucracies. . . . They are not Communists, they are not even remotely disloyal. . . . But they are of a mind-set, as doctrinaire as those on the extreme Right, which makes them singularly vulnerable to the Communist popular-front appeal under the banner of social justice. . . . As soon as the Hiss case broke and well before a bill of particulars was even available, much less open to close critical analysis, they leaped to the defense of Alger Hiss—and to a counterattack of unparalleled venom and irrational fury on his accusers.

By becoming an enemy to this group, Richard Nixon became a hero to the backlash ideologues—a position he consolidated by conducting a slashing anti-Communist campaign against Helen Gahagan Douglas for the Senate in 1950. To be sure, her own Democratic opponents in the primary had referred to her as one of a "small subversive clique of red-hots conspiring to capture, through stealth and cunning, the nerve centers of our Democratic party," and the like. But Nixon did no less, distributing the famous Pink Sheet handbills which pointed out that Helen Gahagan Douglas had voted 354 times the same way as the Communist party-liner Vito Marcantonio. Most of those votes, of course, had nothing to do with any Communist-related issues, yet such, again, was the temper of the times that Helen Gahagan Douglas ended up publicly accusing Nixon of giving "aid and comfort to the Communists. On every key vote Nixon stood with party-liner Marcantonio against America in its fight to defeat Communism." In any case, Nixon won and in the process earned additional love from the Right and additional hatred from the Left.

NIXON AS COSMOPOLITAN

However, if Nixon's reputation as a prime defender of Americanism, the old American virtues, sat well in his Orange County constituency, in the nation's other backlash regions, and in his own mind as a winning political stance, he was also a flawed defender in the eyes of backlash extremists like the leaders of the John Birch Society—flawed by a tendency to cosmopolitanism. In the first place, he had always been an internationalist. From the beginning of his Congressional career, he was deeply committed to and gratified by his work on the Herter Committee which set up the first foreign-aid plans,. even though the concept of foreign aid received a negative poll in his own district. Worse still, he argued during the age of McCarthyism that the Republican party must avoid extremism, a position which he expressed later in these words:

> It is as wrong for the Republican party to become a far-right party as it is for it to become a radical party. As a matter of principle it can never look back and it must never put itself in the position of dividing Americans into classes. To take the far-right viewpoint would destroy it as a national party.

Of course, this attitude was partly a function of political acuity. But cosmopolitanism among political conservatives is, in general, just that: a function of acuity, of enlightened self-interest based on a history-wise understanding of the necessity not just to "look back," but to accept and even promote certain types of social change. The "Eastern Republican establishment," often the educated descendants of the old robber barons, became increasingly cosmopolitan on precisely that basis. Moreover, the cosmopolitan understands that political victory cannot be won in America by a fringe party or an ideologically pure faction, and he understands that majorities only accrue to coalition parties which can engage in political enterprise, which can deal comfortably with some element of change (or with some element of resistance to change, as the case may be: the cosmopolitans in the Democratic party saw that when the Mc-Govern provincials took over from them; and the comopolitans in the Republican party saw it when the Goldwater provincials took over from them).

Conspiracy theories and their attendant political implications are obviously not in the cosmopolitan style. Political cosmopolitans usually know that most grand conspiracy theories have, in fact, been old wives' tales. (Some become so "sophisticated" that they resist accepting even routine little conspiracies when they are proved, such as the Communist party spy rings in Washington which were related to the Alger Hiss case.) They know too that history is being changed by social forces which are not in any prime way subject to manipulation, let alone dependent on conspiratorial master-direction. And they know that the kind of departure from democratic process encouraged by extremist thinking is dangerous and normally does not serve their enlightened self-interest.

To be sure, none of this has prevented cosmopolitans from aligning themselves temporarily under certain circumstances with extremist movements and tendencies. During the early 1950's, for example, just such a marriage of convenience took place between establishment Republicans and Joseph McCarthy, although they always basically disapproved of his extremist provincialism and the methods which flowed therefrom.

Nixon was among those who disapproved. Apparently making a distinction between the way he himself conducted electoral campaigns, and the way he conducted government business, Nixon in office constantly pulled back from McCarthy-like statements. Even when armed during the Hiss investigation with clear evidence that high Democratic officials had, for various political reasons, failed to act on information of espionage activities, Nixon said: "There are some who claim that Administration officials failed to act because they were Communist or pro-Communist. But the great majority of our officials were not in this category, and I cannot accept this accusation as a fair one."

It was in fact Nixon who as Vice President finally engineered the confrontation which sank Joe McCarthy. With the Republican party now in power, McCarthy had, of course, become an embarrassment to it, while Nixon had become a full-fledged member of the cosmopolitan Eastern Republican establishment which had chosen Eisenhower over Taft and had (if somewhat reluctantly) accepted Nixon as Eisenhower's running mate. The result was that Nixon now became an object of attack by the extreme ideologues of the backlash.

Commenting on Nixon's bid for the Presidency in 1960, Robert Welch, the head of the Birch Society, explained that "the Insiders [the conspirators] think they can accomplish far more for the Communist movement, far more safely, with an Eisenhower-type administration, this time under Richard Nixon, than they would with a Kennedy or a Humphrey as President." When Nixon met privately with Nelson Rockefeller in the latter's Fifth Avenue apartment on the Saturday before the 1960 Republican convention, Phyllis Schlafly, a leading Goldwater pamphleteer, denounced him for making "himself acceptable to the New York kingmakers." Goldwater himself predicted that the alliance between Nixon and Rockefeller, who seconded Nixon's nomination at the convention, would "live in history as the Munich of the Republican party." Later, in the California campaign, Joseph Shell, Republican leader of the California Assembly, charged Nixon with being "soft on Communism."

For his part, Nixon denounced the Birch Society, and seemed to settle down as part of the cosmopolitan Republican establishment. He was booed by the California Young Republicans when he said he wanted to study an anti-Communist proposition before endorsing it, and told them: "The American Constitution has to apply even when you're fighting Communism."

TOWARD WATERGATE

For all this, however, Nixon never quite lost his favorable reputation among the ideologues of backlash. To many of them he was a strayed soul, perhaps reclaimable, rather than an ancestral enemy. Conversely, to many cosmopolitan Republicans, he remained suspect for the same reason—in addition to remaining subject to the normal dosage of snobbery against the provincial from Whittier, the same kind of snobbery which some of the Democratic elite directed at Lyndon Johnson.

But most important of all in affecting his future role was the fact that while at his cosmopolitan peak, Nixon suffered two demoralizing defeats: for President in 1960, and for Governor of California in 1962. At the end of that last disaster, he gave vent to one of the least controlled outbursts of his public life, possibly his most quoted words:

. . . as I leave the press, all I can say is this: for sixteen years, ever since the Hiss case, you've had a lot of fun . . . you've had an opportunity to attack me . . . I leave you gentlemen, now, and just think how much you're going to be missing. You won't have Nixon to kick around anymore. . . .

That speech had been festering for a long time. Once, during his campaign for Vice President, when a heckler shouted something about the "secret fund" story which had just broken, in another unprepared outburst, Nixon heatedly replied:

You folks know the work that I did investigating Communists in the United States. Ever since I have done that work, the Communists, the left-wingers have been fighting me with every smear that they have been able to. Even when I received the nomination for the Vice Presidency, I want you to know—and I'm going to reveal it today for the first time—I was warned that if I continue to attack the Communists and the crooks in this government they would continue to smear me. . . .

But the forces he saw unfairly arrayed against him were not restricted to Communists. "The Hiss case," he later wrote,

brought me national fame, but it also left a residue of hatred and hostility toward me—not only among the Communists but also among substantial segments of the press and the intellectual community . . . who have subjected me to a continuous utterly unprincipled and vicious smear campaign.

Nixon's ultimate triumph, his election to the Presidency in 1968, occurred in a sequence of events which could only have served to reinforce his sense of the power of his interlocking opposition. When Hubert

Humphrey left the disastrous Chicago convention, he was 16 percentage points behind Nixon in the polls, in a three-candidate race. Yet by election day, the gap had closed spectacularly, and Humphrey's popular vote was almost equal to that of Nixon. Since polling began in 1936, no Presidential candidate had ever experienced such a precipitous decline. Just as in 1960—so it must have seemed to Nixon—the liberal establishment had again demonstrated its marvelous ability to turn public opinion against him. Little wonder, then, that immediately after taking office in 1969 the administration's chief ideological spokesman, Spiro Agnew, undertook to attack the "effete corps of impudent snobs who characterize themselves as intellectuals," and to complain about news commentators and producers who "to a man . . . live and work in the geographical and intellectual confines of Washington, D.C., or New York City, the latter of which James Reston terms the 'most unrepresentative community in the entire United States.'" The depth of sentiment in high White House circles was expressed even more strongly when Attorney General John Mitchell, after complaining in a press interview in September 1970 about the "stupid kids," feelingly said: "The professors are just as bad, if not worse. They don't know anything. Nor do the stupid bastards who are running our educational institutions. . . ."

Thus while Nixon stood against and resisted blatant backlash extremism, and while he repudiated comprehensive conspiracy theories such as were held by the KKK and then by the Birch Society, he did have a markedly adversary relationship to those elements which have always formed the central core of conspiracy theories: the "intellectual community," the journalists, the Ivy League elite, the "liberals." Furthermore, Nixon explicitly put these elements together into a connected network, which he had indicated was hostile toward him and toward traditional American values. It was ironic that this man, one of whose main political purposes was to contain the excesses of right-wing extremism which he saw as inimical to the Republican party and to his Presidency, should have carried the atmosphere and the logic of that very extremism right into the White House and into the heart of the Republican establishment. Once in the White House, however, it became easy for the logic of that extremism to unfold, especially given the circumstances which the Nixonites found in Washington.

For the Washington they entered was still a Democratic town. Democrats not only held a majority in Congress, they clearly retained the sympathies of the potent civil service, including its upper echelons—not to mention the press corps, particularly those representing the most influential papers and the national TV news programs. The bulk of consultants were heavily liberal, as were the largely government-financed "think tanks," from Brookings to Rand. (Brookings was to be the target of a planned break-in, and Henry Rowen, the then president of Rand, appeared on the enemies list.) And then the evidence began to pile up, in the form of leaks and pilfered documents, that persons in high places in government were in collusion with this elite to expose and frustrate the new administration. As John Erhlichman described the way the administration people saw their situation:

There were a number of holdovers in the executive branch who actively opposed the President's policies. . . . These people conducted a kind of internal guerrilla warfare against the President during his first term, trying to frustrate his goals by unauthorized leaks of part of the facts of a story, or of military and other secrets, or by just plain falsehood. The object was to create hostility in the Congress and abroad and to affect public opinion.

Meanwhile, outside government, there was the anti-war movement. Even though the New Left was obviously exhausted, even though the campuses had begun to quiet down by the fall of 1969 in response to troop withdrawals and the disappearing draft, many in the White House, finding confirmation in the May 1970 demonstration on Cambodia, persisted in believing that the same "extra-parliamentary" forces which had destroyed Lyndon Johnson would, if left unchecked, destroy Richard Nixon too.

It was also believed in the White House that the disruptive forces were being supported by foreign funds. When the FBI and the CIA reported that they could unearth no evidence of significant foreign involvement in the domestic New Left or in the anti-war movement, the White House staffers concluded that a new intelligence operation, controlled by the White House itself, was needed. Arguing for such an operation which would include proposals he himself described as "clearly illegal," a young White House aide, Tom Huston, wrote in a September 1970 memo to Haldeman:

The biggest risk we could take, in my opinion, is to continue to regard violence on the campus and in the cities as a temporary phenomenon. . . . I believe we are talking about the future of this country, for surely domestic violence and disorder threaten the very fabric of our society. For eighteen months we have watched people in this government ignore the President's orders, take actions to embarrass him, promote themselves at his expense, and generally make his job more difficult.

The original plans, though initially approved by the President, were killed by the opposition of J. Edgar Hoover, who apparently saw the scheme as reflecting a negative evaluation of the FBI by the White House. And he was correct in this.

For now even Hoover was suspect. Huston told Haldeman in August

1970 that Hoover "has become totally unreasonable and his conduct is detrimental to our domestic intelligence operation." He particularly singled out FBI campus coverage as inadequate. And in March 1973, Nixon apparently reiterated to Richard Moore the curious myth which had become the in-house explanation, that Hoover could not be relied on to investigate Daniel Ellsberg properly since Ellsberg's father-in-law was a friend of Hoover's, a statement which, though also spread by Ehrlichman and others, was false.

To be sure, the situation with the FBI is clearly complex. Given the enormous number of terrorist bombings and other illegal acts in the late 60's and early 70's, there can be little doubt that the FBI and the assorted state and local police groups which sought to deal with them were largely unsuccessful. Few of the guilty were apprehended. Rarely did the law-enforcement agencies give advance notice of terroristic acts. As compared, for example, to the Israeli secret police, Shin Beth, which seems to know everything about Arab terrorism, the Americans were a failure. And this fact seemingly justified administration proposals to change procedures, and even to create new agencies, the secret domestic intelligence evaluation group, under Robert C. Mardian, located in the Justice Department, and the covert "special investigation unit," under Egil Krogh, in the White House.

Placing blame on the FBI or other investigative agencies for failing to uncover the terrorists, however, ignored the nature of the protests of the 1960's. Unlike the Communist party of earlier decades, or the Arab terrorists today, both with centralized leadership, the recent American "Movement" was composed of literally hundreds, if not thousands, of separate, independent "cells," many bitterly hostile on ideological grounds to one another. There were few national organizations. Most of those which existed—the SDS, the Young Socialist Alliance, the Progressive Labor party, the Spartacus League—did not take part in terrorism, either for ideological or practical reasons. The bombings, the arson, the raids on government offices, were largely conducted by small local groups, often comprising a handful of people. It was quite impossible for the FBI or even the local police to penetrate these cells. And most of them evidently were clever enough not to let anyone in the above-ground anti-war organizations know who they were.

There was, then, no single large conspiracy, there were thousands of small conspiracies. Few of those were in a position to secure foreign funds or help, although some probably did. Alien subversive forces would have had as little luck in locating the American terrorists as did the FBI; and Mardian and Krogh were later equally unsuccessful in finding them. Hence, both the CIA and the FBI were undoubtedly correct in reporting to the White House that foreign-supported conspiracies did not explain the continuation and spread of terrorism.

But such reports did no good, for conspiracy-theory logic had enveloped the White House. Much as extremists, both of the Left and of the Right, found it impossible to accept the fact that Lee Harvey Oswald was a loner linked neither to the CIA nor to Castro, so the White House could not accept a non-conspiratorial interpretation of Daniel Ellsberg's turnabout. Faced with the "betrayal" of a once-trusted supporter of the Vietnam war, they refused to see Ellsberg as a man who has always shown a need for passionate commitment, who, in the words of the CIA psychological profile which they rejected, had always been "either strongly for something or strongly against," and who had now reached a time of life when many men, especially very ambitious ones, "come to doubt their earlier commitments, and are impelled to strike out in new directions." The CIA profile asserted that "There is no suggestion that [Ellsberg] thought anything treasonous in his act. Rather, he seemed to be responding to what he deemed a higher order of patriotism." But in the White House view Ellsberg *had* to be part of a broader conspiracy, and anyone who doubted this—even the CIA or so reliable an ally as J. Edgar Hoover—must either have been misled or somehow corrupted.

THE TWO SIDES OF WATERGATE

In short, the behavior summed up in the name Watergate was typical, at least in form, of American backlash extremism. But if this is so, two important questions still have to be answered. First, how did this syndrome get seated so directly in the White House and in the Republican establishment? There had been other backlash administrations in Washington, but such administrations had usually taken care to separate themselves from extremist behavior while sympathizing with or tolerating it. Even after World War I, when the U.S. Attorney General's office was directly involved in a Watergate-type pattern, the activist-extremist centers like the KKK or the American Defense League were outside the government exerting pressure. Here the activist extremist center was the White House itself, and it was evidently self-starting. But secondly, why, emanating as it did from the highest places, should Watergate have been so pale and tepid an expression of extremist action?

The first question seems troubling, the second comforting—but they are both finally the same question, and the answer to both lies in Richard Nixon's remarkable personification of the American split: convincingly enough provincial, convincingly enough cosmopolitan. Because for enough people he stood for the backlash, while for enough people he stood for the resistance to factional extremism, he managed to reach the White House, and he also managed to prevent the formation of a classic extremist movement. He certainly defused George Wallace, who complained bitterly about it many times. Wallace told a national television audience: "I wish I had copyrighted or patented my speeches. I would be drawing immense royalties from Mr. Nixon and especially Mr. Agnew." In order to defuse the backlash, however, Nixon had to represent it himself, and it was this that brought the extremist syndrome right into the White House. Yet at the same time the "cosmopolitan" climate in which the backlash now had to operate also blunted and made it relatively ineffectual. After World War I Attorney General A. Mitchell Palmer set up an extra-legal intelligence agency, and promptly swept many thousands of people into jail. Nixon's first attempt to set up an extra-legal intelligence agency was shot down by a cross word from Hoover, and he fell back to a "plumbers" operation which was neither massive nor very efficient. Second-story men all over the nation must still be chuckling over the ineptitude of the Watergate break-in itself. The plumbers found out nothing in the office of Ellsberg's psychiatrist, and indeed managed only to guarantee Ellsberg's acquittal. Enemies lists were prepared, but for the most part they ended up in John Dean's files without being acted on. The proposal to deny government research grants to MIT because of the objections of its president, Jerome Wiesner, to administration military and foreign policies was never carried through, apparently because of opposition from the Pentagon and other government agencies. In order to harass people through their income tax, White House staff had to resort to sending anonymous "citizens" letters to the IRS, with scarcely impressive results. They bugged the wrong phones. They tried to "get something" on Daniel Schorr of CBS, but succeeded only in alerting him. Nor did they have a "chilling" effect on anyone, in the way that Joseph McCarthy so often did with an essentially one-man operation.

This is not to minimize the seriousness of these activities, nor to dismiss them as merely inept. Presumably, with more practice, the Watergate group could have improved its skills. In any case, a botched burglary is still a burglary, an unsuccessful assault on constitutional liberties it still an assault. But the point is that the Watergate horrors were perpetrated covertly, in the dark of the night, whereas in the 1920's, the illegal activities of the government were carried out in the open, and apparently with the overwhelming approval of the American people. In the Nixon administration, by contrast, the most elaborate operation was the cover-up, which is itself a measure of the restraining power of the cosmopolitan climate not only within the administration but in the nation at large—in, that is, the growing cosmopolitanization of the American people.

Thus, as compared with the 1920's, for example, the American people today are more willing to accept cultural and political differences. All three Presidents of the 1920's—Harding, Coolidge, and Hoover—publicly expressed themselves in racist terms. Harding supported the immigration restrictions on the basis of inherent "racial differences" and the unassimilability of anyone but Northern Protestants. Coolidge, in an article in *Good Housekeeping*, argued that "biological laws show us that Nordics deteriorate when mixed with other races." Herbert Hoover declared that "immigrants now lived in the United States on sufferance . . . and would be tolerated only if they behaved." Today no major party politician or officeholder could possibly air such views, and racists who hope to be elected are forced to mute their appeal .

On another front, the public receptivity to charges that liberals are "soft on Communism" has declined considerably, and even during the Vietnam war—a war, after all, against Communism—various restrictions of the rights of Communists were struck down by the courts, by universities, and by trade unions, without a serious murmur from the public. Perhaps the best indication of the growth in cosmopolitanism has been Nixon's foreign policy and its acceptance by the bulk of the American population. A quarter of a century of cold-war anti-Communism in which Richard Nixon himself played a key role simply went out the window in the face of its failure to meet the test of reality in Vietnam and in connection with Sino-Soviet relations.

None of this means that fanatical anti-Communism or bigotry has disappeared. What it does mean is that more and more Americans have learned to lace their biases with democratic restraint. *That* is the nature of the cosmopolitan impulse, and its growth in the past fifty years seems to be related to the spread of formal education. The 60's taught us that education can breed a cultural intolerance of its own, but for people coming out of a traditionally anti-modernist milieu, education is still likely to encourage a greater readiness to accept diversity, if only on grounds of enlightened self-interest. On that score, of course, the difference between the American population of the 1920's and that of the 1970's is statistically spectacular. Between 1920 and 1970 the proportion of the college-age population enrolled in higher education jumped from 8 to almost 50 per cent. There were 600,000 college students in 1920; there are 9 million today. College professors alone now constitute a major occupational group, over half-a-million, almost as many as there were students in 1920.

But democratic restraint is not an absolute commitment. It describes a threshold, which in turn relates to level of provocation, level of desperation. Political extremism may be more difficult to make overt than it was in the 1920's, but the dynamic is always there, never expunged. Massive unmet aspirations on the Left—or, as has more often happened in America, unattended status backlash on the Right—can obviously overwhelm democratic restraint under certain conditions, and thus a major function of pragmatic politics in America has always been to prevent those conditions from prevailing. This is why the possibility of a more narrowly ideological national politics seems so ominous.

What Watergate suggests is that just such a withdrawal from cosmopolitan politics may be in store for America. The electorate in general has grown more cosmopolitan largely because of education, but education has also helped to create more ideological fervor at both ends of the political spectrum. According to a study by Everett Ladd, college-educated Democrats are more ideologically liberal and college-educated Republicans are more ideologically conservative than less educated party partisans. And abundant data indicate that well-educated ideologues are the most likely of all to be active in party affairs and to vote in primary elections. When the conservative ideologues captured the Republican party in 1964, the mass of Republicans was in effect disenfranchised, as was the mass of the Democratic electorate when the liberal ideologues captured their party in 1972. To imagine an entirely disenfranchised electorate, we need only imagine a Goldwater-McGovern contest for the Presidency. Watergate has now revealed that we were much closer to such a situation than many thought. McGovern, like Goldwater before him, lost by a landslide because he was seen as a factionalist, an extremist. Nixon, on the other hand, was perceived as a former factionalist who had turned into a pragmatist, a coalition leader, a cosmopolitan. To some extent, this was certainly true of Nixon, but we now know that the provincial, factional, ideological, extremist element in Nixon was also still alive, restrained by his cosmopolitan side but clearly not squelched.

If, then, American society, torn between provincialism and cosmopolitanism, indeed had an appointment with Watergate, it could scarcely have chosen a more likely person to keep that appointment than Richard M. Nixon. The corrolary is that if American society is to avoid backlash extremism in the future, it will have to find ways of preventing the disenfranchisement of the electorate by ideological factionalists, and of making the politics of pragmatism and democratic restraint prevail once again on the national scene.

Although several other chief executives had taped occasional phone conversations and meetings, Richard Nixon attempted to secure a taped record of virtually all his activities. Beginning in 1970 a voice-activated system recorded all that was said in the Oval Office, in the presidential hideaway in the Executive Office Building, in the Cabinet Room, and on several key telephone lines. Ultimately, of course, the so-called Nixon tapes provided the damning material which drove Richard Nixon from office. The following extract is from the White House transcript of a June 23, 1972, meeting between Nixon and his chief aide, H. R. (Bob) Haldeman. This tape revealed the existence of the "smoking pistol," the unequivocal proof that the president had attempted to limit the FBI's investigation of the Watergate break-in and to conceal White House involvement in this illegal action.

The extract also suggests the potential value of the White House tapes for scholars. What does this brief conversation reveal about the way in which the Nixon White House operated? What does it suggest about Nixon's values and priorities? Can you confidently draw a portrait of the Nixon presidency from the handful of tapes which were made public during the Watergate investigation?

House Judiciary Committee

The Nixon Tapes

H. Now, on the investigation, you know the Democratic break-in thing, we're back in the problem area because the FBI is not under control, because [Acting FBI Director L. Patrick] Gray doesn't exactly know how to control it and they have—their investigation is now leading into some productive areas—because they've been able to trace the money—not through the money itself—but through the bank sources—the banker. And, and it goes in some directions we don't want it to go. Ah, also there have been some things—like an informant came in off the street to the FBI in Miami who was a photographer or has a friend who is a photographer who developed some films through this guy [Bernard] Barker [one of the men who broke into Democratic headquarters] and the films had pictures of Democratic National Committee letterhead documents and things. So it's things like that that are filtering in. [John] Mitchell [former attorney general and head of the 1972 re-election committee] came up with yesterday, and John Dean analyzed very carefully last night and concludes, concurs now with Mitchell's recommendation that the only way to solve this, and we're set up beautifully to do it, ah, in that and that—the only network that paid any attention to it last night was NBC—they did a massive story on the Cuban thing.

P. That's right.

H. That the way to handle this now is for us to have [Vernon] Walters [Deputy Director of the CIA and a Nixon appointee] call Pat Gray and just say, "Stay to hell out of this—this is ah, business here we don't want you to go any further on it." That's not an unusual development, and ah, that would take care of it.

P. What about Pat Gray—you mean Pat Gray doesn't want to?

H. Pat does want to. He doesn't know how to, and he doesn't have, he doesn't have any basis for doing it. Given this, he will then have the basis. He'll call Mark Felt [an FBI official] in, and the two of them—and Mark Felt wants to cooperate because he's ambitious—

P. Yeah.

H. He'll call him in and say, "We've got the signal from across the river to put the hold on this." And that will fit rather well because the FBI agents who are working the case, at this point, feel that's what it is.

P. This is CIA? They've traced the money? Who'd they trace it to?

H. Well, they've traced it to a name, but they haven't gotten to the guy yet.

P. Would it be somebody here?

H. Ken Dahlberg.

House of Representatives, *Statement of Information: Appendix III. Hearings before the Committee on the Judiciary to investigate whether sufficient grounds exist for the House of Representatives to exercise its constitutional power to impeach Richard M. Nixon,* U.S. Government Printing Office, 1974.

P. Who the hell is Ken Dahlberg?

H. He gave $25,000 in Minnesota and, ah, the check went directly to this guy Barker.

P. It isn't from the Committee though, from Stans?

H. Yeah. It is. It's directly traceable and there's some more through some Texas people that went to the Mexican bank which can also be traced to the Mexican bank—they'll get their names today.

H. —And (pause)

P. Well, I mean, there's no way—I'm just thinking if they don't cooperate, what do they say? That they were approached by the Cubans. That's what Dahlberg has to say, the Texans too, that they—

H. Well, if they will. But then we're relying on more and more people all the time. That's the problem and they'll stop if we could take this other route.

P. All right.

H. And you seem to think the thing to do is get them to stop?

P. Right, fine.

H. They say the only way to do that is from White House instructions. And it's got to be to [CIA Director Richard] Helms and to—ah, what's his name . . . . . ? Walters.

P. Walters.

H. And the proposal would be that Ehrlichman and I call them in, and say, ah—

P. All right, fine. How do you call him in—I mean you just—well. we protected Helms from one hell of a lot of things.

H. That's what Ehrlichman says.

P. Of course; this Hunt, that will uncover a lot of things. You open that scab there's a hell of a lot of things and we just feel that it would be very detrimental to have this thing go any further. This involves these Cubans, Hunt, and a lot of hanky-panky that we have nothing to do with ourselves. Well what the hell, did Mitchell know about this?

H. I think so. I don't think he knew the details, but I think he knew.

P. He didn't know how it was going to be handled though—with Dahlberg and the Texans and so forth? Well who was the asshole that did? Is it [G. Gordon] Liddy? Is that the fellow? He must be a little nuts!

H. He is.

P. I mean he just isn't well screwed on is he? Is that the problem?

H. No, but he was under pressure, apparently, to get more information, and as he got more pressure, he pushed the people harder to move harder—

P. Pressure from Mitchell?

H. Apparently.

P. Oh, Mitchell. Mitchell was at the point (unintelligible).

H. Yeah.

P. All right, fine, I understand it all. We won't second-guess Mitchell and the rest. Thank God it wasn't [Charles] Colson [a White House Assistant].

H. The FBI interviewed Colson yesterday. They determined that would be a good thing to do. To have him take an interrogation, which he did, and that—the FBI guys working the case concluded that there were one or two possibilities—one, that this was a White House— they don't think that there is anything at the Election Committee— they think it was either a White House operation and they had some obscure reasons for it—non-political, or it was a—Cuban and the CIA. And after their interrogation of Colson yesterday, they concluded it was not the White House, but are now convinced it is a CIA thing, so the CIA turnoff would—

P. Well, not sure of their analysis, I'm not going to get that involved. I'm (unintelligible).

H. No, sir, we don't want you to.

P. You call them in.

H. Good deal.

P. Play it tough. That's the way they play it and that's the way we are going to play it.

H. O.K. . . .

H. Did you get the report that the British floated the pound?

P. No, I don't think so.

H. They did.

P. That's devaluation?

H. Yeah, Flanigan's got a report on it here.

P. I don't care about it. Nothing we can do about it.

H. You want a run-down?

P. No, I dont.

H. He argues it shows the wisdom of our refusal to consider convertibility until we get a new monetary system.

P. Good. I think he's right. It's too complicated for me to get into. (unintelligible) I understand.

H. Burns expects a 5-day percent devaluation against the dollar.

P. Yeah. O.K. Fine.

H. Burns is concerned about speculation about the lira.

P. Well, I don't give a (expletive deleted) about the lira. (Unintelligible)

H. That's the substance of that.

P. When you get in—when you get in (unintelligible) people, say, "Look the problem is that this will open the whole, the whole Bay of Pigs thing, and the President just feels that ah, without going into the details—don't, don't lie to them to the extent to say there is no involvement, but just say this is a comedy of errors, without getting into it, the President believes that it is going to open the whole Bay of Pigs thing up again. And, ah, because these people are plugging for (unintelligible) and that they should call the FBI in and (unintelligible) don't go any further into this case period!

P. Three or four things. Ah—Pat [the First Lady] raised the point last night that probably she and the girls ought to stay in a hotel on Miami Beach. First she says the moment they get the helicopter and get off and so forth, it destroys their hair and so forth. And of course, that is true—even though you turn them off and turn them on so on. The second point is—

H. Could drive over—

P. Well, the point is, I want to check with Dean to be sure what the driving time is. If the driving time with traffic is going to be up to an hour—

H. Oh no.

P. With the traffic—

H. But they have an escort.

P. How long would it take?

H. Half an hour. Less than half an hour. You can make it easy in a half hour without an escort, and they would—they should have an escort. They should arrive with—and they may not like it—it may bother them a little, but that's what people expect—and you know at the Conventions—every county—

P. She has another point though which I think will please everybody concerned. She says, "Now look. You go there—she says as far as she was concerned she would be delighted—the girls would be delighted to every reception—everything that they have there." They want to be busy. They want to do things and they want to be useful. Of course, as you know, our primary aim is to see that they are on television (unintelligible) coming into the hall (unintelligible) shooting the hall (unintelligible) plan on television. My point is, I think it would be really great if they did the delegations of the bit states. Just to stop in you know. Each girl and so forth can do—

H. Sure.

P. The second thing is—just go by and say hello, and they'll do the handshakers (unintelligible) you know (unintelligible).

H. Well, the big point is, there's, there's several major functions that they may want to tie that into.

P. Yeah. Yeah.

H. There's—a strong view on the part of some of our strategists that we should be damned careful not to overuse them and cheapen them. That they should—there is a celebrity value you can lose by rubbing on them too much—

P. I couldn't agree more.

H. and so we have to—their eagerness to participate should not go—

P. California delegation (unintelligible) think I'm here. I mean we're going to have (unintelligible)

P. You understand—they're willing. Have them do things—do the important things, and so forth, and so on.

H. There's the question. Like Sunday night they have the (unintelligible) whether they should go to that—now at least the girls should go. I think I ought to go too!

P. Yep.

H. You know, whether Pat—one thought that was raised was that the girls and their husbands go down on Sunday and Pat wait and come down with you on Tuesday. I think Pat should go down and should be there cause they'll have the Salute—

P. (Inaudible)

H. She should arrive separately. I think she should arrive with the girls. Another thought was to have the girls arrive Sunday, Pat arrive Monday and you arrive Tuesday. I think you're overdoing your arrivals.

P. No, no, no. She arrives with the girls and they—they should go. I agree.

H. But, I don't think you have to be there until Tuesday.

P. I don't want to go near the damned place until Tuesday. I don't want to be near it. I've got the arrival planned (unintelligible) my arrival of, ah—

H. Now we're going to do, unless you have some objection, we should do your arrival at Miami International not at Homestead.

P. Yes, I agree.

H. Ah, we can crank up a hell of an arrival thing.

P. Alright.

P. (unintelligible) is for you, ah, and perhaps Colson probably (inaudible).

P. I was thumbing through the, ah, last chapters of (unintelligible) [Nixon was apparently referring to his earlier memoirs, *Six Crises*] last night, and I also read the (unintelligible) chapters (unintelligible). Warm up to it, and it makes, ah, fascinating reading. Also reminds you of a hell of a lot of things that happened in the campaign—press you know, election coverage, the (unintelligible) etc., etc.

H. Yeah.

P. So on and so on. I want you to reread it, and I want Colson to read it, and anybody else.

H. O.K.

P. And anybody else in the campaign. Get copies of the book and give it to each of them. Say I want them to read it and have it in mind. Give it to whoever you can, O.K.?

H. Sure will.

P. Actually, the book reads awfully well—have to look at history. I want to talk to you more about that later in terms of what it tells us about how our campaign should be run, O.K.?

H. O.K. . . .

H. Yep.

P. (unintelligible) check another thing—gets back? Convention?

H. He was, I'm not sure if he still is.

P. Could find out from him what chapters of the book he worked on. Ah, I don't want coverage of the heartattack thing. I did most of the dictating on the last two but I've been curious (unintelligible). But could you find out which chapters he worked on. Also find out where Moscow is—what's become of him—what's he's doing ten years. Say hello to him (unintelligible) might find it useful (unintelligible) future, despite the (unintelligible). You'll find this extremely interesting, read (unintelligible).

H. Read that a number of times (unintelligible) different context—

P. Ah, I would say another thing—Bud Brown (unintelligible) did you read it? (Unintelligible) candidates. I don't know who all you discussed that with. Maybe it's not been handled at a high enough level. Who did you discuss that with? (Unintelligible)

H. MacGregor and Mitchell. MacGregor and Mitchell, that's all.

P. Yep. (Unintelligible) I don't mind the time—the problem that I have with it is that I do not want to have pictures with candidates that are running with Democrats—or against Democrats that may either be (unintelligible) or might be for us. . . .

P. Yeah. Another point I was going to mention to you, Bod, [sic] is the situation with regard to the girls. I was talking to Pat last night. Tricia and I were talking, and she mentioned—Tricia said that apparently when she was in Allentown there were 20 or 30 thugs— labor thugs out booing.

H. Hmmm.

P. And when she went to Boston to present some art—her Chinese things to the art gallery there—two the (unintelligible) from the press were pretty vicious. What I mean is they came through the line and one refused to shake. One was not with the press. Refused to shake hands, so forth and so on. Tricia (unintelligible) very personal point, (unintelligible) good brain in that head. She said first she couldn't believe that the event that they do locally (unintelligible) understand. You know she does the Boys' Club, the Art Gallery (unintelligible). She says the important thing is to find this type of (unintelligible) to go into the damn town (unintelligible) do television, which of course, they do. (Unintelligible) she says why (unintelligible) control the place. She says in other words, go in and do the Republican group. Now, sure isn't (unintelligible) to say the Republican group, as it is the Allentown Bullies Club? But, that's the paper story. The point is, I think Parker has to get a little more thinking in depth, or is it Codus now who will do this?

H.   They are both working on it.

P.   What's your off-hand reaction on that, Bob?
I do not want them, though, to go in and get the hell kicked (unintelligible).

H.   There's no question, and we've really got to work at that.

P.   Yep. (unintelligible)

H.   Ya, but I think—I'm not sure—if you can't get the controlled non-political event, then I think it is better to do a political event (unintelligible).

P.   For example—now the worse thing (unintelligible) is to go to anything that has to do with the Arts.

H.   Ya, see that—it was (unintelligible) Julie giving that time to the Museum in Jacksonville.

P.   The Arts you know—they're Jews, they're left wing—in other words, stay away.

P.   Make a point.

H.   Sure.

P.   Middle America—put that word out—Middle America-type of people (unintelligible), auxiliary, (unintelligible). Why the hell doesn't Parker get that kind of thing going? Most of his things are elite groups except, I mean, do the cancer thing—maybe nice for Tricia to go up—ride a bus for 2 hours—do some of that park in Oklahoma—but my view is, Bob, relate it to Middle America and not the elitist (unintelligible). Do you agree?

H.   Yep. Sure do.

P.   I'm not complaining. I think they are doing a hell of a job. The kids are willing—

H.   They really are, but she can improve.

P.   There again, Tricia had a very good thought on this, but let's do Middle America.

H.   Yep.

P.   (Unintelligible).

P. I don't know whether Alex told you or not, but I want a Secret Service reception some time next week. I just gotta know who these guys are. (Unintelligible). Don't you think so? I really feel that they're there—that ah, I see new guys around—and Jesus Christ they look so young.

H. Well, they change them—that's one (unintelligible) any reception now would be totally different (unintelligible).

P. Get 100 then—so it's 200 and I shake their hands and thank them and you look (unintelligible) too—(unintelligible). They have a hell of a lot of fellas, let's face it, (unintelligible) friends (unintelligible), but I just think it's a nice—

H. They all—you have such—that's why it's a good thing to do, 'cause they are friends—and they have such overriding respect for you and your family—that a

P. I wouldn't want the whole group—something like (unintelligible). Third point—I would like a good telephone call list for California, but not a huge book, and the kind is—This would be a good time where (unintelligible) and just give thanks to people for their support. For example, Colson had me call (unintelligible) the other day—(unintelligible) thing to do, but, here you could take the key guys that work—I wouldn't mind calling a very few key contributors—maybe, but we're talking about magnitude of ten—very key ten.

H. Ten—you mean ten people?

P. Ya.

H. Oh, I thought you meant $10,000.

P. No, ten. Ten. I was thinking of very key (unintelligible), people like—that worked their ass off collecting money, just to say that—people that—the people that are doing the work—very key political (unintelligible) just to pat them on the back. I mean that means a helluva lot—very key political VIPs, you know, by political VIPs. . . .

The resignation of Richard Nixon brought Gerald Ford into the presidency, but a change in presidents did not necessarily mean changes in policies. Ford's retention of Henry A. Kissinger as Secretary of State implied an endorsement of certain key elements in Nixon's foreign policy: the importance of detente with the Soviet Union, the rapprochement with the People's Republic of China, the attempt to play a peace-making role in the Middle East. In all of these matters, Kissinger appeared to view the world in conventional balance-of-power terms.

But behind balance-of-power politics lay economic realities, and the economic questions which beset the international order by the early seventies came to occupy more and more of Secretary Kissinger's attention. The following speech outlined Kissinger's ideas about the world economic structure. If the past thirty years of rapid economic growth have been as universally beneficial as Kissinger suggests, why do you think some of the so-called third world nations want a restructuring of the world economic system? In attempting to alleviate poverty domestically, the United States has traditionally responded by stressing rapid economic growth rather than redistribution of income. Do you see suggestions of a similar approach in Kissinger's speech? What are the advantages to such an approach on an international level? What are the disadvantages?

Henry A. Kissinger

Strengthening the World Economic Structure

The paramount necessity of our time is the preservation of peace. But history has shown that international political stability requires international economic stability. Order cannot survive if economic arrangements are constantly buffeted by crisis or if they fail to meet the aspirations of nations and peoples for progress.

The United States cannot be isolated—and never has been isolated—from the international economy. We export 23 percent of our farm output and 8 percent of our manufactures. We import far more raw materials than we export; oil from abroad is critical to our welfare. American enterprise overseas constitutes an economy the size of Japan's. America's prosperity could not continue in a chaotic world economy.

Conversely, what the United States does—or fails to do—has an enormous impact on the rest of the world. With one-third of the output of the non-Communist world, the American economy is still the great engine of world prosperity. Our technology, our food, our resources, our managerial genius and financial expertise, our experience of leadership are unmatched. Without us there is no prospect of solution. When we are in recession, it spreads; without American expansion, the world economy tends to stagnate.

For 30 years the modern economic system created at the Bretton Woods conference in 1944 has served us well. Its basic goals—open, equitable, and expanding trade, the stability and orderly adjustment of currencies, coordination in combating inflation and recession—have largely been achieved. World growth has surpassed any prior period of history.

But the system is now under serious stress. It faces shortages and disputes over new issues such as energy, raw materials, and food. And many of its fundamental premises are challenged by the nations of the developing world.

Obvious crises are the easiest to meet; the deepest challenges to men are those that emerge imperceptibly, that derive from fundamental changes which, if not addressed, portend upheavals in the future. These contemporary challenges to the world economic structure must be overcome, or we face not only an end to the growth of the last 30 years but the shattering of the hopes of all of mankind for a better future. Our economic strength is unmistakable. But what is tested now is our vision and our will—and that of the other nations of the world.

The Existing System

The international economic system has been built on these central elements:

Open and expanding trade;

Secretary Henry A. Kissinger before the Kansas City International Relations Council. Kansas City, Mo., May, 1975.

Free movement of investment capital and technology;

Readily available supplies of raw materials; and

Institutions and practices of international cooperation.

Within this framework, over the past quarter century, the industrialized countries have maintained an almost continuous record of economic growth. The developing countries have made unprecedented advances, though their progress has been uneven.

After the experience of the 1930's the post-war system was designed—with the United States playing a leading role—to separate economic issues from political conflict and to subject them as much as possible to agreed multilateral procedures. The rules were designed to restrain unilateral actions that could cause economic injury to others.

The world's economic growth within this framework has been simultaneously the cause and the result of growing interdependence among nations. Revolutions in communication and transportation have shrunk the planet. The global mobility of capital, management and technology, and materials has facilitated the growth of industry. World trade has encouraged specialization and the efficient division of labor, which in turn have stimulated further expansion. The recession and inflation of the last few years—which spread around the world—have reminded us that nations thrive or suffer together. No country—not even the United States—can solve its economic problems in isolation.

Consciousness of interdependence has been most successfully implemented among the industrialized countries. When the energy crisis first hit us the industrial countries agreed that they would not resort to unilateral, restrictive trade measures to make up the payments deficits caused by high oil prices. That pledge was respected and will be renewed this year. And last fall, as the recession worsened, the President held a series of conversations with German, Japanese, British, and French leaders to devise a coordinated strategy for economic recovery. These policies have begun to bear fruit. The advanced industrialized countries have understood the imperative of coordinating their economic policies.

As our economies now turn toward expansion we must ensure that our policies remain coordinated, particularly for the control of inflation with its economic costs and attendant social dangers.

Against this background of cohesion the industrial countries can act with renewed confidence across the entire range of political, economic, and security issues. The annual ministerial meeting later this month of the Organization for Economic Cooperation and Development [OECD] is therefore of great significance. This body—composed of the industrialized countries of North America, Europe, and Asia—will assess where we stand and discuss even closer coordination and joint actions in economic policies. Secretary [of the Treasury William E.] Simon and I will represent the United States.

The Challenge From the Developing World

Global interdependence is a reality. There is no alternative to international collaboration if growth is to be sustained. But the world economic structure is under increasing challenge from many countries which believe that it does not fairly meet their needs.

The challenge finds its most acute and articulate expression in the program advanced in the name of the so-called Third World. This calls for a totally new economic order, founded on ideology and national self-interest. It is stimulated by resentments over past exploitation, and it is sustained by the view that the current system is loaded against the interests of the developing countries. One of the central proposals is that the prices of primary products should be set by international agreements at new high levels and then pegged to an index of world inflation. The objective, as with the oil price increases, is a massive redistribution of the world's wealth.

This challenge has many aspects. At one level it is an effort to make the availability of vital natural resources depend on political decision, particularly with respect to energy, but increasingly involving other materials as well. More fundamentally it is a result of the new dispersion of economic power among developed and developing countries that springs from the unprecedented global economic expansion of the last 30 years.

The United States is prepared to study these views attentively, but we are convinced that the present economic system has generally served the world well. We are prepared to consider realistic proposals, but we are convinced that poorer nations benefit most from an expanding world economy. History has proved the prosperity of each nation requires expansion of global prosperity. This should be the focus of our efforts.

The United States is convinced that an international system overshadowed by the rivalry of nations or blocs will produce instability and confrontation. This will prove disastrous to every nation—but above all to the weakest and the poorest.

The United States therefore is committed to a cooperative approach. We recognize that an international order will be durable only if its members truly accept it. And while the participation of developing countries has increased, it is clear that the energy producers and the emerging nations in Latin America, Asia, and Africa have believed themselves to be outside the system. We have a duty to warn against, and to resist, confrontation. But we are prepared to strengthen and expand the international economic system.